Unsettling Sexuality

Unsettling Sexuality

Queer Horizons in the Long Eighteenth Century

EDITED BY
JEREMY CHOW
SHELBY JOHNSON

NEWARK

Library of Congress Cataloging-in-Publication Data

Names: Chow, Jeremy, editor. | Johnson, Shelby Lynn, 1988– editor.
Title: Unsettling sexuality : queer horizons in the long eighteenth century /
   edited by Jeremy Chow and Shelby Johnson.
Description: Newark, DE : University Of Delaware Press, [2025] | Includes
   bibliographical references and index.
Identifiers: LCCN 2024005275 | ISBN 9781644533482 (paperback ; alk. paper) |
   ISBN 9781644533499 (hardcover ; alk. paper) | ISBN 9781644533505 (epub) |
   ISBN 9781644533512 (mobi) | ISBN 9781644533529 (pdf)
Subjects: LCSH: Gay people—History—18th century. | Civilization,
   Modern—18th century. | Gay studies.
Classification: LCC HQ76.25 .U56 2025 | DDC 306.76/60909033—dc23/eng/20240426
LC record available at https://lccn.loc.gov/2024005275

A British Cataloging-in-Publication record for this book is available from the British Library.

This collection copyright © 2025 by the University of Delaware
Individual chapters copyright © 2025 in the names of their authors
All rights reserved

No part of this book may be reproduced or utilized in any form or by any means, electronic
or mechanical, or by any information storage and retrieval system, without written permission from the publisher. Please contact University of Delaware Press, 200A Morris Library,
181 S. College Ave., Newark, DE 19717. The only exception to this prohibition is "fair use" as
defined by U.S. copyright law.

References to internet websites (URLs) were accurate at the time of writing. Neither the
author nor University of Delaware Press is responsible for URLs that may have expired or
changed since the manuscript was prepared.

⊖ The paper used in this publication meets the requirements of the American National Standard for Information Sciences—Permanence of Paper for Printed Library Materials, ANSI
Z39.48-1992.

udpress.udel.edu

Distributed worldwide by Rutgers University Press

Contents

Acknowledgments   vii

Introduction: Unsettling Sexuality   1
Jeremy Chow and Shelby Johnson

PART I
*Gender Nonconformity: Embodiment,
Sociality, and Politics*

1   Transgender Citizenship and Settler Colonialism
in Aphra Behn's *The Widow Ranter*   21
Ula Lukszo Klein

2   Samson Occom, the Public Universal Friend, and
a Queer Archive of the Elsewhere   38
Shelby Johnson

3   Refashioning Masculinity in Regency England:
Female Fashions Inspired by the Persian Envoy Mirza
Abul Hassan Khan and His Circassian Wife   55
Humberto Garcia

PART II
Novel Intimacies

4   "My sister, my friend, my ever beloved":
Queer Friendship and Asexuality in *The Memoirs
of Miss Sidney Bidulph*   79
Ziona Kocher

5   Redefining the Archive in Queer Historical
    Romance Novels   95
    Cailey Hall

PART III
Queer Ecologies and Cartographies

6   Matters of Intimacy: *The Sugar-Cane*'s
    Asexual Ecologies   111
    M. A. Miller

7   Fantasy Maps and Projective Fictions   129
    Tess J. Given

PART IV
Racializing Affect, Queering Temporality

8   Dark and Delayed Labor: Sex Work and Racialized
    Time in Eighteenth-Century London   147
    Nour Afara

9   Unsettling Happiness: Blackness, Gender,
    and Affect in *The Woman of Colour* and
    Its Media Afterlives   162
    Jeremy Chow and Riley DeBaecke

Coda: Eighteenth-Century Longing   180
Eugenia Zuroski

Notes on Contributors   187
Index   189

Acknowledgments

This collection is indebted to the work that the Queer and Trans Caucus (formerly, the Gay and Lesbian Caucus) of the American Society for Eighteenth-Century Studies seeks to accomplish in shifting the conversations, methods, and modes of interpretation that find a home in eighteenth-century studies. Indeed, our collaboration as coeditors developed out of our work as cochairs for the caucus. We dedicate this collection to the newly minted caucus and its members, especially in their collective aspirations for social, cultural, and epistemological change.

We are grateful to our contributors and their support networks who have believed in this work and labored tirelessly to bring it to fruition. Julia Oestreich has continued to be an advocate for this work, and the University of Delaware Press, under her guidance, has generously provided a home for these collaborative conversations. The transfixing artistry of Kent Monkman and Norval Morrisseau has captivated us—compelling us to reflect and write on them. We are honored by Monkman and the Estate of Norval Morrisseau for granting image permissions.

We remain inspired by Sara Ahmed's provocation, which we take up in the introduction, that "to be part of a collection can be to become a collective." This collection models what collective coalitional camaraderie can accomplish, and we offer this work to further agitate toward such efforts in which we might, together, rail against neocolonial regimes embedded in supremacist values that get their kicks on marginalization and discrimination.

Together, we can unsettle.

Introduction

UNSETTLING SEXUALITY

Jeremy Chow and Shelby Johnson

> *To be part of a collection can be*
> *to become a collective.*[1]
> —*Sara Ahmed,* On Being Included

Unsettling Sexuality: Queer Horizons in the Long Eighteenth Century sets out to revisit, reframe, and upheave the traditional ways that scholarship has approached sexuality, gender nonconformity, and sex (as well as its absence) in eighteenth-century studies, which focuses on a period that we define capaciously to encompass the Restoration, the years 1700 to 1799, and the Romantic period. In nine essays, divided among four distinct yet interconnected sections, and a coda, the authors featured here read transatlantic, European, and global eighteenth-century literary archives in order to:

1. simultaneously construct and deconstruct formations of gender performance, sexuality, community, and identity that emerged and cohered in the long eighteenth century;
2. decenter and delink from the Eurocentricism of eighteenth-century queer and trans studies and its concomitant whiteness, which continues to saturate queer studies writ large;
3. magnify differential methodologies to enlarge what might be valued as queer scholarship in the long eighteenth century;
4. demonstrate the affinities between queer historiography and reading and recent calls for decolonizing eighteenth-century studies; and
5. establish an intentional citational praxis that enriches who gets cited, what is engaged, and how epistemologies circulate.

This collection, at its core, is a commitment to opening and welcoming alternative, renewed, queer, trans, and decolonial horizons for eighteenth-century studies. In so doing, we aim to perform and invigorate intersectional queer readings, methods, and citations.

Consider this painting by Cree artist Kent Monkman as a generative example that takes up many of the evocations prompted by this collection (see Figure 0.1). In *Welcoming the Newcomers* (2019), Monkman queerly provokes by radically subverting colonialist perspectives, and, as a result, imagining ways of unsettling sexuality through queer artistry. The enormous mural—approximately eleven feet by twenty-two feet—currently welcomes museum goers to the Great Hall at New York City's Metropolitan Museum of Art. There, the central figure is Miss Chief Eagle Testickle, Monkman's alter ego, who appears throughout his work as a gender-fluid, time-traveling, and supernatural being (her name puns on "mischief" and "egotistical"). Across Monkman's oeuvre, Miss Chief powerfully challenges both settler gender binaries and linear history, or what José Esteban Muñoz, to whom we will return shortly, refers to as "*straight time*."[2] Monkman recurrently features Miss Chief, whose divested form highlights melanated musculature and vibrant sensuality. Here, Miss Chief sports beaded earrings, a wind-rushed fabric about the waist, and Christian Louboutin stilettos—sartorial depictions that play with denuded Indigeneity, conspicuous capitalist consumption, and drag and gender performativity as an icon of resurgent Two-Spirit traditions within hemispheric Indigenous cultures.[3]

Read from within Cree cultures, Miss Chief in *Welcoming the Newcomers* emblematizes love and kinship—*kisâkihitin* and *wahkotowin* in Cree, respectively—illustrated by the positions of bodies and lines of sight assembled in the painting. Miss Chief gazes at viewers, thereby contesting conventions within settler visual art that represented Indigenous persons—especially Two-Spirit Indigenous persons—as the subjects of a voyeuristic white gaze, perhaps nowhere more prominently than in George Catlin's *Dance to the Berdache* (c. 1835/1837). Instead, Miss Chief reaches toward a Black enchained figure, a gesture of racial solidarity that also counters tropes of abjection through which Euro-American art has represented slavery and Blackness. Rather than the scattered and disarticulated human forms of J.M.W. Turner's *The Slave Ship* (1840), which is implicitly alluded to by the surfacing shark in the painting's top right corner, *Welcoming the Newcomers*'s horizon of possibility testifies to Indigenous and Black resilience against the intertwined forces of anti-Black violence, Indigenous displacement and "disappearance," and the coercive norms of intimate settler life.

Viewers may be disoriented by the frenzied beauty of *Welcoming the Newcomers*, which resists the orthodoxy of the singular, centralized figure so favored by portraiture. While we could argue that Miss Chief is the mural's protagonist, the eye moves easily, if not promiscuously, about the image, locating the vexed and oftentimes subtle intimacies that Monkman crafts. Whereas swelling seas and ship-wrecked colonists and enslavers may portend an apocalyptic vision, the Indigenous figures counter narratives of calamity, ensconced on a shoal of safety otherwise absent from the rising tides that surround—and for this, we draw deliberately from Tiffany Lethabo King's explication of a shoal as "an interstitial and emerging space of becoming," where the "boundaries between the human and Black and

Figure 0.1. Kent Monkman, *Welcoming the Newcomers* (2019). Collection of the Metropolitan Museum of Art. Courtesy of the Artist.

Indigenous bodies continually shift."[4] On the shoal, figures are arrayed in postures of intimacy and embrace, vibrancy and vulnerability: an Indigenous figure gives birth; two others, whose nudity is displayed to viewers, hold one another; a person with bare breasts grasps the arm of a white settler whose hands grope with abandon. Miss Chief embraces only the enchained Black figure, and while her right hand extends openly to others, contact is fluid—imminent but not yet attained. Alongside these captures of haptic, licit, and illicit intimacy, the gazes of the Indigenous figures open up alternative ways of reading queer visualities, temporalities, and histories: what we understand as invitations for alternative, anticolonial queer horizons.

To read Monkman this way is to reckon with transhistorical opacities of queerness and transness. The methodologies of unsettling offered by this collection seek to animate something similar. Put another way, we take Monkman's visual cues as a furtive yet necessary lens for the methods we collaboratively assemble: an imperative to foreground queer, trans, Indigenous, and Black improvisations of gender and sexuality, a mandate to analyze the genres of heteropatriarchal and colonial expansion within the long eighteenth century, and a call to reimagine and decolonize the historical frames we think and write within.

Unsettling Sexuality seeks to expand and enrich our dedications to gender, queer, trans, asexual, and sexuality studies, venues by which we can reimagine sometimes staid or too-comfortable hetero *and* homonormative modes. Many of us in this volume found our work as queer, trans, and gender-nonconforming scholars and our pursuit of queer and trans scholarship through critiques of heteronormativity, others through excoriations of heteronormativity and its entwinement *with* whiteness and coloniality. Yet these trenchant and now well-established critiques can also run the risk of reproducing homonormativity, which, like heteronormativity, tends to be fixed *to* whiteness and coloniality. While these currents have sustained scholarly discussions, working groups, and caucus meetings, this collection endeavors to resist both the static and echoed criticisms of heteronormativity and evade the potential pitfalls of homonormative thinking. The contributors, in other words, chart new waters and cartographies by which eighteenth-century studies can benefit from a necessary unsettling that exists in multidimensional horizons, as Monkman depicts.

Queer horizons are germane to our past, presents, futures, hopes, and worries: temporal, affective, and sensory experiences that enflesh how we might understand queerness and epistemologies of the horizon. Queer horizons in the long eighteenth century may first appear oxymoronic, but we home in on these semantics to offer ways of reading that might play with lines of sight, branches of scholarship, and situated positions. These horizons are also about genre and disciplinarity; they enable us to meditate on recent trends in queer and sexuality studies and new realms of engaging the period's literature, art, performance, and culture. They allow us to consider how the eighteenth century is repeatedly reanimated in contemporary biopics, historical fiction, and museum and archival exhibits. Queer horizons do not flatten historical time as the image of a horizon might putatively suggest; we are not interested in "straightening" anything. Instead, queer horizons locate positionality, intimacy, and geography as sites of knowing that can disrupt the notion of horizons as somehow straight and thereby normative.

We wager that a horizon is not something strictly in front of us. A queer horizon can be behind, beside, adjacent to, and in front of us. Other queer directions, orientations, and prepositions abound. We seek them out—we eke them out—here. A queer horizon does not exist in a single temporal scape. It is not linear. It is not hierarchical. It is not an ontology. It defers stable signification. In this way, queer horizons may be understood through their antinomic placement. They are subversive geographies bound up in hope and promise—perhaps antinomies to the surfeit of anti-queer and anti-trans rhetoric and legislation that saturates the political landscapes in which we persevere and pen this collection.

Queer horizons bleed across borders, electrify rhizomes, resist taxonomic objectification, and spread among transhistoric and transcorporeal kin networks unencumbered by blood or genealogy. By thinking with queer horizons, we are of course thinking with José Esteban Muñoz's *Cruising Utopia: The Then and There of Queer Futurity* (2009), which urges scholars of gender and sexuality not to tether queerness solely to matters of political pragmatism. As important as issues of marriage equality, housing discrimination, or media representation might be, queer and trans possibilities, Muñoz argues, lie in the future. Queerness is *not yet here*. Muñoz's invocation of queerness as a potentiality relies on a rejection of the reproductive futurist present, in which queerness is somehow quotidian or tethered to the logics of hetero- and homonormativity. By offering queer temporalities and future horizons, Muñoz refuses the linearity of straight time by proposing queer temporalities in which "queerness's ecstatic and horizonal temporality is a path and a movement to a greater openness to the world."[5] The ecstasy of revising the horizon lies in imagining, even occupying, the multidimensional.

Queer horizons unsettle. They are not beholden to normative scales or temporal structures. They resist rigidity and welcome sexuality as something that can likewise resist rigidity. In the chapters that follow, contributors toggle between queer, gender, and sexuality studies, not to conflate their purviews but because they offer important vectors by which to think through coherences, productive tensions, and sometimes fissures of possibility. Neither gender nor sexuality studies is a monolith, and we uphold them as promiscuous fields of cross-contamination that motivate our collection-*cum*-collective, as Sara Ahmed reminds us. Some chapters may initially not appear queer to readers because they favor discussions of sexuality that incorporate heteronormative models. And yet discussions of racialized sexuality, such as those approached by Nour Afara and by Jeremy Chow and Riley DeBaecke, are often eclipsed because of their intersectional positioning. These three navigate dimensions of racialized sexuality to address the insinuations of race and sexuality prompted by critiques from feminists of color and queer of color intellectuals. Other authors may not appear to address sexuality because they channel queer gender or asexual discourses. As M. A. Miller, Tess Given, and Ziona Kocher demonstrate, the currently operationalized conceit within sexuality studies is predicated on forms of compulsory sexuality that marginalize other sexualities, especially asexuality, in favor of a spectrum that is recurrently limited in scope. We thus prioritize unsettling as a keyword throughout; by "unsettling," we mean to reimagine the aforementioned queer spectrum that has found a home in cultural criticism, as well as reposition and rework how supremacist constructs contour understandings of race, indigeneity, sex, sexuality, affect, and place.

To this end, the nine chapters and coda here are not a standardization tool by which to assess how queer and sexuality studies *should* be conducted in eighteenth-century studies. Instead, they produce a series of rigorous dialogues that invite readers to consider the sinews of our current discourses and open ways of thinking otherwise. This is precisely why readers will not find a static definition of "queer" here or throughout; while we do not intend to evacuate meaning from the term, identity, and politic (leaving it an empty husk of significance), we also maintain a committed reaction against any definition that may only serve to pigeonhole the utopianism we seek in, embody with, read within, and attribute to queerness. For those interested in a barebones definition of queerness as a metric that might approximate legitimated acceptability politics and epistemological consonance, this collection may not be for them.

The queerness of this collection, in other words, invites readers to find its unsteady, unsettled meanings and frameworks in the chapters that follow. *Unsettling Sexuality* draws inspiration from previous collections to address how sexuality, gender, queerness, and transness emerge from long-eighteenth-century archives or are theorized from within them.[6] And in conversation with these interlocutors, we uphold queer horizons as a desire to behold and be held by alternatives that have otherwise been refused us. We seek queer horizons that allow us to unify (not unanimize) in our aspiration for a collection that, as Ahmed inspires, "can become a collective."[7] In queer horizons, we find manifold worlds of prospective desires and intimacies.

Queer History | Queer Citation

Scholars of eighteenth-century gender and sexuality have principally examined how institutions and discourses of disciplined desire in Europe were reproduced throughout the colonized world. Literary scholars and historians, such as Jonathan Goldberg, Madhavi Menon, Valerie Traub, Abdulhamit Arvas, and Jen Manion, among others, have sought to recover historical queer identities, moving beyond an earlier emphasis on gay and lesbian desire to explore transgender, nonbinary, asexual, and gender fluid positions, and interrogate intimacies that existed beyond the norms of heteropatriarchal Euro-American cultures among the broader and longer early modern world.[8] Yet, we acknowledge the methodological obstacles of extricating desire from eighteenth- and nineteenth-century archives, which largely reflect the material conditions of surveillance that governed identity and intimacy. These conditions produced, as Mark Rifkin argues, a narrowly defined "common sense" that elided other possibilities for expressing gender and sexuality.[9]

INTRODUCTION

As a method for moving through and beyond the heteronormativity of colonial records, we turn often to representations of alternative sensations—sight, sound, touch, taste—as illustrated so powerfully in Monkman's subversion of the gaze and portrayal of haptic connections between Indigenous and Black figures in *Welcoming the Newcomers*. We are thereby influenced by Elizabeth Freeman's *Beside You in Time* (2019), which attends to notions of sense, what Freeman identifies as "sense methods," in continuation of the project to map queer temporality, what we see as a necessary tenet of queer horizons. For Freeman, "sense methods" engender "a queer theory of relationality and sociability" that imagines queerness as "a drive toward connectivity, conjugation, and coalescence"—a powerful counter to the colonial "common sense" Rifkin describes.[10] If we accept the provocation that queer methodologies can promote a temporal and phenomenological hypersociality, then we can embrace opportunities to, as Freeman puts it, "rearrange the relations between past and present, linking contemporary bodies to those from other times in reformulations of ancestry and lineage."[11] In this embrace of *sense*—common, queer, methodological, transhistorical—we welcome new formations of history and desire, temporality and intimacy, embodiment and identity, and queerness and transness that can account for our ardent intent to unsettle, reimagine, and re-enliven.

In our own exercise of sense methods, these essays bring to the fore questions of citationality. While citation is too often considered *de rigeur*, or pursued merely performatively, we acknowledge that citation is a deliberate practice that telegraphs inclusion, exclusion, appropriateness, and appropriation. Citational circulation is a craft and technique of always deliberate (even if purportedly unintentional) relation. Scholarship *as* citational accountability and responsibility makes evident to readers who is cited, how they are cited, and the extent of that citation. In *Living a Feminist Life* (2017), Ahmed invokes the verb "to path" as a means of establishing an intersectional and antiracist citation that lays out "paths we call desire lines."[12] Katherine McKittrick, in this same vein, writes in *Dear Science and Other Stories* (2021): "I am not interested in citations as quotable value. I want to reference other possibilities such as, citations as learning, as counsel, as sharing."[13] Ahmed and McKittrick identify concerns that bespeak conversations at eighteenth-century conferences, especially in caucuses, panels, or roundtables that incorporate marginalized voices.

To that end, this collection is committed to giving voice to scholars whose work, presence, or placement in the academy have long been marginalized, providing a useful place of theorizing and recuperating. Marginalia, indeed, can be harnessed for queer liberation. This is why the authors included here represent a wide spectrum of academic placements and, of course, the precarities experienced therein. While academics who have found a home through the ladder system are featured here, so too are individuals who are in the throes of doctoral candidacy or those who have thrived in contingent roles. A few are independent scholars. Other contributors are publishing for the first time; one is even an undergraduate coauthor. By welcoming junior, emerging, and established scholars, we want to give voice and allow others to find their own. In our commitment to polyvocality, *Unsettling*

Sexuality desires an assemblage that endeavors to deprivilege hierarchies of domination that too often are reified through the academy and its publishing arms.

We are, to be certain, responding to concerns over citation that have surfaced in our field, though these feelings and anima have undoubtedly simmered below the surface for decades. Sal Nicolazzo, for example, questions how to decenter whiteness and its pernicious historical instantiations in eighteenth-century studies. Drawing from Roderick Ferguson's queer of color critique, Nicolazzo contends that "the field, in its citational practices, its orientation toward knowledge, its definition of expertise, and—most crucially—its relation to the distribution of material resources (both within the university and beyond)" often reaffirms the status quo of whiteness through a citational circulation that operates through/as epistemology (and vice versa).[14] Megan Peiser (Choctaw Nation) has similarly addressed how conventional academic modes of citationality and publication reproduce settler colonialism.[15] Through her experience as an Indigenous scholar, Peiser rightfully demands more accountability in oftentimes cursory or half-hearted attempts at decolonizing the fields in which we are embedded and complicit. To truck with the academy is to commit to systems of white supremacy and settler colonialism that were (and continue to be) engineered on the premise of exclusion. And in another reflection published by *Eighteenth-Century Fiction*, one of this volume's editors, Jeremy Chow, has recently called for an "enlightened citational praxis" that perverts the Enlightenment's hegemony and "invites us to circulate our own work—the work that honours difference, identity, relationality—among one another because you are my audience, you are my ally, and you are my advocate."[16] These collective calls for action are motivated by experiences of marginalization and actively broadcast a desire to shift the adamantine structures of our profession in hopes of refusing unabashed, even if unintentional, white supremacy and its alibi of "good-intentions."[17]

Our goal remains, as we noted previously, to produce a concerted and intentional citational praxis for the purpose of enrichment that follows unsettling the ontological and epistemological regimes that shape the study of eighteenth-century sexuality and gender. The citational models promoted by this collection speak both to the primary and secondary sources we approach. For instance, several authors interrogate narratives that have been deified as pillars of the canon, while others introduce popular or marginalized figures who have only recently become part of scholarly conversations. Rather than holding canonicity harmless, we path with intellectual interlocutors—many outside of eighteenth-century studies, as Monkman or Norval Morrisseau, whose work graces this collection's cover, are—who may help us revisit critical conversations and modes of inquiry that are too important to belong to only the fields of contemporary theory, literature, or art. We stage possibilities of *listening to* archives that exist across historical periods and genres. Queer horizons demand these types of transversal and transhistorical *longings*—a critical concept with which Eugenia Zuroski concludes this collection.

Unsettling Sexuality draws from recent and emerging criticism in Middle Eastern and Asian studies, African American studies, and Native American and Indigenous studies to argue that colonial modernity imbricated both European settlers and people of color into a narrow uniform of sexuality as part of the colonizing project, strictly organized around the nuclear family, patriarchal property relations, and the cultural reproduction of colonial norms.[18] Put differently, we argue that sexuality and gender are expressed within a matrix of colonial modernity, which Catherine E. Walsh and Walter Mignolo remind us is an epistemological settler projection that seeks to segregate relationality in favor of the fictions of autonomy and ontology.[19] These fictions are predicated on the coloniality of being—structures and recognitions of the colonial matrix of power—which is reinforced and subtended by racism, sexism, able-bodiedness, and anti-queerness. In response, we take up María Lugones's contention that what is required from us is to improvise a vibrant "decolonial feminism," which in its intersectional outlook cannot be unmoored from queerness, queer gender, and sexuality.[20]

One intervention of this collection is to explore how racial embodiment becomes a material site for conflicts over intimacy, desire, and kinship. Essays by Humberto Garcia, Shelby Johnson, Nour Afara, and Jeremy Chow and Riley DeBaecke take up Iranian travelers, a Mohegan pastor and a nonbinary white preacher, dark-complexioned sex workers, and mixed-raced women, respectively, to interrogate how people of color in the long eighteenth century understood and resisted their conscriptions into what Rifkin calls a "competent" performance of modernity.[21] While not every essay in the collection overtly takes up racial embodiments or colonial settings, we collectively acknowledge that settler structures shaped all acts of literary production in this period, in large and small ways.

And we hope to open new questions and methods for continuing the work of this volume in future collections, projects, and critical conversations. This is precisely what Walsh and Mignolo mean when they, like Aníbal Quijano before them, name coloniality—a violent, immuring logic and infrastructure left in the wake of colonialism that determines governance, surveillance, and identity, as well as distinguishes the human from the nonhuman.[22] In our efforts to center decoloniality through an ethics of citation, we are mindful that these frameworks are grounded in Indigenous and postcolonial sovereignty struggles, and thus have dimensions far beyond academic research. This is part and parcel of the desire to make this collection open access, which has been generously supported by the University of Delaware Press's investment in this work. In addition, we are invested in thinking through decoloniality not only for Indigenous, African diasporic, Middle Eastern, and Pan-Asian experiences in the early modern period but also for canonical texts of the eighteenth century.[23] We thus share a commitment to unsettling academic disciplinarity itself.[24] In this way, the collection provides new insights into how queer persons and writers of color contest—*unsettle*—the intimate colonization of their bodies, minds, spirits, and communities.

INTIMATE METHODS

Queer horizons inhabit the intimate. This collection centers *intimacy*—as intersubjective proximities, as material and tactile sensations, as modes of desire and yearning, as everyday routines of being and belonging, as well as quotidian communal formations, in their plural refractions in transatlantic and global eighteenth-century literatures. For this work, we think with Lisa Lowe's *The Intimacies of Four Continents* (2015), which defines intimacy as "a means to observe the historical divisions of world processes into those that develop modern liberal subjects and modern spheres of social life."[25] Recently, Lowe has reflected on responses to "intimacies as method" and argues: "Intimacies as method emphasizes relation, convergence, and interdependency, and attends to residual and emergent knowledges that may be elided by the dominant disciplines in which we work."[26] Lowe further suggests that "identifying such connections often means breaking with customary modes for organizing history," prompting us to rethink the canons, geographies, vocabularies, and conceptual frames that principally organize eighteenth-century literary studies.[27] Queer horizons extend alternative methods. In this way, we hope to build on Lowe's interventions by channeling scholars such as Ariella Aïsha Azoulay, who urges us to attend to alternative forms of life, which exist as "persisting and repressed forms and formations of being in the world, shaped by and through intimate knowledge of the world and its secrets, of its multiple natural, spiritual, political, and cosmological taxonomies preserved and transmitted over generations."[28] Queer histories are often secret, hidden, implicit. They thus urge us to unsettle dominant regimes of legibility and visibility in the archive.

The essays in this collection cultivate intimacy as method by addressing how varied cultural formations and lived experiences become differential entry points into representations of race, gender, and sexuality in the archive. Indeed, intimacy in this volume often arises from messy proximities to borders and boundaries— the tactile and sensuous lines between skin and air, water and soil, human and nonhuman bodies, nations and empires, temporal periods and chronological experiences. The essays featured here turn to encounters like these to unsettle imperial systems and illuminate ways of living otherwise, a project we see recast in *Welcoming the Newcomers*. Contributors to *Unsettling Sexuality* thus consider manifold formations of eighteenth-century gender and sexuality but at scale, shaped by intimate histories, geographies, cultures, and contacts. For this, we draw from historians and literary scholars working in queer of color critique, Black feminist studies, and Native American and Indigenous studies.[29] As Leanne Betasamosake Simpson (Michi Saagiig) argues from the perspective of Nishnaabeg thought: "Heteropatriarchy isn't just about exclusion of certain Indigenous bodies, it is about the destruction of the intimate relationships that make up our nations, and the fundamental systems of ethics based on values of individual sovereignty and self-determination. The more destruction our intimate relationships carry, the more destruction our political systems carry, and the less we are able to defend and protect our lands, and the easier it is to dispossess."[30] Acknowledging how and where eighteenth-century archives are complicit in these dispossessive maneuvers— and where queer and trans figures imagine liberatory alternatives—is part of the path this collection pursues.

While scholars who work in historically inflected fields might contemn these methods as presentist or ahistorical, the praxis at work intercedes in Western understandings of time, which principally center a linear *telos* of historical "progress" that refuses non-Western, non-European, and Indigenous formations of embodiment, kinship, and intimacy. Katherine Binhammer contends that the "long eighteenth century" that frames this collection reflects a vexed colonial periodization that frequently elides global Indigenous epistemologies—a decolonial provocation that we aim to take up.[31] We also heed Kwakwaka'wakw scholar Sarah Hunt, who reminds us that "the potential for Indigenous ontologies to unsettle dominant ontologies can be easily neutralized as a triviality, a case study, or a trinket, as powerful institutions work as self-legitimating systems that uphold broader systems of (neo)colonial power."[32] Essays by Shelby Johnson and Ula Lukszo Klein, for instance, engage with methods in Native American and Indigenous studies to address settler colonialism as a structure that violently elides non-Western gender rituals and imposes narrow norms on lived Indigenous subjectivities.

Transhistorical methods are not limited to interventions in Indigenous studies, of course. Scholars in early modern and eighteenth-century sexuality studies have improvised historically supple and "unhistorical" methods, including David Halperin in *One Hundred Years of Homosexuality* (1989) and, more recently, Susan S. Lanser in *The Sexuality of History: Modernity and the Sapphic* (2014) and Heather Love in *Underdogs: Social Deviance and Queer Theory* (2021). In this vein, Carolyn Dinshaw argues that placing texts in promiscuous, transhistorical proximities can illuminate new possibilities for approaching the past—"a queer touch across time"—while warning that this method may also only reveal what we desire to know about queer lives and pleasures in the past.[33] Ziona Kocher's essay, to this point, unsettles received historical methods to re-encounter eighteenth-century literature by taking up Frances Sheridan's epistolary novel *The Memoirs of Miss. Sidney Bidulph* (1761) as a text that challenges chrononormative structures reflected in Sidney's intense desire to return to a time before her unhappy marriages. In particular, Kocher argues that Sidney's asexual yearning for union with her friend Cecelia counters heteronormative orientations to time and conjugality.

Turning to transhistorical methods to illuminate queer possibilities and pleasures is not without risks. From the perspective of Black Studies, we take seriously Saidiya Hartman's contention that the subjunctive—"a grammatical mood that expresses doubt, wishes, and possibilities"—can enable a speculative practice that she names "critical fabulation," which reflects an intention "both to tell an impossible story and to amplify the impossibility of its telling."[34] In this sense, "critical fabulation" must "reckon with the precarious lives which are visible only in the moment of their disappearance," but can never entirely repair archival aporia.[35] Hortense Spillers and Christina Sharpe likewise call us to recognize how eighteenth-century archives are constitutively shaped by violence.[36] Recent scholarship on the Black Atlantic, as in work by Jessica Marie Johnson,

Jennifer L. Morgan, and Alexis Pauline Gumbs, among others, has taken up Black women's improvisations of resistant intimacy across time and space, thus modeling methods for reading within these aporia for Black feminist, queer, and trans thinking.[37] Critics like Omise'eke Natasha Tinsley, for example, have turned to "queer imaginings of the Middle Passage" to recover how "unnamed rebellions took place . . . in *erotic* resistance, in interpersonal relationships enslaved Africans formed with those imprisoned and oozing beside them."[38] For many of our contributors, our positionalities as queer and trans scholars and/or as scholars of color differently inflect our efforts to model speculative engagements with the long eighteenth century, and we draw from citational conversations across an array of fields to pursue these reparative undertakings.

Intimacy as method animates not only our attention to lived experiences for queer and trans figures of the long eighteenth century but also to the lived environments within which decolonial struggle occurred (and is occurring still). Given histories of colonial expansion and settlement at work across eighteenth-century trade networks and global connections, several contributors explore the imbrication of gender and sexuality within the intimacies of environments. They build on scholars like Greta LaFleur, who describes discourses of "environmental sexuality" whereby Euro-American scientific writing and fiction came to portray racial and sexual difference as the products of discrete ecologies and climates—discourses, in other words, within which white settlers became vulnerable to degeneration.[39] Chapters by M. A. Miller and Tess Given, in concert, explore differently desired forms of life in Caribbean settings that countered colonial efforts to bound intimacy, specifically by interrogating how the homogenizing presumptions of Western settlement and plantation projects encountered human and more-than-human resistances.

In these and other interventions, *Unsettling Sexuality* is influenced by intellectuals such as Melissa K. Nelson (Métis and Anishinaabe), who engages with "eco-erotic" practices whereby Indigenous oral traditions, among other non-European traditions, model alternative reproductive processes—what Nelson calls "a messy, visceral, eco-erotic boundary-crossing entanglement of difference that can engender . . . a lived environmental ethic."[40] Furthermore, scholars in Black studies, such as Sylvia Wynter, Katherine McKittrick, and Tiffany Lethabo King, have traced modes of Black "being human" habituated within "an unstable ecozone and nervous landscape," where human and nonhuman persons encountered each other in new, tense, and complicated formations.[41] The intersections of new materialism, environmental humanities, and gender and sexuality studies thus generate invaluable perspectives on how subjugated human and nonhuman figures cultivated disordered worlds queerly recalcitrant to eighteenth-century colonial aspirations for managed lands and bodies.

Above all, what different essays in *Unsettling Sexuality* strive to do is center queer and sexual creativity, intimacy, and joy, even while acknowledging and tracing how imperial violence and settler colonialism sought to govern and surveil queer persons (and especially Black, Brown, and Indigenous queer and Two-Spirit

INTRODUCTION

persons). This is the impossible story at the heart of this collection's improvisation of intimate methods. Chow and DeBaecke, for instance, read the anonymously published *The Woman of Colour* (1808) to interrogate the sociocultural and literary conditions that made happiness an exclusive attainment largely unavailable to mixed-race women. Moreover, Cailey Hall engages with contemporary queer historical romances set in the long eighteenth century as counternarratives to established conventions in which queer relationships uniformly ended in tragedy. Too often in eighteenth-century studies the emphasis is on mourning—on grieving Black enslavement, Indigenous displacement, anti-queer and transphobic violence—but criticism that ends with a metonymic association of queerness with death or loss may only reinscribe these correspondences and deny other possibilities for queer being and belonging in myriad geographies of the eighteenth century. We seek here not rose-colored optimism but also not a mind-numbing nihilism; if such a happy medium is possible, *Unsettling Sexuality* reaches for it. The volume's critical emphasis on a multitude of lives and pleasures ultimately reflects variations on what Deborah Miranda (Chumash/Esselen), writing of the difficulties of excavating Indigenous intimacies from settler archives, calls an "indigenous reading" praxis: a method "that enriches Native lives with meaning, survival, and love."[42] Broadly, *Unsettling Sexuality* turns to intimacy—a way of placing archives, temporalities, persons, communities, and ecologies into promiscuous proximity—to reimagine the methods we assemble and mobilize.

CHAPTER OVERVIEW

The essays in this collection are organized into four categories, which reflect new directions in canons, frameworks, and methods in eighteenth-century gender and sexuality studies: "Gender Nonconformity: Embodiment, Sociality, and Politics," "Novel Intimacies," "Queer Ecologies and Cartographies," and "Racializing Affect, Queering Temporality."

The essays in "Gender Nonconformity: Embodiment, Sociality, and Politics" employ different entry points, including Indigenous and Persian studies, for analyzing Anglo-American eighteenth-century iterations of masculinity and gender-nonconformity as challenges to dominant configurations of social and political affiliation. In chapter 1, "Transgender Citizenship and Settler Colonialism in Aphra Behn's *The Widow Ranter*," Klein draws on formulations of Indigenous nonbinary and transgender identities in Native scholarship to take up Aphra Behn's *The Widow Ranter: or, The History of Bacon in Virginia* (1676) as a drama that, in Behn's depictions of cross-dressing Indigenous and British characters, foregrounds the imbrication of imperial whiteness and queerness with the imperatives of settler expansion.[43] Klein suggests that terms like "cross-dressing" are colonialist projections that cannot fully account for Indigenous transgender routines and rituals.

In chapter 2, "Samson Occom, the Public Universal Friend, and a Queer Archive of the Elsewhere," Johnson reads Mohegan pastor Samson Occom's encounters with white nonbinary preacher the Public Universal Friend, which were facilitated by the ongoing legacies of Indigenous land theft. Johnson argues that Occom and the Friend embraced, in different ways, queer intimacies at odds with emerging early American norms of gender and sexuality, and these norms were significantly shaped by histories of population displacement and resettlement in the aftermath of the American Revolution. Their experiences of communal displacement and hope for new organizations of social life inflect the queerness of their writings, what Johnson denotes a "queer archive of the elsewhere."

In chapter 3, "Refashioning Masculinity in Regency England: Female Fashions Inspired by the Persian Envoy Mirza Abul Hassan Khan and His Circassian Wife," Humberto Garcia turns to Mirza Abul Hassan Khan, envoy extraordinary and minister plenipotentiary from the Qajar ruler Fath 'Ali Shah. Tracing reactions to Abul Hassan in British periodical culture of the day, Garcia argues that Abul Hassan's fashionable clothing unsettles and restructures heteronormative sexualities in Regency England in such a way that fashion came to entail a normative pull. In this way, Garcia trenchantly reorients our understanding of how Islamicate fashion could both signify gender nonnormativity and recalibrate Regency formations of heterosociality in Britain.

In the essays included in "Novel Intimacies," Ziona Kocher and Cailey Hall engage with critical conversations on epistolary fiction and romance novels, respectively, to trace transhistorical orientations to intimacy improvised in both eighteenth- and twenty-first-century novels. In chapter 4, "'My sister, my friend, my ever beloved': Queer Friendship and Asexuality in *The Memoirs of Miss Sidney Bidulph*," Ziona Kocher considers the asexual potential of both the themes and form of Frances Sheridan's epistolary novel. Kocher argues that the novel presents a critique of compulsory sexuality that hinges on Sidney's failed attempts at marriage while her relationship with her closest friend Cecilia illustrates the potential joy of queer friendship. Though Sidney is unable to pursue a life outside of marriage, the centrality of her relationship with Cecilia highlights possibilities beyond compulsory sexuality, a structure that proves destructive not only to the novel's protagonist but also to numerous other characters within the text.

Chapter 5, Cailey Hall's "Redefining the Archive in Queer Historical Romance Novels," pivots to contemporary reimaginings of eighteenth- and nineteenth-century intimacies in recent queer romance novels. Hall considers Olivia Waite's Regency romance novel, *The Lady's Guide to Celestial Mechanics* (2019), as an exemplum of the recent turn to queer historical romance within romance publishing. For Hall, Waite's novel offers a counternarrative to the assumption that queer historical love stories are inevitably tragic and, in doing so, meditates on the affordances and limits of reparative archival practices that inflect romance novels' speculative dimensions.

Essays in "Queer Ecologies and Cartographies" turn to Caribbean settings—real and imagined—to survey how ecologies and nonhuman beings shaped intimacy in the long eighteenth century. The two chapters draw from recent scholarship in ecocriticism on the imbrication of race and sexuality in imperial projects to suggest how eighteenth-century texts are central to the crises of our environmental present. Chapter 6, M. A. Miller's "Matters of Intimacy: *The Sugar-Cane*'s Asexual Ecologies" turns to vegetal and soil life in and beyond James Grainger's georgic poem *The Sugar Cane* (1764) to explore forms of life that exceed and transgress efforts to manage their reproduction. By tracking the porous entanglements between soil and "the proliferating scales of life and vitality that soil attends to," Miller "unearth[s] responses and resistances to sexualities of containment produced by colonial acts of enclosure during the Plantationocene."

Following, chapter 7, Tess J. Given's "Fantasy Maps and Projective Fictions," begins with a reading of the fictionalized map that prefaces Daniel Defoe's *Robinson Crusoe* (1719). Using this map as an entry point that opens a gap between projection and perception, Given explores the ways in which mapping projects necessarily have an embedded "erotics of non-relation" that occlude the possibility of relations as a form of colonial power. These erotics, Given argues, shape how relations are captured, spatialized, and made "real."

Our last section, "Racializing Affect, Queering Temporality," demonstrates that attention to race, gender, and sexuality must account for differential affects and temporalities as they appear throughout eighteenth-century archives. Chapter 8, "Dark and Delayed Labor: Sex Work and Racialized Time in Eighteenth-Century London" by Nour Afara, reshapes considerations of sex work in the eighteenth century, which have heretofore prioritized white women and eclipsed intersectional discussions of racialized sex work. Afara conceptualizes idleness as a racialized affect to recover evidence of dark-skinned sex workers in the fictionalized collection of memoirs *The Histories of Some of the Penitents in the Magdalen-House, as Supposed to be Related by Themselves* (1760). This archival work reveals important connections between eighteenth-century understandings of racialization and what were considered valid or invalid types of work and embodiment.

Chapter 9, Jeremy Chow and Riley DeBaecke's "Unsettling Happiness: Blackness, Gender, and Affect in *The Woman of Colour* and Its Media Afterlives," considers how the marriage plot reinforces formations of happiness that are whitewashed through hetero-domesticity. Chow and DeBaecke read Olivia Fairfield as one model to think through "Blackened happiness," which, in its attempt to unsettle whitewashed notions of happiness, accounts for an intersectional experience by Black and mixed-race women in which happiness exists outside of or in contradistinction to the marriage plot. They trace this pattern and its complications further in Amma Asante's *Belle* (2013) to reveal alternative horizons for racialized affects, especially happiness, that are constructed along racial and sexual vertices in the Caribbean and England.

Eugenia Zuroski's "Coda: Eighteenth-Century Longing" concludes this collection by returning to Muñoz and the prospect of queer utopianism. In conversation with Theodor Adorno and Ernst Bloch on the utopian imaginaries of sausage, this coda-*cum*-conclusion proposes a series of questions that invite us to consider what is at stake in a project such as this one, in which collective (be) longing is proffered and established. Has, Zuroski asks, the long eighteenth century now—decades into the twenty-first century—become too long, and how might any attempt at coherence reflect a neo-imperial impulse at enclosure? For Zuroski, queer utopianism is one such skeleton key through which we might resist the territorialization of the long eighteenth century in favor of indeterminacy, unsettling, and queer longing.

In seeking to extricate whiteness from queer studies and reimagine it while also accounting for how decolonial reckonings do not exist on the fringe, *Unsettling Sexuality* intends to establish new directions in queer, sexuality, and decolonial eighteenth-century studies by examining their mutually informative crosshatchings. Through their jointure, new horizons can flourish, and this volume sets the stage for innovation, ingenuity, interdisciplinary, and insights aplenty. By moving toward and upon these queer horizons, this collection aspires, as Ahmed teaches us, to become collective—not as a homogenous monolith but rather as a fluid body leaching out for connection and alternative paths of contact.

NOTES

1. Sara Ahmed, *Living a Feminist Life* (Durham, NC: Duke University Press, 2017), 15.

2. José Esteban Muñoz, *Cruising Utopia: The Then and There of Queer Futurity* (New York: New York University Press, 2019), 22.

3. "Two-Spirit" was adopted in 1990 at the Native American/First Nations Gay and Lesbian Conference in Winnipeg, and rejects previous terms projected onto Native cultures by settler anthropologists. Qwo-Li Driskill, Chris Finley, Brian Joseph Gilley, and Scott Lauria Morgensen argue in their introduction to *Queer Indigenous Studies: Critical Interventions in Theory, Politics, and Literature* (Tucson: University of Arizona Press, 2011), 1–28, that Two-Spirit is not a stable referent for "authentic" Native culture but "was designed as a logic and method to confound such desires. Displacing a prior generation's interest in anthropological authority, *Two-Spirit* became frustrating, complicating, and exciting by shifting the terms on which knowledge of Indigenous people would be produced" (17).

4. Tiffany Lethabo King, *The Black Shoals: Offshore Formations of Black and Native Studies* (Durham, NC: Duke University Press, 2019), 3, 78.

5. Muñoz, *Cruising Utopia*, 25.

6. Chris Mounsey, ed., *Developments in the Histories of Sexualities: In Search of the Normal, 1600–1800* (Lewisburg, PA: Bucknell University Press, 2015); Robin Runia, ed., *The Future of Feminist Eighteenth-Century Scholarship* (New York: Routledge, 2017); Jolene Zigarovich, ed., *TransGothic in Literature and Culture* (New York: Routledge, 2017); Greta LaFleur, Masha Raskolnikov, and Anna Klosowska, eds., *Trans Historical: Gender Plurality before the Modern* (Ithaca, NY: Cornell University Press, 2021).

7. Sara Ahmed, *On Being Included: Racism and Diversity in Institutional Life* (Durham, NC: Duke University Press, 2012), 13.

8. Jonathan Goldberg and Madhavi Menon, "Queering History," *PMLA* 120, no. 5 (Oct. 2005): 1608–1617; Valerie Traub, *Thinking Sex with the Early Moderns* (Philadelphia: University of Pennsylvania Press, 2015); Jen Manion, *Female Husbands: A Trans History* (Cambridge: Cambridge University Press, 2020); and Abdulhamit Arvas, "Performing and Desiring Gender Variance in the Ottoman Empire," in *Trans Historical: Gender Plurality Before the Modern*, ed. Anna Klosowska, Masha Raskolnikov, and Greta LaFleur (Ithaca, NY: Cornell University Press, 2021), 160–177.

9. Mark Rifkin, *Settler Common Sense: Queerness and Everyday Colonialism in the American Renaissance* (Minneapolis: University of Minnesota Press, 2014), 3–6. For a discussion of "common sense" in eighteenth-century British philosophy, especially the work of Jeremy Bentham, see Carrie D. Shanafelt, *Uncommon Sense: Jeremy Bentham, Queer Aesthetics, and the Politics of Taste* (Charlottesville: University of Virginia Press, 2022), 11–15, 21–24.

INTRODUCTION

10. Elizabeth Freeman, *Besides You in Time: Sense Methods and Queer Sociabilities in the American Nineteenth Century* (Durham, NC: Duke University Press, 2019), 12–13.

11. Freeman, *Besides You in Time*, 15.

12. Ahmed, *Living a Feminist Life*, 15.

13. Katherine McKittrick, *Dear Science and Other Stories* (Durham, NC: Duke University Press, 2021), 26.

14. Sal Nicolazzo, "Another 1987, or Whiteness and Eighteenth-Century Studies," *Eighteenth-Century Fiction* 33, no. 2 (Winter 2021): 233–238 (234). See also Roderick Ferguson, *Aberrations in Black: Toward a Queer of Color Critique* (Minneapolis: University of Minnesota Press, 2003).

15. Megan Peiser, "We Have Always Been Here: Indigenous Scholars in/and Eighteenth-Century Studies," *Eighteenth-Century Fiction* 33, no. 2 (Winter 2021): 181–188.

16. Jeremy Chow, "Queer Rage against the (Eighteenth-Century) Machine," *Eighteenth-Century Fiction* 34, no. 3 (Spring 2022): 333–346 (344).

17. See Ta-Nahisi Coates on the grotesque masquerade of good intentions, which exonerates hegemonic whiteness and its oppression of people of color, especially Black and enslaved descendants in the United States. Coates, *Between the World and Me* (New York: Spiegel and Grau, 2015), 33–34.

18. Scott Lauria Morgensen, *Spaces between Us: Queer Settler Colonialism and Indigenous Decolonization* (Minneapolis: University of Minnesota Press, 2011), 1.

19. Catherine E. Walsh and Walter Mignolo, *On Decoloniality: Concepts, Analytics, and Praxis* (Durham, NC: Duke University Press, 2018), 3. On decolonial methods and Indigenous studies, see also Linda Tuhiwai Smith, *Decolonizing Methodologies: Research and Indigenous Peoples*, 2nd ed. (London: Zed Books, 2012), 12–13; and Zoe Todd, "An Indigenous Feminist's Take on the Ontological Turn: 'Ontology' Is Just Another Word for Colonialism," *Journal of Historical Sociology* 29, no. 1 (March 2016): 4–22.

20. María Lugones, "Toward a Decolonial Feminism," *Hypatia* 25, no. 4 (Fall 2010): 742–759.

21. Mark Rifkin, *When Did Indians Become Straight?* (Oxford: Oxford University Press, 2010), 36.

22. Aníbal Quijano, "Coloniality of Power, Eurocentrism, and Latin America," trans. Michael Ennis, *Nepantla: Views from the South* 1, no. 3 (Summer 2000): 533–580.

23. On recovering African American queer and trans lives, see Saidiya Hartman, *Wayward Lives, Beautiful Experiments: Intimate Histories of Social Upheaval* (New York: W.W. Norton, 2019). On the sometimes fraught intersections between Indigenous and queer studies, see Jodi Byrd, "What's Normative Got to Do with It?: Toward Indigenous Queer Relationality," *Social Text* 38, no. 4 (December 2020): 105–123; and Elizabeth Povinelli, *Empire of Love: Toward a Theory of Intimacy, Genealogy, and Carnality* (Durham, NC: Duke University Press, 2006). For queer Middle Eastern and South Asian studies and the recuperation of queer and trans lives, see Gayatri Gopinath, *Impossible Desires: Queer Diasporas and South Asian Public Cultures* (Durham, NC: Duke University Press, 2005); Joseph Massad, *Desiring Arabs* (Chicago: Chicago University Press, 2007); and Afsaneh Najmabadi, *Professing Selves: Transsexuality and Same-Sex Desire in Contemporary Iran* (Durham, NC: Duke University Press, 2013). These scholars represent vital citational nodes for this collection.

24. Eve Tuck and K. Wayne Yang, "Decolonization Is Not a Metaphor," *Decolonization: Indigeneity, Education & Society* 1, no. 1 (Spring 2012): 1–40.

25. Lisa Lowe, *The Intimacies of Four Continents* (Durham, NC: Duke University Press, 2015), 17.

26. Lisa Lowe, "Response: Intimacies as Method," *Eighteenth-Century Fiction* 34, no. 2 (Winter 2022): 207–213 (207).

27. Lowe, "Response"; and Elizabeth Freeman, *Time Binds: Queer Temporalities, Queer Histories* (Durham, NC: Duke University Press, 2010).

28. Ariella Aïsha Azoulay, *Potential History: Unlearning Imperialism* (New York: Verso Books, 2019), 388.

29. For queer embodiments and intimacies and early African American literature, see C. Riley Snorton, *Black on Both Sides: A Racial History of Trans Identity* (Minneapolis:

University of Minnesota Press, 2017); Brigitte Fielder, *Relative Races: Genealogies of Interracial Kinship in Nineteenth-Century America* (Durham, NC: Duke University Press, 2020); and Elahe Haschemi Yekani, *Familial Feeling: Entangled Tonalities in Early Black Atlantic Writing and the Rise of the British Novel* (London: Palgrave Macmillan, 2021). For early Indigenous Two-Spirit embodiments and relations, see Deborah Miranda, "Extermination of the *Joyas*: Gendercide in Spanish California," *GLQ: A Journal of Gay and Lesbian Studies* 16, no. 1–2 (April 2010): 253–284; Rifkin, *When Did Indians Become Straight?*; Kai Pyle, "Naming and Claiming: Recovering Ojibwe and Plains Cree Two-Spirit Language," *TSQ: Transgender Quarterly* 5, no. 4 (November 2018): 574–588; Leanne Betasamosake Simpson, *As We Have Always Done: Indigenous Freedom through Radical Resurgence* (Minneapolis: University of Minnesota Press, 2017), 119–144; and Qwo-Li Driskill, *Asegi Stories: Cherokee Queer and Two-Spirit Memory* (Tucson: University of Arizona Press, 2016). For a theorization of colonial gender, see María Lugones, "The Coloniality of Gender," in *The Palgrave Handbook of Gender and Development*, ed. W. Harcourt (London: Palgrave Macmillan, 2016), 13–33.

30. Simpson, *As We Have Always Done*, 123.

31. Katherine Binhammer, "Is the Eighteenth Century a Colonizing Temporality?" *Eighteenth-Century Fiction* 33, no. 2 (Winter 2020–2021): 199–204.

32. Sarah Hunt, "Ontologies of Indigeneity: The Politics of Embodying a Concept," *Cultural Geographies* 21, no. 1 (January 2014): 27–32 (30).

33. Carolyn Dinshaw, *Getting Medieval: Sexualities and Communities Pre- and Postmodern* (Durham, NC: Duke University Press, 1999), 3. For an early American context, see also Jordan Alexander Stein, "American Literary History and Queer Temporalities," *American Literary History* 25, no. 4 (Winter 2013): 855–869.

34. Saidiya Hartman, "Venus in Two Acts," *Small Axe* 12, no. 2 (June 2008): 1–14 (11).

35. Hartman, "Venus in Two Acts," 12.

36. Hartman, "Venus in Two Acts," 12–13; Hortense J. Spillers, "Mama's Baby, Papa's Maybe: An American Grammar Book," in *Black, White, and in Color: Essays on American Literature and Culture* (Chicago: University of Chicago Press, 2003), 203–229; and Christina Sharpe, *In the Wake: On Blackness and Being* (Durham, NC: Duke University Press, 2016).

37. See Jennifer L. Morgan, *Reckoning with Slavery: Gender, Kinship, and Capitalism in the Early Black Atlantic* (Durham, NC: Duke University Press, 2021), 6–10; Jessica Marie Johnson, *Wicked Flesh: Black Women, Intimacy, and Freedom in the Atlantic World* (Philadelphia: University of Pennsylvania Press, 2020), 8–10; and Alexis Pauline Gumbs, *Spill: Scenes of Black Feminist Fugitivity* (Durham, NC: Duke University Press, 2016).

38. Omise'eke Natasha Tinsley, "Black Atlantic, Queer Atlantic," *GLQ: A Journal of Gay and Lesbian Studies* 14, no. 2–3 (June 2008): 191–215 (198).

39. Greta LaFleur, *The Natural History of Sexuality in Early America* (Baltimore, MD: Johns Hopkins University Press, 2018), 60.

40. Melissa K. Nelson, "Getting Dirty: The Eco-Eroticism of Women in Indigenous Oral Literatures," *Critically Sovereign: Indigenous Gender, Sexuality, and Feminist Studies*, ed. Joanne Barker (Durham, NC: Duke University Press, 2017), 229–260 (232).

41. For Black "human-being," see Sylvia Wynter and Katherine McKittrick, *On Being Human as Praxis* (Durham, NC: Duke University Press, 2014); King, *The Black Shoals*, 78, 114; and Zakiyyah Iman Jackson, *Becoming Human: Matter and Meaning in an Anti-Black World* (New York: New York University Press, 2020), 1–8.

42. Miranda, "Extermination of the *Joyas*," 256.

43. On the imbrications of settler colonialism with whiteness and queer embodiments, see Morgensen, *Spaces Between Us*, 11–13; and Jasbir K. Puar, *Terrorist Assemblages: Homonationalism in Queer Times*, 2nd ed. (Durham, NC: Duke University Press, 2017), 39–40.

PART I

Gender Nonconformity

EMBODIMENT, SOCIALITY,
AND POLITICS

CHAPTER 1

Transgender Citizenship and Settler Colonialism in Aphra Behn's *The Widow Ranter*

Ula Lukszo Klein

Set in Jamestown, Virginia, Aphra Behn's tragicomedy *The Widow Ranter; or, the History of Bacon in Virginia* was her last play, produced posthumously, in 1689. Framed by Bacon's Rebellion, a resistance movement against the British colonial administration led by Nathaniel Bacon, *The Widow Ranter* portrays the fraught alliances forged between dissident English settlers and members of Indigenous communities surrounding Jamestown, including the Pamunkey, Powhatan, and Mattaponi nations. The two principal characters—the Widow Ranter, an English settler, and Semernia, an Indigenous woman—cross-dress to participate in the military skirmishes that characterized Bacon's Rebellion and to engage in erotic pursuits. As with Behn's earlier *Oroonoko* (1688), *The Widow Ranter* is contradictory, its investments unclear, offering an implicit critique of imperial violence against the racialized Indigenous Other, and yet unable to disavow the imperial project.[1]

This chapter attempts to unpack the queer potentialities and trans capacities of the play while also keeping in mind that the greatest opportunities for the queer and trans characters of the play lie with the settler characters who find ways of playing with gender norms in the New World setting.[2] Whether the play endorses that result or presents it rather as the reprehensible yet logical outcome of colonial violence, though, is ambiguous. The play posits a new kind of royal subject in the British colonies: that of the transgender citizen, who embodies masculine strength and courage with the feminine ability to reproduce once the local Powhatan Indigenous community—represented in the play as a racial double—is eliminated.[3] Thus is transgender capacity racialized in the New World context, giving rise to imperial genders reliant on racial and national homogeny, even as the play endorses and comically exploits cross-class movement.[4] Further, the transgender *citizen*, as opposed to subject, foreshadows other formations of citizenship predicated on whiteness, Europeanness, and a compulsory heterosexuality that both rely on and obscure queer and trans identity formations.[5]

Scholarship on the play has burgeoned in the last fifteen years, with much of it examining how the play functions as a mirror for England or as an exploration of Behn's royalist sympathies.[6] Queer and trans readings of Behn's oeuvre have attempted to unravel some of what makes her works so potentially subversive and endlessly fascinating to modern readers. Scarlet Bowen, Hannah Chaskin, Jennifer Frangos, and Kirsten T. Saxton have argued for different ways to understand how Behn's works disrupt conventional understandings of sexuality and gender identity in the past while perhaps even disrupting or satirizing entire established genres and their conventions.[7] In her reading of Behn's amatory fictions, though, Saxton notes that the queer potentialities of Behn's texts are often vacated by their end: "Queer possibility . . . open[s] spaces for queer potentials that the narrative consistently forecloses."[8] Saxton finds meaning in the possibilities that the text "suggests, but cannot reach."[9] It is with this idea in mind that I turn to *The Widow Ranter* and the possibilities it holds out but also forecloses when we consider the play in terms of not only its queer possibilities but also its transgender capacity— that is, as David Getsy reminds us, as a "site where dimorphic and static understandings of gender are revealed as arbitrary and inadequate."[10]

Recent work has also emphasized the critical relevancy of trans studies to the long early modern period. Joseph Gamble has traced a trans philology to the seventeenth century with words like *transexion* and *transfeminate*; a 1656 dictionary entry for *transfeminate* defines it as "to turn from woman to man, or from one sex to another."[11] The case of Thomas/Thomasine Hall, which came before a Virginia court in 1629, has recently been revisited by both Frangos and Kathryn Wichelns as part of a conversation on how early colonial records reckoned with a person deemed "both man and woeman."[12] More broadly, though, collections of essays like *Trans Historical: Gender Plurality before the Modern* (2021), the special issue "Early Modern Trans Studies" in the *Journal for Early Modern Cultural Studies* (2019), and the special issue "Beyond the Binaries in Early America" in *Early American Studies* (2014) all point to "the persistence of gender crossings over historical time and geographical space" as part of the critical project "to historicize and assert the long-time existence of transgender people."[13] While the play's primary characters, the Widow and Semernia, are both characterized as cisgender women, assigned female at birth, who cross-dress only temporarily, current work in trans studies has opened up new ways of thinking about such transmasculine performances and how they might function as an index of trans capacity.[14]

In thinking about the queer and the trans in *The Widow Ranter*, I am consciously playing with strategic anachronism. While subjecthood was the primary way of thinking of national belonging in the seventeenth century, the word "citizen" and its meaning as both a free inhabitant of a city or urban area, as well as its denotation of a "legally recognized subject or national of a state" and "person considered in terms of his or her acceptance or fulfilment of the duties and responsibilities of a member of society" circulated at the same time.[15] According to Luc Borot, "'citizen' is anachronistic in the modern, political sense," and yet concepts of citizenship were critical to seventeenth-century English debates on property ownership, commonwealth membership, and the rise of republican ideology.[16] Although Borot does not discuss the Ranters per se, he writes about religious dissenters and Levellers, specifically, as among those citizens of England who could not see themselves as *subjects* to the king because they felt they served a higher power: God and their country.[17] Debates regarding citizenship and the concept of universal citizenship continued throughout the Interregnum, though they were never satisfactorily resolved. I argue that the modern concept of citizenship is indeed relevant to *The Widow Ranter* from this perspective, but also from the perspective of birthright citizenship, which became law in the American republic a century later. As Stephanie Degooyer explains, *Calvin's Case* of 1608 established English subjecthood for those born in Scotland after the Unification, specifically; its long-lasting effects were to lay the foundation for birthright citizenship for white citizens in the United States.[18] The successes the Widow Ranter has in Virginia are, therefore, centered around concepts of modern citizenship and national belonging not necessarily relating to subjecthood to a distant monarch.

By contrast, Semernia's Indigenous identity and subjecthood to a non-European monarch, Cavarnio, are cause for elimination from the play, which thematizes how English colonization and imperial expansion worked to establish not just Englishness but also whiteness more generally as an underlying, foundational principle of American citizenship. It is important here to note that indigeneity does not unproblematically link to "race" in today's context, as Indigenous scholars have increasingly argued for such a categorization as a colonial imposition. In many ways, in fact, the term "race" is, like citizenship, transness, or queerness, an anachronistic term; I am aware of these linguistic and cultural divergences, and I argue that *The Widow Ranter*, like *Oroonoko*, participated in defining the boundaries of race (as well as gender and national belonging) in its time. Throughout the play, Behn racializes Indigenous characters through stereotyped, exoticized representations that I discuss later. It may also be relevant to note here that, as early as 1670, Virginia law grouped Indigenous people and those of African descent together, though ostensibly they were linked together as non-Christians in opposition to Christians. A 1667 Virginia law declared that a child born of an enslaved person who was baptized into the Christian faith was still considered not free. The laws of the time, then, appear to be grappling with precisely the notion of "race" as an inborn yet somehow also undefinable (but immediately recognizable) quality that blended both national origins, cultural or religious background, as well as physical characteristics.

The power vacuum in *The Widow Ranter* is a strategic choice by Behn that enables consideration of the role of citizenship in the colonial space rather than or in addition to subjecthood. The lack of a direct representative of the English king in Virginia in the form of a governor renders subjecthood to the English crown tenuous, and English law is made to appear arbitrary when Friendly declares that Bacon's actions are "noble" and are only "criminal for want of a law to authorise them."[19] By the end of the play, although Bacon and his rebellion have been quelled and the colony corralled under the control of the Crown, both Cavarnio and Bacon—characters that the play depicts as in possession of sovereignty, as Melissa Mowry defines them—are killed.[20] Their aspirations to sovereign power expire too, and the ending of the play, with its various couplings and implied colony-building that is really also family-building, leaves the audience with a sense of a new world order predicated on white European reproduction rooted in a growing middle-class citizenry.

We might, then, consider how the play imagines settler colonial belonging in the heterotopic space of the play through transgender citizenship—that is, where persons assigned female at birth take precedence in shaping the colony's future by appropriating a transmasculine persona while retaining the ability to birth future obedient subject-citizens for the colony.[21] In proposing the notion of transgender citizenship, I propose "citizenship" as a term that encompasses both the legal conception of the word and its sociocultural elements, which together anticipate the Foucauldian concepts of biopower and biopolitics as structuring elements of modern government.[22] By extension, Semernia's plight reinforces the concept of transgender citizenship as one that is defined by settler colonist identity: her transing of gender leads to her death.

In what remains, I explore how the play posits the white-settler, middling-class, transgender citizen as a potential ideal inhabitant of the colonies whose rise comes explicitly at the expense of the racialized and exoticized Other. The play juxtaposes the desires of Semernia, an Indigenous woman involved in an adulterous romance, with those of the Englishwoman, the Widow Ranter, a former indentured servant pursuing unrequited love. Both women use cross-dressing to enter the scene of battle, rendering their stories parallel. The play's representation of cross-dressing functions to highlight the importance of gender-fluid identities to empire building. This trans doubling emphasizes the trans capacity of the play and Behn's playful approach to gender when it comes to the Widow, but the play's inability to find playfulness in the representation of Semernia renders her more noble than the Widow but also without a future in the colonies. As I argued in *Sapphic Crossings*, cross-gender performance is one type of transgender representation that, in the long eighteenth century, was often used as shorthand for same-sex desires but also for desires of freedom and mobility.[23] In the case of *The Widow Ranter*, the desires at play are not just romantic but also nationalistic, as the play considers how trans characters like the Widow and Semernia combine notions of masculine and feminine traits necessary for their survival, while also demonstrating how romantic desires and the desire for power are entangled in the colonial setting.

TRANS DOUBLING AND THE HETEROTOPIA OF ILLUSION IN *THE WIDOW RANTER*

In the play, both the Widow Ranter and Semernia dress in men's clothing to disguise themselves in the scene of battle. This trans doubling creates an opportunity for thinking about the intersections of queerness, transness, and racial fungibility.[24] Both characters also portray elements of cross-cultural characteristics. For example, the Widow smokes tobacco, even though, as Edith Snook argues, "Tobacco . . . is central to many Native American stories and sacred rituals . . . Yet, in the play, tobacco belongs only to the Settlers."[25] By contrast, Semernia is given elements of English monarchical grandeur.[26] This mixing of gender and racial characteristics is part of the play's depiction of the colony as a space of experimentation and unconventionality. Ultimately, the play is unable to sustain a space in which settlers and Indigenous people can coexist, and in a move that feels remarkably contemporary, it makes space for settler trans representation (the Widow) even as it kills off the trans person of color who is also an Indigenous woman (Semernia).[27] The play thus reinforces C. Riley Snorton's argument in *Black on Both Sides* that "the condensation of transness into the category of transgender is a racial narrative," while also epitomizing the "impasse" between Indigenous studies and queer studies that Chickasaw scholar Jodi Byrd characterizes as "an erasure that shadows the dispossessive regimes of settler colonialism that has already conditioned Indigenous presence, knowledge, and livability."[28] The queerness of works like *The Widow Ranter* and the trans capacity of the play are entwined with the discourses of imperial conquest, white supremacy, slavery, and genocide, even as its queerness and trans capacity offer moments of resistance to discourses of racial and national hegemony.

Cavarnio speaks to Bacon about his people's prior claims to the Virginia land in terms that, like Oroonoko's indictments of slavery, appear to offer such a moment of resistance: "We were monarchs once of all this spacious world, till you an unknown people landing here, distressed and ruined by destructive storms, abusing all our charitable hospitality, usurped our right, and made your friends your slaves."[29] His speech here is one such moment that initially appears to "activate an Indigenous perspective" in the play, to use Dawn Morgan's figuration.[30] However, the power of Cavarnio's claim is undercut by much of the rest of the action of the play, in which the land remains in the hands of the usurpers. Part of the complexity of *The Widow Ranter* lies in its queer failure to make good on the promises that the heterotopia of the colony and the theater hold out.[31]

Foucault's heterotopia describes a real space that is somehow also unreal; in the heterotopia, "all the other real sites that can be found within the culture, are simultaneously represented, contested and inverted."[32] And yet, *The Widow Ranter* cannot fully reject or criticize the growing European interests in defining racial and national hierarchies in which Indigenous people figure as inferior. If, as Byrd argues, the constraints of queer studies and Indigenous studies create "an assertion of de/colonial difference enacted as and for the real," then the heterotopia of the play and the trans doubling of Ranter and Semernia within it draw attention to the de/colonial difference between Indigenous women and settler women—a difference that cannot be resolved within the heterotopia of the play.[33] The Virginia colony is not a heterotopia of compensation, as Foucault theorizes colonial spaces; instead, it is the heterotopia of illusion: "Their role is to create a space of illusion that exposes every real space, all the sites inside of which human life is partitioned, as still more illusory."[34] Indeed, Behn's heterotopia reveals the illusory nature of gender and class, positing a fluid space in which to play with both, rendering the theatrical space one of experimentation and critique wherein power, social hierarchies, the law, and social structures like marriage are exposed as mere social constructs. Race and nationality, however, act as the two constants that cannot be made playful or revealed as illusory, and, in fact, the play constructs the national differences between the Indigenous and the English as racial.

Another aspect of the play's complexity and its opacity pertains to the specificity in choosing to set the action within the historical events of Bacon's Rebellion, and the changes that Behn makes to historical facts.[35] Behn's play removes Virginia governor William Berkeley from the action of the play, creating a power vacuum that the rebel Nathaniel Bacon wishes to fill. Similarly, *The Widow Ranter* portrays Bacon as a romantic hero in love with the Indian Queen Semernia. The play depicts the colonial tensions in broad strokes, eliding or omitting some of the Indigenous groups of Virginia that were involved in the conflict, such as the Doeg and the Susquehannock, but alludes to at least one group overtly, the Pamunkey, in a reference that is both historically accurate but also mired in Pocahontas mythology:[36] Semernia explains to her servant Anaria that she first met Bacon "at twelve years old—at the Paumungian court I saw this conqueror."[37] Some scholars have also drawn attention to the potential historical basis for Semernia, the Pamunkey queen Cockacoeske who served as leader of the Pamunkey from 1656 until her death and was an ally of the English Crown but also a skilled diplomat.[38] The play merges fact and allusion with fantasy and poetic license while also engaging Restoration Era theater norms and their penchant for breeches parts, which allowed for the appearance of scantily clad actresses on stage in men's clothing.[39] Taken together, the play offers up a dizzying array of gender-bending possibilities and queer desires that ultimately reinforce reproductive futurity and imperial racial hierarchies.

TRANSING GENDER, SETTLER COLONIALISM, AND THE WIDOW RANTER

Despite her small role in the grand scheme of events in the play, the Widow Ranter's role within this heterotopia of illusion is notable, as she reveals just how tenuous gender binaries are in the colony. Her cross-gender representation begins long before she dons men's clothing. She is coarse, unrefined, and given to ranting, in both the modern sense as well as in the sense of the religious dissenters, the Ranters, of the mid-1600s, whose women were often caricaturized as loud-mouthed and sexually liberated viragos.[40] When she enters the stage in Act I, Scene 3, one of the first actions she takes is to order a boy to go get her "some pipes and a bowl of punch" for "I must smoke and drink in a morning, or I am maukish all day."[41] Though "maukish" here may signal a parodic indictment of the confines of womanhood, there is much in the Widow's characterization that can be read as refusing genteel femininity: she smokes tobacco, drinks punch in the morning, swears, threatens, and is belligerent. In speaking of the man she loves, the Widow states, "I hope I shall not find that rogue Daring here, sniveling after Mrs Chrisante: if I do, by the Lord, I'll lay him thick. Pox on him, why should I love the dog."[42] Her language is brash and full of bravado even when speaking of her feelings for Daring and her fears for Daring's life, exhorting Friendly, who fights against Bacon, "Hark ye, Charles, by heaven if you kill my Daring I'll pistol you."[43]

Her aggressive masculine bluster combined with her boldness and bravery contrasts with the cowardice of many of the men of the colony, including the Justices of the Peace Timerous, Whimsey, Whiff, and Boozer. Male-bodiedness, as many texts of female soldiers in subsequent decades suggest, does not directly correlate with masculine qualities such as bravery, boldness, or patriotism.[44] The figure of the Widow epitomizes the trans capacity of the play by destabilizing gender binaries through her refusal of stereotypical feminine norms, while her butch description also has a sapphic resonance that cannot be erased by her declarations of love for Daring.

Ranter's cross-gender appearance in the battle scene further cements the play's representation of white, transmasculine citizenship in the service of settler colonialism. Ranter dresses in men's clothing to find Daring during the battle, but also to pull him away from Chrisante. She presents herself to Daring and his friend Fearless, masquerading as a lover to Chrisante. Daring is initially unaware of the trick; once Fearless explains to Daring that the lover is in fact Ranter in disguise and that she loves *him*, Daring comes around. He begins to play along, mocking Ranter while still pretending he does not recognize her. Only after teasing her into anger does Daring reveal that he knows she is the Widow and that she loves him. Daring, who only recently was sighing after Chrisante, suddenly declares his love for the Widow and persuades her to marry him immediately—without her changing back into women's clothing. He explains, "Nay, prithee, take me in the humour, while thy breeches are on—for I never liked thee half so well in petticoats."[45] His desire for her in breeches functions as a humorous critique of gender roles: for all his protestations, Daring is happy to exchange the virginal and rather boring Chrisante for the masculine virago Ranter. Later, in the final scenes of reconciliation among all parties, Ranter, who had been taken prisoner by Hazard, is returned to Daring. When Ranter complains to her love that he abandoned her "scurvily in Battel," Daring replies, "That was to see how well you cou'd shift for your self, now I find you can bear the brunt of a Campaign you are a fit Wife for a Soldier."[46] Daring's preference for a partner who is "fit" to be a soldier's mate, along with his earlier desire that Ranter remain in breeches, reinforces the idea that certain trans identities may in fact be ideal for the survival of the colony.

Ranter's eventual union with Daring, one of the heroes of the play, signals a union of competing but equally important qualities for the survival of the colony: boldness and daring, loyalty and tenderness. From another perspective, though, the Widow herself is all these things even without Daring. She embodies the ideal colonial citizen by combining masculine-coded heroism and resourcefulness with the female-bodied ability to birth children who will be future citizens of the colony, revealing how transgender citizenship is invested in reproductive futurity. The Widow survives and thrives in the American colonies. The resourceful white Englishwoman becomes, in fact, the building block of the colonies and Britain's power abroad. Moreover, the colonies, as portrayed in the play, are a dangerous space for men, who may die of disease or in battle, thus leaving their wives and daughters unprotected—or available to remarry with money to burn. Though the white women captured by Bacon's troops remind us that the colonies held dangers for women as well, Behn's play centers the conveniences and possibilities open to the white female colonists. Madame Surelove runs her own business, Chrisante's father must eventually allow her to marry the man of her choice, and the Widow has money, bad manners, and the man of her dreams. Semernia stands in stark contrast to these women, as her choices are contained by the colonial space rather than expanded by it. She must stand by her husband Cavarnio and by her people, unable to act on her passion for Bacon except when it is too late, and her actions lead to her death. In the case of Ranter, we see Saxton's argument that the queer potentials of Behn's work are "consistently foreclosed" confirmed. Ranter's status as a gender outlaw is made comic and finally neutralized by marriage to Daring, and Ranter and Daring, as surprisingly suitable partners, symbolize a middle-class settler colonist family structure built on the qualities of transgender citizenship.

TRANSING GENDER, QUEER SUBJECTS, AND SEMERNIA

The spectacle of cross-dressing by women of two different races in a colonial setting sets up a contrast between these women, whose different ultimate fates, tragic and comic, reveal who has a future in the colonies and who does not. However much lip service the play may give to Indigenous sovereignty in the form of Cavarnio's one short speech, it is impossible to overlook the stereotyped, essentializing, and exoticizing representation of Indigenous people, especially in a play where the Indigenous characters are all dead by the end. *The Widow Ranter* can be understood as a text that "discursively vacates the Indigenous from the Indigenous" in that it homogenizes disparate Indigenous groups, emphasizes stereotyped tropes of Native women who desire white men, and removes tobacco from its Indigenous context and reassigns it to the settler colonial lifestyle, as Lenape scholar Joanne Barker describes.[47] Finally, the play erases the Indigenous woman from the action of the play doubly: first, by equating her with a white woman via cross-dressing and secondly by having her die, by the hand of her white lover, no less. The doubling of cross-dressing similarly "translates [Semernia] into normative gendered and sexed bodies" of the colonizer.[48] Mi'kmaq scholar Robbie Richardson, writing of *The Female American*, a 1767 novel that stages similar normative horizons, concludes that "The Indian-Briton [Unca Eliza] (or perhaps Briton-Indian) of *The Female American* does not function in a way meant to appropriate the virtues of the Indians, but rather to introduce European virtue among them."[49] Notably, *The Widow Ranter* assigns noble European virtues to Cavarnio and Semernia as part of their role as King and Queen of their people; there is very little "Indian" about them to begin with. According to Rebecca Lush, "Behn even attempts to portray a polyvocal perspective; however, the Indians of Behn's play merely ventriloquize English colonial ideas despite the significant sections of dialogue assigned to them."[50] The play merges European class-based virtues into the colonial context to create characters whose deaths, like those of Oroonoko and Imoinda, are tragic because of the characters' status but also because of the inevitability of their deaths.

Like Ranter, Semernia also appears in men's clothing in the second half of the play to enter the scene of battle in disguise. For Semernia, though, cross-dressing leads to her demise.[51] Dressed as an "Indian man" along with her maid and several other of her people, she attempts to flee the English, only to have her guards surprised by Bacon and his men. Unlike the Widow, Semernia declares that she is not war-like and "ha[s] no Amazonian fire about [her]."[52] Yet, when the Indian men with her declare they will shoot poison arrows at Bacon, Semernia, who cannot stand the thought of Bacon's dying, runs into the fray, shouting, "Hold, hold, I do command ye."[53] She is courageous—but only when the life of her lover is on the line. The stage directions inform us that subsequently, "Bacon flies on them as they shoot and miss him, and fights like a Fury, and wounds the Queen in the disorder."[54] Semernia's masculine disguise is partly responsible for her death even as it reminds us, however briefly, of the fluidity of gender roles and the trans capacity of the play.

At the same time, though, the word "Amazonian" conjures up stereotyped, exoticized accounts of Indigenous women by white imperialists of earlier decades. As Sydnee Wagner notes, early English reports from the Americas described "the Amazonian cannibal woman [as] a transmasculine figure."[55] Sir Walter Raleigh's 1596 account of *The Discoverie of Guiana* presents "Amazonian cannibal women [as] gender-deviant as well as fierce, savage, and hypersexual; as such, they were entirely outside the ideals of white femininity."[56] Such characterizations of Indigenous women were common; Byrd argues that "the Indigenous is always already queer to the normative settler," and Qwo-Li Driskill explains that "within dominant European worldviews *all* Cherokees were characterized as gender-nonconforming and sexually deviant."[57] What makes Behn's representation of Semernia so striking, then, is that Semernia is so entirely *inside* the ideals of white femininity with her focus on honorable behavior and language of a much higher register than that of Ranter, her stage double. Thus, while the play can be read as "part of the work of recovering transhistoricity" and specifically its nonwhite representations, it also reminds us of Snorton's argument that transness is always already a racialized category.[58] Semernia's transgender citizenship equals death, as she best serves the imperial project in her non-being.

Semernia's death contrasts starkly with the Widow's happy ending. In many ways, her fate functions as synecdoche for the fate of a whole race caught in the crossfire of empire and the violence of colonization while clearly forming a component of the canon of literature that embraces the "vanishing Indian" trope. The play's ending suggests that Indigenous people and cross-racial romance must die or be eliminated in order to make room for white settlers. As Margaret Ferguson puts it, "The widow and Daring acquire their license to live at the *price* of their doubles' [Semernia and Bacon's] deaths."[59] In many ways, the finale of *The Widow Ranter* is a foregone conclusion, as earlier moments in the play portray the Indigenous people as mere caricatures. It is impossible to ignore the haunting stage directions to Act IV, Scene I, that describe "a temple, with an Indian god placed upon it . . . all bow to the idol . . . the Priest and Priestesses dance about the idol, with ridiculous postures and crying (as for incantations). Thrice repeated, 'Agah Yerkin, Agah Boah, Sulen Tawarapah, Sulen Tawarapah,'" after which, Cavarnio invokes "the god of our Quiocto."[60] Suvir Kaul describes these elements of the play as "colonial fantasies [that] are designated to delineate cultural difference, but also . . . to render imaginable (and thus *manageable*) faraway places and peoples."[61] For contemporary readers and scholars, however, these stage directions suggest a deeply uninformed, exoticizing, bigoted view of Indigenous peoples and their culture on the part of the playwright.

Beyond those fantastic and offensive descriptions, Semernia's cross-dressing does not merely make her the Widow's "double"; it also eroticizes and exoticizes her as an individual, playing into Restoration era trends of attracting audiences by dressing women performers in men's clothes, while her Indigenous dress is not historically accurate.[62] The image of Anne Bracegirdle as Semernia, depicted in an exoticized manner, her light skin a stark contrast to the short, dark-skinned servants or slaves fanning her, represents an image of a sexually available feminine Indigeneity that is still acceptably English and white (see Figure 1.1). This image reminds us that the Indigenous characters in *The Widow Ranter* would have been played by English actors. The visuals of the play are a mix of stereotyped exotic qualities and barely disguised Englishness. Semernia's trans embodiment, like the overall portrayal of her indigeneity in the play, reflects imperial desires for consuming Indigenous people rendered exotic.

Transness and Reproducing Empire

As the titular character of the play, the Widow Ranter's character and story is central to the play's construction of meaning. Her ability to cross class boundaries illustrates the possibilities for a new start in the colonies for former citizens of the imperial center, while her transing gender successfully reveals how the play is attuned to the possibilities of imperial romance for those who have majoritarian attributes. In addition to emphasizing the moral characteristics necessary for a successful bi-gender colony, the play also suggests that the Widow, in particular, embodies transgender citizenship through her ability to both fight like a man and give birth to future (white) colonists. Although children do not play a central role in *The Widow Ranter*, several allusions throughout suggest one of the crucial objects to establishing imperial supremacy: the reproduction of independent, resilient, but governable subject-citizens.

Figure 1.1. A character in the play "The Widdow Ranter": Semernia, a Native American queen, with two pageboys. Mezzotint by W. Vincent. [1690?] Credit: Wellcome Collection.

The play posits the colony as a heterotopia, with its subversion of colonial leadership and cast of characters whose status bespeaks a world-upside-down mentality. Colonies often functioned as male homosocial spaces to which women needed to be imported.[63] *The Widow Ranter*, however, presents Virginia as a space inhabited by many single women (or functionally single in the case of Madame Surelove). By the end of the play, these women have been successfully matched to the "excess" men of the cosmopolitan center of the colony, second sons of impoverished upper-class families in England. These romantic relationships have a specific goal: to build the colony's economic power through successful reproduction, growing the colony's governing power.

From the beginning, the play establishes the idea that men like Friendly and Hazard will be helping themselves—and the colony—by marrying and siring children. As he urges Hazard to pursue Madame Surelove, Friendly explains, "This country wants nothing but to be peopled with a well-born race to make it one of the best colonies in the world."[64] And while his passive construction "to be peopled" obscures the process through which that will happen, his encouragement to Hazard in the very first scene of the play, his emphasis on the good (or acceptable) "breeding" among the available women, and his own focus on the possibility of financial successes in the colony paint a picture that equates reproduction of "appropriate" colonists with personal success not only for himself and his friend but also for the colony and the English empire. His use of the phrase "well-born race" again reminds us of how whiteness is becoming constructed as a racial category. The play ends on a similar note when Chrisante's father Downright blesses her union with Friendly. He consents to the union but notes to Friendly: "Here, take her young man and with her all my fortune—when I am dead, sirrah—not a groat before—unless to buy ye baby clouts."[65] Downright's refusal to bequeath his money until after his death is softened by the mention of future grandchildren, as the play reminds us at its conclusion that heterosexuality and reproductive futurity are the goal in these pairings.[66]

The deaths of Bacon and Semernia ultimately make way for an overflow of English/white heterosexuality and its consequent reproducibility. Differences of class, fortune, and rank become erased among the settler colonists, as if the play were overcompensating for its homosociality: much of the play revolves around the friendship of Friendly and Hazard, the loyalty of Daring to Bacon, the broken alliance between Bacon and Cavarnio, and the tenuous alliance of the inadequate justices of the peace. Bacon and Semernia die before consummating their love and do not reproduce in the colonies. Notably, Semernia and Cavarnio also do not mention any children in their union—their reproductive lack may be read as a consequence of a lack of sexual desire between them, or as symbolic for what the play anticipates as the impending obliteration of Indigenous societies with the continued waves of settlers. While the play ends in a way that reinforces Mark Rifkin's notion of "settler common sense," I argue that the fate of Semernia leaves a ghostly impression over the final scene, inflecting this "common sense" with a bloody pall.[67] Her transgender performance and that of the Widow cannot be separated at the end of a play in which their stories have run so clearly parallel to one another.

The reproducibility of empire is that performance's main objective, and once the Indigenous characters are purged, transgender citizenship comes to mean one thing specifically: white settler resilience combined with the ability to reproduce implicitly white, English subject-citizens for the economic benefit of the colonizer. Behn's vision of trans citizenship ends up, as much of her work likewise models, reproducing British imperialism and whiteness, and whatever possibilities for gender nonnormativity are extended by the play are safely contained by its ending.[68] The brief moments of trans embodiment highlight how only certain forms of gender crossing are permitted as part of the imperial project: they must be temporary, situated through white bodies, and put into the service of heteronormative familial relations. The homosocial bonding among settler colonists is part of settler colonialism and settler common sense, even as this bonding and heterosexual monogamy are revealed as built on a foundation of queer desires and transgender embodiments.

The transmasculine performances of Ranter and Semernia structure the transgender capacity of *The Widow Ranter*, as their cross-dressing and melding of binarized gender norms within single characters do indeed create what Getsy suggests is a "site where dimorphic and static understandings of gender are revealed as arbitrary and inadequate."[69] Within the colonial heterotopia, the gender binary is revealed as a construct that likewise pushes on the categories of race and nationality. The play exposes a far earlier understanding of transness as a racialized category by giving new meaning to Indigenous transitivity. Transitivity, which Snorton borrows from Claire Colebrook, "is the condition for what becomes known as *the* human."[70] While *The Widow Ranter* as a work is problematic, and its final erasure of Indigenous characters stereotypical to say the least, it is also true that in giving Semernia a central role, and in giving her speeches the full majesty of tragedy, Behn allows her to articulate the humanity of herself and the other Indigenous characters, however fleetingly. However, it is Semernia's transing of gender that triggers her death, her removal from the human. The play posits, to paraphrase Snorton, that indigeneity is "a condition of possibility for the modern world" while also "articulat[ing] the paradox of nonbeing."[71] In this way, as in so many others, Behn's work holds out the possibility of destabilizing gendered and racial norms before, disappointingly, foreclosing them yet again. It is perhaps this essential contradiction of the play that has made it so popular to read and study, and so impossible to stage.

NOTES

Acknowledgment: I'd like to thank the editors of the collection and the anonymous reviewers for their feedback on this essay and Emily M. N. Kugler for her assistance in editing. I'd like to thank Emily, Amanda Johnson, and Nicole Garret for feedback on an early version of this essay. I'd also like to thank my research assistant Jennifer Porter for her assistance on this project, as well as the students in Celia Barnes's fall 2020 drama course at Lawrence University for their thought-provoking questions on transness in this play. Finally, thank you to Margaret Huettl for helping me think through some of the more tangled elements of Indigenous representation in this work.

1. Jonathan Elmer, in writing about the play and *Oroonoko*, argues that "these texts are tonally hybrid and notoriously ambiguous about their values," while Srinivas Aravamudan calls *Oroonoko* "an ironic text," and I would venture to say the same of *The Widow Ranter*. Similarly, Adam Beach and Sara Eaton have also noted that the play poses a challenge for readers, as it, like *Oroonoko*, refuses any single interpretation of its aims or politics. Elmer, *On Lingering and Being Last: Race and Sovereignty in the New World* (New York: Fordham University Press, 2008), 23; Aravamudan, *Tropicopolitans: Colonialism and Agency, 1688–1804*

(Durham, NC: Duke University Press, 1999), 33; Beach, "Anti-Colonist Discourse, Tragicomedy, and the 'American' Behn," *Comparative Drama* 38, no. 2 (Summer/Fall 2004): 213–233; and Eaton, "'A Well-Born Race': Aphra Behn's 'The Widow Ranter; or The History of Bacon in Virginia' and the Place of Proximity," in *Indography: Writing the "Indian" in Early Modern England*, ed. Jonathan Gil Harris (New York: Palgrave Macmillan, 2012), 235–248.

2. I turn here to David J. Getsy's entry on "transgender capacity" in the collection on "Keywords for Transgender Studies"; I discuss my use of this term more fully in the rest of the chapter. See David J. Getsy, "Capacity," *TSQ: Transgender Quarterly* 1, no. 1–2 (May 2014): 47–49.

3. I use the term "citizen" here purposefully to highlight the coming change from subject to citizen that *The Widow Ranter*, I argue, is anticipating.

4. Jennifer Frangos argues that *The Widow Ranter* specifically reveals the "transformative power and queer potential of the early modern Atlantic world," an argument I also make about the stories of Anne Bonny and Mary Read in my article "Busty Buccaneers and Sapphic Swashbucklers on the High Seas" in *Transatlantic Women Travelers, 1688–1843*, ed. Misty Krueger (Lewisburg, PA: Bucknell University Press, 2021), 95–113. See Frangos, "The Early Modern Queer Atlantic: Narratives of Sex and Gender on New World Soil," in *The Edinburgh Companion to Atlantic Literary Studies*, ed. Leslie Elizabeth Eckel and Clare Frances Elliott (Edinburgh: Edinburgh University Press, 2016), 164–175 (163).

5. In this way, Behn's play anticipates Jasbir Puar's concept of homonationalism as elaborated in *Terrorist Assemblages: Homonationalism in Queer Times* (Durham, NC: Duke University Press, 2007).

6. See, for example, Elliott Visconsi, "A Degenerate Race: English Barbarism in Aphra Behn's 'Oroonoko' and 'The Widow Ranter,'" *English Literary History* 69, no. 3 (Fall 2002): 673–701; Jenny Hale Pulsipher, "'The Widow Ranter' and Royalist Culture in Colonial Virginia," *Early American Literature* 39, no. 1 (Spring 2004): 41–66; Melissa Mowry, "'Past Remembrance or History': Aphra Behn's 'The Widdow Ranter,' or How the Collective Lost Its Honor," *English Literary History* 79, no. 3 (Fall 2012): 597–621; and Denys Van Renen, "Reimagining Royalism in Aphra Behn's America," *Studies in English Literature, 1500–1900* 53, no. 3 (Fall 2013): 499–521.

7. See Scarlet Bowen, "Queering the Sexual Impasse in Seventeenth-Century 'Imperfect Enjoyment' Poetry," *GLQ: A Journal of Gay and Lesbian Studies* 19, no. 1 (January 2013): 31–56; Frangos, "The Early Modern Queer Atlantic," 163–175; Hannah Chaskin, "Masculinity and Narrative Voice in Aphra Behn's *Love Letters between a Nobleman and His Sister*," *Women's Writing: The Elizabethan to Victorian Period* 28, no. 1 (July 2021): 75–89; and Kirsten T. Saxton, "'[T]hat Where One Was, There Was the Other': Dreams of Queer Stories in Aphra Behn's *The History of the Nun, or, the Fair Vow-Breaker* (1689)," *Women's Writing: The Elizabethan to Victorian Period* 28, no. 2 (April 2021): 160–176.

8. Saxton, "'[T]hat Where One Was,'" 164.

9. Saxton, "'[T]hat Where One Was,'" 164.

10. Getsy, "Capacity," 47–49.

11. Joseph Gamble, "Toward a Trans Philology," *Journal for Early Modern Cultural Studies* 19, no. 4 (Fall 2019): 26–44 (26).

12. Quoted in both Frangos, "The Early Modern Queer Atlantic," 165, and Kathryn Wichelns, "From 'The Scarlet Letter' to Stonewall: Reading the 1629 Thomas(ine) Hall Case, 1978–2009," *Early American Studies* 12, no. 3 (Fall 2014): 500–523 (501).

13. Greta LaFleur, Masha Raskolnikov, and Anna Kłosowska, "Introduction: The Benefits of Being Trans Historical," in *Trans Historical: Gender Plurality Before the Modern*, ed. Greta LaFleur, Masha Raskolnikov, and Anna Kłosowska (Ithaca, NY: Cornell University Press, 2021), 1–24 (5).

14. See, for example, Susan Stryker, "Foreword," in *TransGothic in Literature in Culture*, ed. Jolene Zigarovich (New York: Routledge, 2018), xi–xvii.

15. "citizen, n. and adj.," *OED Online* (Oxford: Oxford University Press, March 2022). For more discussion on the uses of "subject" vs "citizen" in the seventeenth century, see Luc

Borot, "Subject and Citizen: The Ambiguities of the Political Self in Early Modern England," *Revue Française de Civilisation Britannique* 21, no. 1 (July 2016): 1–15.

16. Borot, "Subject and Citizen," 1–2.

17. In "'Past Remembrance or History,'" Mowry argues convincingly that Behn would have been aware of Leveller ideologies and, further, that her thoughts on sovereignty were "so nuanced and profound, it suggests a substantive intellectual engagement with mid-century radicalism" (600).

18. Stephanie Degooyer, *Before Borders: A Legal and Literary History of Naturalization* (Baltimore, MD: Johns Hopkins University Press, 2022), 40–41.

19. Behn, *The Widow Ranter*, 268. All references to *The Widow Ranter; or, the History of Bacon in Virginia* are from *Oroonoko, The Rover, and Other Works*, ed. Janet Todd (London: Penguin Books, 2003), 249–327. All references to the play will be referenced by page number, rather than act or line number. I use the modernized spellings as per this edition.

20. Mowry, "'Past Remembrance or History,'" 614.

21. I discuss my use of Foucault's concept of heterotopia more fully in subsequent paragraphs.

22. As elaborated by Michel Foucault in *The History of Sexuality, Vol. 1: An Introduction* (New York: Vintage, 1990), biopower is a theory that makes visible how political power and knowledge structures turn to biological life as a site of control, governance, and surveillance. As European nations shifted from monarchical forms of governance to increasingly complex bureaucratic institutions, attempts to control biological life became invested in educational, medical, and policing systems. Biopolitics, moreover, is a term Foucault utilizes to describe how these systemic shifts seep into and penetrate everyday life (120).

23. Ula Lukszo Klein, *Sapphic Crossings: Cross-Dressing Women in Eighteenth Century British Literature* (Charlottesville: University of Virginia Press, 2021), 10–13.

24. In "'[T]hat Where One Was,'" Saxton identifies "queer doubling" in Behn's *History of the Nun*, writing, "These doublings work structurally with other formal effects to queer gender itself, revealing the limits of hetero- cisgendered categories" (164). I extend Saxton to consider trans doubling in the Widow and Semernia's cross-dressing.

25. Edith Snook, "English Women's Writing and Indigenous Medical Knowledge in the Early Modern Atlantic World," in *A History of Early Modern Women's Writing*, ed. Patricia Phillippy (Cambridge: Cambridge University Press, 2018), 382–397 (386).

26. Rebecca M. Lush, "The Royal Frontier: Colonist and Native Relations in Aphra Behn's Virginia," in *Before the West Was West: Critical Essays on Pre 1800 Literature of the American Frontiers*, ed. Amy T. Hamilton (Lincoln: University of Nebraska Press, 2014), 130–160.

27. Trans persons of color, particularly Black trans women, are today at the highest risk of violent death in the United States of all trans and nonbinary people. According to the Human Rights Campaign (HRC), "It is clear that fatal violence disproportionately affects transgender women of color—particularly Black transgender women." See "Fatal Violence against the Transgender and Gender Non-Conforming Community in 2022," Human Rights Campaign, accessed July 28, 2023, https://www.hrc.org/resources/fatal-violence-against-the-transgender-and-gender-non-conforming-community-in-2022. Additionally, the Missing and Murdered Indigenous Women movement has brought attention to the crisis of violence facing Indigenous women both in North America and around the globe.

28. C. Riley Snorton, *Black on Both Sides: A Racial History of Trans Identity* (Minneapolis: University of Minnesota Press, 2017), 8; and Jodi A. Byrd, "What's Normative Got to Do with It?: Toward Indigenous Queer Relationality," *Social Text* 38, issue 4, no. 145 (December 2020): 105–123 (106).

29. Snorton, *Black on Both Sides*, 269.

30. Dawn Morgan, "Indigenous Perspectives in Eighteenth-Century Literature," *Eighteenth-Century Fiction* 33, no. 2 (Winter 2021): 209–219 (214).

31. Michel Foucault, "Of Other Spaces," trans. Jay Miskowiec. *Diacritics* 16, no. 1 (Spring 1986): 22–27.

32. Foucault, "Of Other Spaces," 24.

33. Byrd, "What's Normative Got to Do with It?," 105.

34. Foucault, "Of Other Spaces," 27.

35. For more information about Nathaniel Bacon and his political views, see Laura Doyle, *Freedom's Empire: Race and the Rise of the Novel in Atlantic Modernity, 1640–1940* (Durham, NC: Duke University Press, 2008), especially chapters 2 and 3. For an in-depth history of the rebellion, see James D. Rice, *Tales from a Revolution: Bacon's Rebellion and the Transformation of Early America* (Oxford: Oxford University Press, 2012).

36. For information about Bacon's Rebellion and the Indigenous groups involved, see Kathleen M. Brown, *Good Wives, Nasty Wenches, and Anxious Patriarchs: Gender, Race, and Power in Colonial Virginia* (Chapel Hill: University of North Carolina Press, 2012), 159.

37. Behn, *Widow Ranter*, 317. Heidi Hutner has read this exchange as channeling the myth of Matoaka. See Heidi Hutner, *Colonial Women: Race and Culture in Stuart Drama* (Oxford: Oxford University Press, 2001), 90–91.

38. Hutner, *Colonial Women*, 99. For more on Cockacoeske, see Martha W. McCartney, "Cockacoeske, Queen of Pamunkey: Diplomat and Suzeraine," in *Powhatan's Mantle: Indians in the Colonial Southeast*, rev. and ex. ed., eds. Gregory A. Waselkov, Peter H. Wood, and Tom Hatley (Lincoln: University of Nebraska Press, 2006), 245–249. Willow White (Métis Nation of Alberta) also gave a presentation on teaching Cockacoeske, Behn's *Widow Ranter*, and Bacon's Rebellion at the ASECS 2022 annual meeting (Pedagogy Roundtable: The Indigenous Eighteenth Century, Baltimore, MD, April 1, 2022).

39. Felicity Nussbaum discusses the popularity of breeches roles on the Restoration and eighteenth-century stage. See Nussbaum, *Rival Queens: Actresses, Performance, and the Eighteenth-Century British Theater* (Philadelphia: University of Pennsylvania Press, 2010), 195.

40. For how the Widow's personality reflects English ideas about the Ranters, a religious minority, see Mowry, "'Past Remembrance or History,'" 606.

41. Behn, *The Widow Ranter*, 265.

42. Behn, *The Widow Ranter*, 265.

43. Behn, *The Widow Ranter*, 268.

44. See Scarlet Bowen, "'The Real Soul of a Man in Her Breast: Popular Opposition and British Nationalism in Memoirs of Female Soldiers, 1740–1750,'" *Eighteenth-Century Life* 28, no. 3 (Fall 2004): 20–45.

45. Behn, *The Widow Ranter*, 310.

46. Behn, *The Widow Ranter*, 323.

47. Joanne Barker, "Introduction: Critically Sovereign," in *Critically Sovereign: Indigenous Gender, Sexuality, and Feminist Studies*, ed. Joanne Barker (Durham, NC: Duke University Press, 2017), 1–44 (7).

48. Barker, "Introduction: Critically Sovereign."

49. Robbie Richardson, *The Savage and the Modern Self: North American Indians in Eighteenth-Century British Literature and Culture* (Toronto: University of Toronto Press, 2018), 143. See also Unca Eliza Winkfield, *The Female American*, 2nd ed., ed. Michelle Burnham (Peterborough, ON: Broadview Press, 2014).

50. Lush, "The Royal Frontier," 131.

51. Semernia's cross-dressing may reflect aspects of Powhatan performances of gender and social role. Anthropologist Margaret Holmes Williamson argues that the Powhatan considered some persons "both male and female" in their navigation of social norms. Individuals assigned male at birth, for instance, might display behaviors or appearances more typical of women (such as engaging in agricultural labor or leaving long hair on the left side of the head while the other side remained shaved, typical for men). "This ambiguity of gender," she argues, "corresponds exactly to ambiguity of status; this is, a man's gender . . . was contingent on the social context in which he found himself. As a husband, he was male; as a subject, he was female to his chief's masculinity" (220). See Williamson, *Powhatan Lords of Life and Death: Command and Consent in Seventeenth-Century Virginia* (Lincoln: University of Nebraska Press, 2003).

52. Lush, "The Royal Frontier," 131.

53. Lush, "The Royal Frontier," 131.

54. Behn, *The Widow Ranter*, 317–318.

55. Sydnee Wagner, "Racing Gender to the Edge of the World: Decoding the Transmasculine Amazon Cannibal in Early Modern Travel Writing," *Journal for Early Modern Cultural Studies* 19, no. 4 (Fall 2019): 137–155 (137).

56. Wagner, "Racing Gender to the Edge of the World," 138.

57. Byrd, "What's Normative Got to Do with It," 105; and Qwo-Li Driskill, *Asegi Stories: Cherokee Queer and Two-Spirit Memory* (Tucson: University of Arizona Press, 2016), 41.

58. Wagner, "Racing Gender," 137.

59. Margaret W. Ferguson, *Dido's Daughters: Literacy, Gender, and Empire in Early Modern England and France* (Chicago: University of Chicago Press, 2003), 354.

60. Behn, *The Widow Ranter*, 299. Janet Todd discusses the difficulty of editing a text like *The Widow Ranter* by drawing attention to this reference to Quiocto and the challenge in knowing whether Behn knew of the Quiocto people and how consciously or not she was making that reference. See Janet Todd, "'Pursue that Way of Fooling, and Be Damn'd': Editing Aphra Behn," *Studies in the Novel* 27, no. 3 (Fall 1995): 304–319 (312).

61. Suvir Kaul, *Eighteenth-Century British Literature and Postcolonial Studies* (Edinburgh: Edinburgh University Press, 2009), 54.

62. I discuss this trend in some detail in Chapter 4 of *Sapphic Crossings*, 145–148.

63. Eve Kosofsky Sedgwick, *Between Men: English Literature and Male Homosocial Desire* (New York: Columbia University Press, 1985, 2015), 3.

64. Behn, *The Widow Ranter*, 256.

65. Behn, *The Widow Ranter*, 322.

66. This ending, with its overflow of heterosexual unions, should put readers in mind of similar endings, such as in Shakespeare's *Twelfth Night* where the sheer numbers of couplings overwhelm but do not completely suppress the prior queerness of desires expressed in the action of the play.

67. Mark Rifkin, *Settler Common Sense: Queerness and Everyday Colonialism in the American Renaissance* (Minneapolis: University of Minnesota Press, 2014), xvi.

68. Again, as in *Twelfth Night*, or even, much later, Maria Edgeworth's *Belinda*, the heterosexual couplings at the ending cannot quite erase the queer desires and trans embodiments in the rest of the text—desires and embodiments that ultimately provide the foundation for heterosexual union.

69. Getsy, "Capacity," 48.

70. Quoted in Snorton, *Black on Both Sides*, 5.

71. Snorton, *Black on Both Sides*, 5.

CHAPTER 2

Samson Occom, the Public Universal Friend, and a Queer Archive of the Elsewhere

Shelby Johnson

We proceeded to form into a Body Politick—we Named our Town by the Name of Brotherton in Indian Eeyawquittoowauconuck ... [and] concluded to live in Peace, and in Friendship.
—Samson Occom, Journal 12 (1785)[1]

The Public Universal Friend adviseth all, who desire to be one *with the* Friend *in spirit, to be wise unto salvation.*
—The Friend, The Universal Friend's Advice (1785)[2]

On March 7, 1786, two of the most famous eighteenth-century colonial preachers, Mohegan minister Samson Occom and the Public Universal Friend, born Jemima Wilkinson, met at a funeral near Mystic, Connecticut.[3] Occom briefly wrote of their encounter in his journal: "Jamima Wilkinson was Speaking; and I coud not get near so as to See her, the People Crouded so, after while I got so as to see her, but She did not Speake long She sat down, and there was another and another one after another, I saw and heard ten six Women and four men, some spoke repeatedly, Jamima got up 3 times and I spoke & others did so,—after a long Time, they shook hands which was a conclution of their ... meeting."[4] After an illness in 1776, the Friend claimed they died, only to be reanimated by a spirit of God. While the Friend never dressed entirely in male attire, they, as one believer put it, were "not to be supposed of either sex" and "neither man nor woman." They eschewed female pronouns and their birth name for the rest of their life, choosing instead to be called the Friend and the Comforter.[5]

On first reading, Occom's journal entry—tantalizing but brief—appears dubious over this unruly rehearsal of gender. Yet it would perhaps be too easy to interpret Occom and the Friend's positions as diametrically opposed, where Occom expresses a seemingly conventional conception of masculinity and the Friend a nascent refusal of narrow gender scripts. On a second reading, Occom's conclusion—"after a long Time, they shook hands"—introduces some ambiguity, where "they" could refer either to a plurality of mourners or only to the Friend. Given this possibility, his writings may index ways of recovering Indigenous perspectives on non-normative personhood that come into further relief when we trace his own confessions of dismay and discomfort with becoming interpellated within colonial gender norms.

Indeed, Occom's writings often reveal his awareness that colonial heteronormativity and land dispossession were interlocking systems of power that threatened Indigenous bodies.[6] When Occom's Wampanoag friend Moses Paul was condemned for fatally striking Moses Cook, a white miller, outside a tavern in New Haven, Connecticut, in December 1771, Occom lamented that Paul had been "unmanned" by his surrender to alcohol—that he had "lost [his] substance," as he called it in his *Sermon on the Execution of Moses Paul*, his most widely read and circulated text (1772).[7] A vexed text, Occom there grapples with settler beliefs that Indigenous men were denied the ability to inhabit masculine norms of self-willed sobriety. In response, he shows that Paul's "unmanning" was driven by systems of colonial violence, what he elsewhere names the processes by which English settlers "want to render us as Cyphers in our own land."[8] Ultimately, Occom transgresses the normative ground of colonial masculinity in the text when he draws on Genesis 2:23 (a verse long recalled in marriage rites) to tell Paul, "You are the bone of my bone and flesh of my flesh."[9] Occom's queer citation of Adam's first words to Eve reconstitutes the circumstances of colonial violence by naming a shared relation to Paul's beloved body. In his encounter with the Friend at a funeral, then, Occom navigates an instance of settler nonnormativity when the "substance" of Indigenous relations is nearly always subject to erasure.

This chapter turns to Occom and the Friend's brief meeting as a lens for addressing two iterations of gender embodiment—and of bodies becoming worlds—in the late eighteenth century.[10] For Occom and the Friend, body and flesh can index an ungovernable surrender to an array of precarities endemic to life on the colonial frontier, both quotidian (illness, addiction, poverty) and metaphysical (sin), even while it extends possibilities for supernatural reanimation and collective worldmaking. Their careers similarly reflect their attempts to restore a "Body Politick" after the upheavals of the American Revolution, where Occom led a multi-tribal migration to Brothertown on gifted Oneida lands, while the Friend organized a retreat to a town they named Jerusalem, built on Seneca territory. Both exercises in social assembly bear further resemblances: they occurred only a few years apart—Brothertown in 1785 and Jerusalem in 1791—and were located on Haudenosaunee lands in New York. And both figures' writings reconceive what counts as grievable life when nonnormative bodies are placed at risk: Occom's late journals detail his continual presence at funerals, and the *Death Book of the Society of Universal Friends* (1773–1830), a major archival source for the Society's history, retells members' deathbed confessions.

Yet despite these similarities, Occom and the Friend's political experiments have never been read together, perhaps an outcome of divergent emphases in early American studies and Indigenous studies. Because of this, their careers coordinate differently legible histories of gender and sexuality, as the Friend has seen a resurgence of critical interest in queer and trans studies, while Occom's negotiations of a racialization of sexuality has provoked comparatively less investigation. We know from scholars in Black and Indigenous studies that one of my primary terms—flesh—carries a vexed history that reflects these differential conditions of experience, embodiment, and worldmaking.[11] For Hortense Spillers, Black flesh reflects the semiotic domain through which the economic and libidinal systems of slavery unfold, emerging as an "ungendering" or "severing of captive body from its motive will, its active desire."[12] When Black bodies are rendered fungible, then "the female body and the male body," as well as queer bodies, as she traces in later work, "become a territory of cultural and political maneuver."[13] Although the political systems conscripting Native Nations found different expression in law and custom, Indigenous bodies also underwent a radical undoing of pre-contact practices of gender, kinship, and sovereignty, as settler discourses sutured Indigenous flesh to discourses of the "savage."[14] As Chickasaw critic Jodi Byrd trenchantly contends, settler occupation enfolds the nonnormative in agendas of settler expansion: property laws reformat Indigenous flesh as moveable and disposable, while deliberately rendering resulting violences illegible and *ungrievable*.[15] The outcome, as Mark Rifkin argues, is that Indigenous flesh became marked as deviant and nonnormative—and unable to inhabit modernity.[16]

Given the violent processes through which Indigenous bodies were ungendered and unmoored, I wonder if pathways exist for recovering decolonial improvisations of vibrant flesh and grievable life in heterodox acts of community-building—for what Tiffany Lethabo King calls a "not-yet form" of freedom—in eighteenth-century archives.[17] In a field-defining exploration of the co-constitution of Blackness and transness, C. Riley Snorton suggests that histories of coercive fungibility, mobility, and transit could animate "a kind of being in the world where gender . . . was not fixed but fungible, which is to say revisable," and this may open "possibilities for valorizing—without necessarily redeeming—different ways of knowing and being, as it is also invested in reviving and inventing strategies for inhabiting unlivable worlds."[18] Read at the intersection of racialized embodiment and settler futurity, the Friend's heterodox embodiment mediates a nascent iteration of what, from the perspective of a later historical period, Scott Lauria Morgensen terms "queer settler colonialism," a coordination of whiteness and nonnormativity with the imperatives of settler-national expansion.[19] The Friend's negotiation of personhood and place is thus implicated in the creation of an "unlivable world" by participating in the occupation of Indigenous lands, evacuating queerness of its transgressive potential. Decolonial queer theory may enable us to chart Occom and the Friend's vexed negotiations of race and gender, while pushing us to acknowledge *where* and *how* colonial structures differently impinged on their community's futures—Jerusalem faded after the death of the Friend, while Brothertown remains, although denied sovereign status.

Put differently, their writings coordinate what I am calling *an archive of the elsewhere*—a reservoir of their yearnings for a "Body Politick" under conditions of unfulfilled promise.[20] By calling this "an archive of the elsewhere," I am drawing on José Esteban Muñoz, who argues that queer performances can open interstitial moments of utopian possibility he calls a "then and there," whose temporal imperatives call us "to desire differently, to desire more, to desire better" in *anticipation* of a future world, as Jeremy and I explored in this collection's introduction.[21] In another sense, however, Occom's writings echo Fred Moten's point that Blackness figures as an "elsewhere and elsewhen" that diasporic communities must not only inhabit but come to desire, where Indigeneity similarly encompasses a historically conditioned set of relations and a proleptic embodiment whose arrival is indefinitely forestalled.[22] To that end, although Occom's journals and the Friend's *Death Book* were not intended for publication, I orient to this archive as more than merely occasional, but as opportunities to trace how their desires for a new future emerge in scenes of writing that refuse closure—in unfinished sentences, in stutters of anaphora, and in grammars of transitivity. Indeed, transitivity's multiple meanings—a grammatical mechanic whereby a subject requires a direct object to complete an action, a condition of change and transformation, a movement to another place—animate this essay's investigations of social experiments as sites of queer possibility and foreclosure. In what follows, I argue that their writings about Jerusalem and Brothertown press on what *elsewhere* could mean at all, where "elsewhere" indexes a trans embodiment or a racialized sexuality at moments of profound grief.

"My dear Redeemer; I love; I love; I love"

Scholars of early American sexuality have variously taken up the Friend's unruly performance of radical prophecy and gender nonnormativity as sites of contestation in imagining social reproduction. Susan Juster has underscored Wilkinson's role as a "female prophet" in an era that saw a surge in transatlantic women preachers, including Ann Lee, the founder of the United Society of Believers in Christ's Second Appearing ("Shakers") in New York, and Joanna Southcott, who published a series of infamous pamphlets from her home in Devon, England, in the early nineteenth century.[23] Early national discourses around republican motherhood, as elaborated by figures like Abigail Adams and Judith Sargent Murray, also centered (white) women's labor in the reproduction of virtuous future citizens. At the same time, several early heterodox leaders, including Ann Lee, mandated celibacy and embodied what Elizabeth Freeman calls an "experimental kinship" that was "neither reproductive nor forward-moving" in their liturgical dance practice, in which "they danced their way out of genital sex and into embodied, holy communion with one another and with God."[24] While the Friend did not command celibacy from their followers, they de-prioritized marriage and the reproduction of the nuclear family and domestic citizenship, values vital to early national norms.

Although this earlier scholarship on the Friend has reflected the contexts of women's prophecy and republican motherhood, I am interested in exploring how trans readings of the Friend expand critical inquiry to unsettle a gender binary. For example, Scott Larson and Paul B. Moyer clarify that the Friend is merely assigned female at birth, rather than a "female prophet."[25] Read this way, the Friend imagined Jerusalem as a social experiment outside heteronormative scripts of re/production, even while the queer future it evoked participated in ongoing Indigenous removal after the American Revolution. Much of the language the Friend deployed to describe their fleshly reanimation and prophetic office aligns with a vocabulary of possession and occupation that powerfully reverberates with colonial expansion. Indeed, the Friend was born in 1752 in Cumberland, Rhode Island, on lands belonging to the Narragansett and Wampanoag nations. The Friend's grandfather, John Wilkinson, acquired territory through the Rehoboth North Purchase from Pokanoket Wampanoag leader Wamsutta (Alexander), while Wilkinson's more well-known contemporary Mary Rowlandson and her family also occupied territory through this land deal.[26] In the aftermath of the cataclysmic conflict now known as King Philip's War (1675–1676), the Friend's father, Jeremiah Wilkinson, cultivated a small holding of orchards he inherited from the Rehoboth North Purchase, where the Friend and their brothers and sisters—twelve siblings in total, with the Friend the eighth—were born.

In 1776, while still inhabiting lands scarred by Wampanoag displacement, the Friend fell ill with what residents colloquially called "Columbus fever" (likely typhus) and in the aftermath of the fever, the Friend claimed that Wilkinson had left time and had her body reanimated by a spirit. This spirit then proclaimed to gathered witnesses: "Room, Room, Room, in the many Mansions of eternal glory for Thee and for everyone."[27] Here, the Friend's use of anaphora draws on the language of John 14:2 ("In my father's house are many mansions") to signal Wilkinson's death, and yet this spatial imagery also reflects colonial cultures of domesticity that routinely criticized Indigenous peoples for their itinerancy. As the Friend describes their illness, this grammar of transitive possession becomes more overt, when they "droppt the dying flesh & yielded up the Ghost. And according to the declaration of the Angels, the Spirit took full possession of the Body it now animates."[28] The Friend's theology of resurrection negotiates a paradoxical vocabulary of subjectivity, where flesh is at once a site of self-possession and at risk of holy occupation—an iteration of embodiment that registers differently from the perspective of colonized people of color, who could rarely exert custodianship over their own bodies and communities.

When the Society of Universal Friends finally procured land for the long awaited community, the title was part of the Nathaniel Gorham and Oliver Phelps Purchase, land speculators who acquired millions of acres of Haudenosaunee territory through a complicated scheme premised on anticipated state boundaries between New York and Massachusetts. Phelps and Gorham paid the colony of Massachusetts $1,000,000, while compensating members of the Haudenosaunee Confederacy only $5,000 for a preemptive right to the land title. When rising land prices caused Phelps and Gorham to default on their payments to Massachusetts, American financier Robert Morris purchased the title under the understanding that the Haudenosaunee's land claim had been irrevocably extinguished because of Mohawk support for the British during the American Revolution.[29] In the 1790s, moreover, the state borders between Massachusetts and New York shifted multiple times, and government officials could not agree on who held property in which jurisdiction. Given this transitive property title, the tract for the Society of Universal Friends initially included either fourteen thousand or eleven hundred acres, depending on which state line a surveyor followed. Eventually the Society obtained an additional ten thousand acres, but they had to repurchase this land when the preemption line moved again.[30]

In 1794, secretary of state Timothy Pickering engaged in negotiations with the Haudenosaunee Confederacy over land rights not under the purview of the Gorham/Phelps purchase. Diplomats met at Canandaigua, a Seneca town only fifteen miles from Jerusalem. While there, American diplomats affirmed the Confederacy as a sovereign entity, a recognition recorded in both the Treaty of Canandaigua and in the George Washington wampum belt held by the Onondaga Nation. One leader at these negotiations was Sganyodaiyo, or Handsome Lake, a Seneca prophet who inspired a revitalization movement. As with the Friend's encounter with Occom, the treaty meeting placed figures like Sganyodaiyo in proximity to non-binary settlers like the Friend, where they represented political views alternative to conventional U.S. policy. The Friend spoke at the treaty conference, at one point offering a long sermon (and an even longer prayer). Their presence was unusual, at least from the perspective of American observers, who interpreted the Friend as a woman speaking in a diplomatic context in which white women rarely participated, although Haudenosaunee councils included and valued the counsel of clan mothers.[31] William Savery, a Quaker preacher who attended several meetings, reported of the Friend's sermon: "[One] of the white women had yesterday told the Indians to repent; and they now called the white people to repent."[32] Savery's observation depicts the Friend as potentially dangerous for the treaty councils and recognizes the Haudenosaunee as savvy negotiators willing to adapt Christian rhetoric to critique ongoing settler incursions on their sovereign territories.

Despite observers' views on the Friend's disruptiveness, their presence at these councils replicates a logic of American expansion, even while the social order they cultivated challenges one typically reproduced within colonial heteronormativity.[33] Jerusalem's archive also reflects these dynamics and extends intricate expressions of intimacy between Society members and the Friend. Their intimacies contour the settlement's improvisation of a grammar of futurity—nowhere clearer than in *The Death Book of the Society of the Universal Friends,* which reports the last words for individual members in the Society, many of them unmarried women who sought to imagine forms of communal futurity beyond marriage. Indeed, one of the longest entries reflects the loss of the Friend's closest confidant, Sarah Richards, who renamed herself "Sarah Friend" in a queer reworking of dominant, exogamous practices where a woman takes her husband's last name. Instead, her new name as "Sarah Friend" delineates her intense attachment to the All-Friend and to their religious community. In addition, the entry in the *Death Book* indexes a syncopated syntax that reflects the Friend's acute grief in the loss: "Sarah Friend or Sarah Richards...Expired! And left Her weeping friends to mourn for themselves!" As the entry unfolds, the Friend improvises a queer theology of grievable life: "The Friend attended Her Funeral, and Preach'd a very great Sermon. The exhortation began thus, It is better to go to the house of Mourning than to the house of feasting, for that is the end of all men, and the living will lay it to heart."[34] In this claim that "the living will lay" their losses "to heart," the *Death Book* archives how shared mourning navigates intricate understandings of death and reanimation, and embodiment and community.

Another entry, one that memorializes Lucy Holmes's life and death, extends an even more complex record of nonnormative intimacy. Lucy Holmes, who "left Time, 11th of the 8th Mo 1790," renders an extravagant representation of heterodox desire: "This departed Saint, as the avenues of mortal life were closing, lifted up her hands in Prayer, said Glory to God in the highest, and unto the Lamb, forever and ever! Saying (with an emphasis which no mortal language can describe) Looking at the Friend, My dear Redeemer; I love; I love; I love. She was."[35] Here, the inscriber struggles to devise a grammar to encompass Lucy's religious experience, including an affective aura that "no mortal language can describe." In addition, I want to suggest that Lucy's spiritual attachment seems not only directed at "the Lamb of God" but also at the Friend, both of whom seem to be invoked when she calls out, "My dear Redeemer; I love; I love; I love"—a repetition that perhaps calls back to the Friend's use of "Room, Room, Room" in their transitive description of their bodily possession by a holy spirit.

In some ways, the *Death Book*'s account of Lucy's passing "out of time" reverberates beyond an expression of intense attachment and toward an articulation of heterodox community. Madhavi Menon argues that formations of queer desire and trans embodiments are nearly always in excess of fixed categories, whether identarian or political: "Whether it is libidinal desire for someone who falls outside the bounds ... or a longing that stretches the borders of our politics, desire does not respect limits."[36] Drawing from Menon, I wonder if Lucy's desire illuminates something queerly embodied about the *Death Book*'s dissenting grammar for loss. Even from a theological perspective, "My dear Redeemer; I love; I love; I love" evinces a certain slippage—is "My dear Redeemer" Christ or the Friend? Although the Friend never claimed to be Christ, the challenge they extended to conventional Christian doctrine enables a queer excess of desire in a way that "does not respect limits." At the same time, although "I love; I love; I love" functions as an archival site of excess, the entry for Lucy is also unfinished, trailing off after "She was ..." In this sense, the *Death Book* reflects an attachment never fully enfleshed within space and time, in stark contrast to settler property enclosures. Within that unfinished entry resides not only a queer archive of the elsewhere—indexed on the borders of Lucy's flesh and spirit—but also a blank space where colonial laws and treaties erased Indigenous sovereignty.

"I heard a heard Heavy news"

In contrast to Jerusalem, the Brothertown settlement project was a response both to decades of slow settler encroachment—what Jean O'Brien (Anishinaabe) calls "dispossession by degrees"—and to the immediate crises of the American Revolution.[37] From the mid-seventeenth century, a series of land sales circumscribed Mohegan hunting and farming grounds, while a land case that contested these encroachments, *Mohegan Indians v. Connecticut* (1705–1773), dragged on for decades.[38] In 1773, when the Mohegan lost their land claim and were confined to a small reservation, they were confronted with the agonizing choice of whether to stay or make a future elsewhere. Occom joined others in the community, including his brothers-in-law, David and Jacob Fowler, and his son-in-law Joseph Johnson (who married Occom's daughter, Tabitha), in planning a separate town as a means of communal survival.[39] Even so, their efforts were disrupted by the American Revolution, a conflict so destructive to Indigenous Nations that it accentuated the need for Brothertown and halted its planning, as military enlistment and wartime upheaval killed nearly half of Mohegan young men, including Johnson, who died sometime between 1776 and 1777. In addition, American general John Sullivan's 1779 genocidal incursions into western New York, near Brothertown's proposed settlement, devastated Haudenosaunee communities, crucial allies to Occom and his cohort.[40] In a 1783 letter, he deeply grieves these losses: "This war has been the most Distructive to poor Indians of any wars that ever happened in my Day."[41] Brothertown's planning documents—"Concluded to live in Peace, and in Friendship"—and settlement's name, Eeyawquittoowauconuck, turn to an idiom of kinship as a counterweight to imperial violence. These documents, however, also index a more formal grammar from the unfinished sentences and raw emotions of Occom's journals, which archive his pained efforts to reimagine grievable life and communal futurity during the beleaguered 1770s and 1780s.

By exploring Occom's depictions of losses and communion with the dead, I want to press on normative conceptions of space and time as a heuristic for addressing Native nation-building.[42] Byrd argues that the aims of Indigenous and queer studies are often in divergence: "The two fields act as if the one does not exist at all for the other, not least because of queer investments in ongoing settler colonialism on the one side and an Indigenous commitment to illegibility and outright refusal of recognition on the other."[43] Byrd further presses on the affordances of normativity itself when "it is either presumed that the Indigenous is always already queer to the normative settler or that the colonizing queer cannot and should not encapsulate Indigenous identities."[44] Occom's journals reflect how figurations of grievable life, with their portrayals of intense sensations, extend methodological difficulties when engaging with Indigenous archives, which are framed by different grammars for orienting to time and space at the very moment formations of U.S. settler-national status are unfolding within an independence campaign from Great Britain. These texts show how Occom turns sovereign conceptions of flesh and community projects to remain rooted to the earth and to each other.

Reading Occom's late works requires critical frameworks that draw from Indigenous feminist and queer paradigms to survey the improvisation of Algonquian sovereignty against settler projects of expansion, while also tracing the queering of Indigenous intimacies in an era of displacement. Occom's writings from just before and during this period, including his "Account of the Montauk Indians" (1761) and his extensive journals (1743–1790), primarily index these as struggles to survive imperial wars, painfully reflected in frequent notices of his attendance at funerals. A brief text, Occom's "Account of the Montauk Indians" (1761) spans only five pages in modern editions and portrays "some of the ancient customs and ways of the Montauk Indians."[45] Occom does this in part through descriptions of mortuary rituals, which offer normative scripts—what Erik R. Seeman calls collective mourning practices or "deathways"—of social belonging and would thus seem a counterintuitive place to find practices for intimacy otherwise.[46] Yet, Montaukett burial rites reveal the generational endurance of dense community traditions. While Occom initially composed the text as an aid for English missionaries, his historiographic perspective is shaped by his position as a kinsman participant in Montaukett life through his marriage to Mary Fowler. He begins by observing that the Montaukett bury objects that "belonged to the dead" or "give [them] away" to surviving kin: "And they use to bury a great many things with their dead, especially the things that belonged to the dead, and what they did not bury they would give away."[47] These objects ground a grammar of nonpossession different from colonial norms, revealing how the very ground inhabited by the Montaukett exists as an interconnected series of repositories that bond the community with land and ancestors.

In "Account of the Montauk Indians," sorrow also embraces a consensual refusal to speak the dead relative's name until surviving family members bestow it on a child. As Occom writes: "Neither will the mourners mention the name by which their dead was called, nor suffer any one in the whole place to mention it till some of the relations is called by the same name."[48] The transmission of names signals how members "become entangled—through the name—in the life histories of others," as Barbara Bodenhorn and Gabrielle vom Bruck argue.[49] Burial objects and funeral liturgies in "An Account of the Montauk Indians" thus retain Algonquian chronologies that are deeply at odds with the imperatives of early U.S. temporality, based on territorial expansion and Native vanishing, to materialize geographies not only as repositories of collective memory but also as grounds for the reproduction of communal futurity. In this text, Occom shows how Algonquian communities continue to pursue sovereignty by adapting quotidian exercises of land inhabitance and family life, which conflict with settler-national time.[50]

Even so, extricating Native mourning practices as a counter-national grammar becomes more difficult when displacement fractures Indigenous communities. As part of a growing Algonquian diaspora, Occom had to negotiate what Abenaki scholar Lisa Brooks calls "the rememberment of a fragmented world" by reconstituting Mohegan unity even when the nation split between two locations in Brothertown, New York, and New London, Connecticut.[51] Occom's journals record his extensive travels as an itinerant clergyman in the years between 1785 and 1789 as part of this effort, when the Occoms had not yet settled in Brothertown but traveled there often.[52] Indeed, Brooks calls Occom's personal writings "journey journals," for they "document a network of relations" with "mnemonic geographic and social markers that often correlate with communal narratives."[53] On June 26, 1785, for instance, he describes one journey spent ministering to the ill in New Concord, where he attended "a large number of people . . . with great Solemnity."[54]

The entry abruptly transitions, however, as Occom records the death of his own daughter, Tabitha: "Next Morning after Breakfast went on and got home about 9 found my Well three Days ago I heard a heard heavy News, my poor Tabitha is Dead & Buried, the Lord the Sovereign of the Universe Sanctify this Dispensation to me and to all my Family—."[55] Overall restrained, the entry's narrative of Tabitha's death is profoundly raw and abrupt, its syncopated rhythms refusing closure in myriad ways. For one, his narrative of the journey past "my Well" delays his arrival home by layering temporalities—"next morning," "breakfast," "about 9," "three days ago"—relative to the present in which he writes. These temporal markers, which appear simultaneously, slow the sentence's momentum toward its conclusion, when he learns of Tabitha's death: Occom, in other words, cannot seem to bear writing until three days after hearing the "heavy News." Finally, because the entry ends with a dash, Occom suggests that his cry to the "Sovereign of the Universe" remains an ongoing—and unfinished—prayer.

Given that Tabitha's loss reflects a rupture in kinship and futurity, Occom's grief brings into relief larger questions of Indigenous survivance under colonialism, specifically in the strange repetition of "I heard a heard."[56] Because his belated arrival prevented Occom from attending to Tabitha in her passing, "I heard a heard" figures as a performative stand-in for the burial litany he was unable to say over his daughter. As Occom pauses his record of a preaching circuit only to try to account for Tabitha's death, "I heard a heard" renders grief as surrogation, as Joseph Roach describes: "Into the cavities created by loss through death or other forms of departure . . . survivors attempt to fit satisfactory alternatives."[57] For Occom, that "satisfactory alternative" is constituted through an unfinished prayer and a grammatical stutter—an anguished call to the "Sovereign of the Universe" and a repetition of "I heard a heard." In a syntactic excess that echoes (with a difference) the "heavy News" of Tabitha's death, the entry stresses the alienations that accompany Occom's itinerancy: his physical distance from his family, the linguistic hesitations that put off the moment he scripts Tabitha's passing, his inability to touch her or her belongings in mourning or in burial. For all the ways "I heard a heard" might seem like a simple error, it remains the surest sign of Occom's presence in the journals, not in the way it records an event, for it continually retreats from offering any full account of the "Heavy news," but in how it archives a lived experience of grief. In its orientation to bodies and worlds, the journal reckons with what it means to be present *with* Native kin across time and space.

Questions of proximity and distance, sensation and chronology, and transitive embodiment and movement also reverberate in another account of profound loss in Occom's journals. In April 1786, not long after Tabitha's death, Occom recorded an extraordinary dream where he is encounters the British preacher, George Whitefield, who died years earlier in 1770:

> Last Night I had a remarkable Dream about Mr Whitefield, I thought he was preaching as he use to, when he was alive . . . and I had been Preaching, and he came to me, and took hold of my wright hand and he put his face to my face, and rub'd his face to mine and Said,—I am glad that you preach the Excellency of Jesus Christ yet, and Said, go on and the Lord be with thee, we shall now Soon done. and then he Stretched himself upon the ground flat on his face and reach'd his hands forward, and made a mark with his Hand, and Said I will out doe and over reach all Sinners, and I thought he Barked like a Dog, with a Thundering Voice . . . [and then] I awoke, and behold it was a dream.[58]

Occom's "remarkable dream" lingers with the tangibility of Whitefield's spectral face and hands, an unusual scene when skin often figures as a boundary that registers ruptured relations to land and kin in early Indigenous writing.[59] Instead, Whitefield's touch is rooted in Christian and Algonquian religious vernaculars, where he reflects dimensions of evangelical charisma, while dogs and wolves are significant in Northeast Indigenous cultures as mediators of spiritual power. Moreover, the vision indexes a transitive dimension in Whitefield's body, as he moves from standing upright to prostration on the ground and turns from touching Occom to barking like a dog.[60] Claire Colebrook defines transitivity as "the condition for what becomes known as *the* human," as flesh becomes a site out of which difference emerges.[61] In Occom's dream, however, Whitefield's movements index a more disruptive and vibrant formation of coextensive life, as the vision's somatic qualities embrace a queer kinship with human, more-than-human, and nonhuman life—a point that Ula Lukszo Klein similarly takes up in chapter 1.

In one sense, Whitefield's cry that he will "out doe and over reach all Sinners" evinces an unsettling excess of desire in keeping with many of his sermons, such as "Christ the Best Husband," which often drew from what Richard Rambuss calls a "sacred erotics" to mark conversion as a marital union with Christ.[62] Derrick R. Miller points out that in some formations of evangelical theology "all souls were female since all souls were similarly situated in marriage to Christ," with Whitefield's caress of Occom's face manifesting what Carolyn Dinshaw calls a "queer touch across time."[63] His expression of a profligate similarity *with* Christ thus marks a possibility for queer union *and* a re-gendering of the pastor. In another sense, Whitefield's claim of boundless sin indexes his aural affiliation to the creaturely—with him "[barking] like a Dog." Yet here, Occom's dream also exceeds a colonial racialization of gender, often evoked in a material and metonymic deracination of Indigenous persons *as* dogs, to instead reflect an Algonquian cosmology, where in some stories a "great dog" guards the path to the afterlife.[64] If we read Whitefield's barking as a sensuous call from across the afterlife—and thus as a recuperation of enfleshed relations between human and nonhuman existence across time—then the vision's conclusion that Occom "shall now Soon done" reflects a promise that his efforts toward Indigenous survivance in Brothertown will be fulfilled in the near future.

What Futures Now?

In their accounts of funeral sites and mourning rites, Occom and the Friend's writings signal upheavals endemic to the American Revolution's aftermath, even as settler foreclosures of nonnormative intimacies amplified their experiences of loss. And while state refusals of Indigenous sovereignty additionally constrained Brothertown's future, Brothertown has endured when Jerusalem did not, illuminating the vexed contours of futurity indexed in different separatist projects. The Society of Universal Friends entered a long decline after the Friend's death in 1819. The Friend's considerable personal charisma sustained the sect, and, given their lack of emphasis on marriage and family, the Society never succeeded in replacing members as they died. In contrast to these theological emphases, colonial and early national laws tended to constrain Indigenous futurity. Indeed, Occom's marriage to Mary Fowler, a member of the Montaukett nation, in 1751 illustrates a different iteration of settler regulations to Algonquian generational endurance. Their relationship conspicuously repudiated New York laws from 1712 and 1754 forbidding exogamous marriages between members of the Montaukett nation and other Native communities—"laws designed," according to Joanna Brooks, "to hasten Indigenous population decline."[65] While the Occom's marriage would seem like an exemplary instance of conjugal partnership, its very illegality reveals one way that colonial codes aimed at foreclosing Indigenous futurity. The Brothertowners encountered additional difficulties in the work of creating an Indigenous future. Under pressure from land-hungry settlers eager to move closer to the Great Lakes, the Brothertown residents, together with members of the Stockbridge-Munsee and Oneida nations, moved west to Wisconsin in the 1830s.[66] Many of the Brothertowners live there still but have been unsuccessful in gaining federal recognition for their tribal sovereignty.[67]

Put simply, Occom and the Friend bear witness to the devastating conditions of settler regulations of intimacy at a critical point of transition from colonial to early national governance in the United States. Yet their vocabularies for mourning also require critical frameworks attentive to the transitive convergences and divergences in lived experiences of gender and racial embodiment that their careers exemplify. In a small way, we might see this in Occom's journal entry on the funeral where he first met the Friend: "But She did not Speake long She sat down, and there was another and another one after another, I saw and heard ten six Women and four men, some spoke repeatedly, Jamima got up 3 times and I spoke & others did so." Here, Occom's syncopated account emphasizes the fleeting nature of the Friend's funeral remarks, as well as the polyphonic rhythms of the ceremony itself, as multiple members of the gathered community speak. Likewise, across Occom and the Friend's writings, fragmented voices reflect both the collective nature and the incompleteness of community projects, as different speakers extend acts of social assembly into a deeply desired but still unfulfilled future. In this way, the political strivings Occom and the Friend differently exemplify signify an *ongoing* elsewhere and elsewhen—or "then and there," to riff on Muñoz—of nonnormative life. Ultimately, their acts of fleshing out grievable bodies and heterodox worlds summon a series of alternative futures toward which eighteenth-century settlement projects tremulously aspire.

NOTES

Acknowledgment: I am deeply grateful to a community of friends and colleagues, including Alyssa Hunziker, Rafael Hernandez, Jeff Menne, and Lindsay Wilhelm, who thoughtfully engaged with this chapter. Conversations with Jeremy Chow, Sari Carter, Don Rodrigues, and Scott Larson generously pushed me toward clarity.

1. Samson Occom, *Journal 12* (1785), in *The Collected Writings of Samson Occom, Mohegan*, ed. Joanna Brooks (Oxford: Oxford University Press, 2006), 308–309.

2. The Friend, *The Universal Friend's Advice*, in *Pioneer Prophetess: Jemima Wilkinson, the Publick Universal Friend*, ed. Herbert A. Wisbey (Ithaca, NY: Cornell University Press, 1964), 107.

3. Early accounts of the Friend, such as Herbert A. Wisbey's *Pioneer Prophetess: Jemima Wilkinson, the Publick Universal Friend* (Ithaca, NY: Cornell University Press, 1964), use female pronouns. Given the Friend's assertion of genderless identity, I use they/them pronouns, drawing from Jen Manion's call to foreground fluid performances of identity in *Female Husbands: A Trans History* (Cambridge: Cambridge University Press, 2021), 10–13 and 265–266. For the Friend in the context of trans and nonbinary scholarship, see also Rachel Hope Cleves, "Beyond the Binaries in Early America: Special Issue Introduction," *Early American Studies* 12, no. 3 (Fall 2014): 459–468; Scott Larson, "'Indescribable Being': Theological Performances of Genderlessness in the Society of the Publick Universal Friend, 1776–1819," *Early American Studies* 12, no. 3 (Fall 2014): 576–600; Paul B. Moyer, *The Public Universal Friend: Jemima Wilkinson and Religious Enthusiasm in Revolutionary America* (Ithaca, NY: Cornell University Press, 2015); T. Fleischmann, *Time Is the Thing a Body Moves through* (Minneapolis: Coffee House, 2019); and Kit Heyam, *Before We Were Trans: A New History of Gender* (New York: Seal Press, 2022), 216–218.

4. Samson Occom, *Journal 15* (1785–1786), in *The Collected Writings of Samson Occom, Mohegan*, 325–335 (331).

5. Quoted in Moyer, *The Public Universal Friend*, 9.

6. For the queering of Native bodies and relations under early American settler colonialism, see Mark Rifkin, *When Did Indians Become Straight?: Kinship, the History of Sexuality, and Native Sovereignty* (Oxford: Oxford University Press, 2011).

7. Samson Occom, *Sermon on the Execution of Moses Paul* (1772), in *The Collected Writings of Samson Occom, Mohegan*, 176–196 (192).

8. Samson Occom, "Mohegan Tribe to Sir William Johnson" (1764), in *The Collected Writings of Samson Occom, Mohegan*, 144–145.

9. Occom, *Sermon on the Execution of Moses Paul*, 188.

10. Vincent Lloyd contends that political theology, as an analytic attuned to power, sovereignty, and the exception, could do more to account for racial ideologies lurking within grammars of flesh. See Vincent Lloyd, ed., *Race and Political Theology* (Stanford, CA: Stanford University Press, 2012), 1–21.

11. On flesh, see Hortense J. Spillers, "Mama's Baby, Papa's Maybe: An American Grammar," in *Black, White, and in Color: Essays on American Literature and Culture* (Chicago: University of Chicago Press, 2003), 203–229; Frank B. Wilderson III, *Red, White, & Black: Cinema and the Structure of U.S. Antagonisms* (Durham, NC: Duke University Press, 2010), 17–18; and Tiffany Lethabo King, *The Black Shoals: Offshore Formations in Black and Native Studies* (Durham, NC: Duke University Press, 2019), Chapter 3.

12. Spillers, "Mama's Baby, Papa's Maybe," 204.

13. Spillers, "Mama's Baby, Papa's Maybe," 206. For Spillers's rethinking of "ungendered" bodies in the context of queerness, see Michelle M. Wright, *The Physics of Blackness: Beyond the Middle Passage Epistemology* (Minneapolis: University of Minnesota, 2015), Chapter 2.

14. Wilderson, *Red, White, and Black*, 28.

15. Jodi Byrd, *The Transit of Empire: Indigenous Critiques of Colonialism* (Minneapolis: University of Minnesota Press, 2011), xv.

16. Rifkin, *When Did Indians Become Straight?*, 36–38. See also Qwo-Li Driskill, *Asegi Stories: Cherokee Queer and Two-Spirit Memory* (Tucson: University of Arizona Press, 2016), 41.

17. King, *The Black Shoals*, 54. For grievable life, I am also thinking with Judith Butler in *Frames of War: What Is Grievable Life?* (New York: Verso Books, 2009).

18. C. Riley Snorton, *Black on Both Sides: A Racial History of Trans Identity* (Minneapolis: University of Minnesota Press, 2017), 59, 7.

19. Scott Lauria Morgensen, *The Spaces between Us: Queer Settler Colonialism and Indigenous Decolonization* (Minneapolis: University of Minnesota Press, 2011), 11–13. See also Jasbir K. Puar, *Terrorist Assemblages: Homonationalism in Queer Times*, 2nd ed. (Durham, NC: Duke University Press, 2017), 39–40.

20. For flesh, space, and time, I am influenced by what Sara Ahmed names a queerly "migrant orientation," a phenomenology for inhabiting space and time "as if they extend our skin. At the same time, for queer projects, this is an extension of embodiment that never quite arrives" (10). I am also drawing from Mikhail Bakhtin's exploration of time and temporality in the chronotope, or in moments where "time, as it were, thickens, takes on flesh, becomes artistically visible; likewise, space becomes . . . responsive to the movements of time, plot, and history" (84). See Ahmed, *Queer Phenomenology: Orientations, Objects, Others* (Durham, NC: Duke University Press, 2006); and Bakhtin, *The Dialogic Imagination: Four Essays*, trans. Caryl Emerson and Michael Holquist, ed. Michael Holquist (Austin: University of Texas Press, 1981).

21. José Esteban Muñoz, *Cruising Utopia: The Then and There of Queer Futurity* (New York: New York University Press, 2009), 189.

22. Fred Moten, "Blackness and Nothingness (Mysticism) in the Flesh," *South Atlantic Quarterly* 112, no. 4 (Fall 2013): 737–780 (746). In *The Physics of Blackness*, Wright also argues that Blackness is not reducible to inherent biology (a "what") but is historically conditioned (a "when" and "where"), 1–3.

23. Susan Juster, *Doomsayers: Anglo-American Prophecy in the Age of Revolution* (Philadelphia: University of Pennsylvania Press, 2003); and Catherine A. Brekus, *Strangers and Pilgrims: Female Preaching in America, 1740–1845* (Chapel Hill: University of North Carolina Press, 2000).

24. Elizabeth Freeman, *Beside You in Time: Sense Methods and Queer Sociabilities in the American 19th Century* (Durham, NC: Duke University Press, 2019), 28–29.

25. See Larson, "'Indescribable Being,'" 580–583, and Moyer, *The Public Universal Friend*, 9–10.

26. For Mary Rowlandson and King Philip's War, see Lisa Brooks, *Our Beloved Kin: A New History of King Philip's War* (New Haven, CT: Yale University Press, 2018).

27. Quoted in Larson, "'Indescribable Being,'" 577.

28. Quoted in Larson, "'Indescribable Being,'" 577.

29. Laurence M. Hauptman, *Conspiracy of Interests: Iroquois Dispossession and the Rise of New York State* (Syracuse, NY: Syracuse University Press, 2001), 58–89.

30. See Moyer, *The Public Universal Friend*, 121–128.

31. On Haudenosaunee women and clan councils, see E. Pauline Johnson, "The Lodge of the Lawmakers," in *Tekahionwake: E. Pauline Johnson's Writings on Native North America*, eds. Margery Fee and Dory Nelson (Peterborough, ON: Broadview Press, 2015), 42–45.

32. Quoted in Fleischmann, *Time Is the Thing*, 83.

33. See Beth Piatote, *Domestic Subjects: Gender, Citizenship, and Law in Native American Literature* (New Haven, CT: Yale University Press, 2013).

34. Wisby's *Pioneer Prophetess* reproduces *The Death Book of the Society of Universal Friends* in Appendix I, 187–195. For Sarah Friend's inscription, see *Death Book*, 191.

35. *Death Book*, 188–189.

36. Madhavi Menon, *Indifference to Difference* (Minneapolis: University of Minnesota Press, 2015), 16.

37. Jean M. O'Brien, *Dispossession by Degrees* (Lincoln: University of Nebraska Press, 2003).

38. For the Mohegan land case, see Mark D. Walters, "Mohegan Indians v. Connecticut (1705–1773) and the Legal Status of Aboriginal Customary Laws and Government in British North America," *Osgood Hall Law Journal* 33, no. 4 (Winter 1995): 785–829; Amy Den Ouden, *Beyond Conquest: Native Peoples and the Struggle for History in New England* (Lincoln: University of Nebraska Press, 2005), 1–3, 68–99; Lisa Brooks, *The Common Pot: The Recovery of Native Space in the Northeast* (Minneapolis: University of Minnesota Press, 2008), 53–80, 83–100; Jean M. O'Brien, *Firsting and Lasting: Writing Indians Out of Existence in New England* (Minneapolis: University of Minnesota Press, 2010), 159–170; David Silverman, *Red Brethren: The Brothertown and Stockbridge Indians and the Problem of Race in Early America* (Ithaca, NY: Cornell University Press, 2010), 46–51; and Craig Bryan Yirush, "Claiming the New World: Empire, Law, and Indigenous Rights in the Mohegan Case, 1704–1743," *Law and History Review* 29, no. 2 (May 2011): 333–373.

39. Anthony Wonderley, "Brothertown, New York, 1785–1796," *New York History* 81, no. 4 (December 2000): 457–492 (464); and Hilary Wyss, *Writing Indians: Literacy, Christianity, and Native Community in Early America* (Amherst: University of Massachusetts Press, 2000), 126–127.

40. For the American Revolution and the Mohegan, see Silverman, *Red Brethren*, 109–117.

41. Samson Occom, "Letter to John Bailey" (1783), in *The Collected Writings of Samson Occom, Mohegan*, 118–120 (119).

42. For this, I am influenced by Deborah Miranda's essay on Chumash and Esselen burial rites, which was largely the purview of Two-Spirit individuals within the community. While Miranda's tribal-national context is very different from Occom's, I take up her provocation to resist a mode of interpretation that turns exclusively to idioms of tragedy to describe Indigenous experiences under colonialism, instead embracing idioms that "enrich Native lives with meaning, survival, and love." See Miranda, "Extermination of the *Joyas*: Gendercide in Spanish California," *GLQ: A Journal of Lesbian and Gay Studies* 16, no. 1–2 (April 2010): 253–284 (256).

43. Jodi Byrd, "What's Normative Got to Do with It?: Toward Indigenous Queer Relationality," *Social Text* 38, no. 4 (Winter 2020): 105–123 (105).

44. Byrd, "What's Normative," 107–108.

45. Samson Occom, "Account of the Montauk Indians" (1761), in *The Collected Writings of Samson Occom, Mohegan*, 47–51 (47).

46. Erik R. Seeman, *The Huron-Wendat Feast of the Dead: Indian-European Encounters in Early North America* (Baltimore, MD: Johns Hopkins University Press, 2011), 2–3.

47. Occom, "Account of the Montauk Indians," 50.

48. Occom, "Account of the Montauk Indians," 50.

49. Barbara Bodenhorn and Gabriele vom Bruck, "'Entangled in Histories': An Introduction to the Anthropology of Names and Naming," in *The Anthropology of Names and Nam-*

ing, ed. Barbara Bodenhorn and Gabrielle vom Bruck (Cambridge: Cambridge University Press, 2006), 1–30 (3).

50. See Mark Rifkin, *Beyond Settler Time: Temporal Sovereignty and Indigenous Self-Determination* (Durham, NC: Duke University Press, 2017), x–xi.

51. Brooks, *The Common Pot*, xxii.

52. Linford Fisher, *The Indian Great Awakening: Religion and the Shaping of Native Cultures in Early America* (Oxford: Oxford University Press, 2014), 184.

53. Brooks, *The Common Pot*, 226.

54. Samson Occom, *Journal 11* (1785), in *The Collected Writings of Samson Occom, Mohegan*, 293–301 (294).

55. Occom, *Journal 11*, 295.

56. On queer futurity, see Lee Edelman, *No Future: Queer Theory and the Death Drive* (Durham, NC: Duke University Press, 2004), and Rebekah Sheldon, *The Child to Come: Life after the Human Catastrophe* (Minneapolis: University of Minnesota Press, 2016).

57. Joseph Roach, *Cities of the Dead: Circum-Atlantic Performances* (New York: Columbia University Press, 1996), 2.

58. Occom, *Journal 15*, 334. On this dream, see Bernd Peyer, *The Tutor'd Mind: Indian Missionary Writing in Antebellum America* (Amherst: University of Massachusetts Press, 1997), 97–98; Joanna Brooks, *American Lazarus: Religion and the Rise of African-American and Native American Literature* (Oxford: Oxford University Press, 2003), 84–86; Keely McCarthy, "Conversion, Identity, and the Indian Missionary," *Early American Literature* 36, no. 3 (Fall 2001): 353–369; and Jessica M. Parr, *Inventing George Whitefield: Race, Revivalism, and the Making of a Religious Icon* (Oxford: University of Mississippi Press, 2015), 103–104.

59. William Apess's *An Indian's Looking-Glass for the White Man* is exemplary here. See Apess, *On Our Own Ground: The Complete Writings of William Apess, A Pequot*, ed. Barry O'Connell (Amherst: University of Massachusetts Press, 1992), 155–161.

60. For queer human-canine kinships, see Donna Haraway, *The Companion Species Manifesto* (Chicago: University of Chicago Press, 2003), and *When Species Meet* (Minneapolis: Minnesota University Press, 2007). For dogs and histories of race, see Colin Dayan, *The Law Is a White Dog* (Princeton, NJ: Princeton University Press, 2013), and *With Dogs at the Edge of Life* (New York: Columbia University Press, 2016); Deborah Bird Rose, *Wild Dog Dreaming: Love and Extinction* (Charlottesville: University of Virginia Press, 2012); Bénédicte Boisseron, *Afro-Dog: Blackness and the Animal Question* (New York: Columbia University Press, 2018); Joshua Bennett, *Being Property Once Myself: Blackness and the End of Man* (Cambridge, MA: Harvard University Press, 2020); and Zakiyyah Iman Jackson, *Becoming Human: Matter and Meaning in an Antiblack World* (New York: New York University Press, 2020).

61. Claire Colebrook, "What Is It Like to Be Human?," *TSQ: Transgender Studies Quarterly* 2, no. 2 (May 2015): 227–243 (228).

62. Richard Rambuss, *Closet Devotions* (Durham, NC: Duke University Press, 1998), 1–4. For a reading of Whitefield's queer sermons, see also Misty G. Anderson, *Imagining Methodism in Eighteenth-Century Britain: Enthusiasm, Belief, and the Borders of the Self* (Baltimore, MD: Johns Hopkins University Press, 2012), 70–75.

63. See Derrick R. Miller, "Moravian Familiarities: Queer Community in the Moravian Church in Europe and North America in the Mid-Eighteenth Century," *Journal of Moravian History* 13, no. 1 (Spring 2013): 54–75 (57); and Carolyn Dinshaw, *Getting Medieval: Sexualities and Communities Pre- and Postmodern* (Durham, NC: Duke University Press, 1999), 3.

64. For the deracination of Indigenous persons as dogs, we must look no further than Occom's own life. On one occasion, he was not able to fulfill a preaching engagement in New Haven, but at least one attendee mistook a white minister for Occom and grumbled, "See how the black dog lays it down," an incident described by William Sprague, *Annals of the American Pulpit*, 3 vols. (New York: R. Carter and Brothers, 1859), 2:40. However, dogs and wolves are significant emblems of power, with the Mohegan Vision Statement proclaiming: "We are the Wolf People, children of Mundo," which is included in Melissa Tantaquidgeon Zobel (formerly Fawcett) and Gladys Tantaquidgeon's *Medicine Trail: The Life and Lessons of*

Gladys Tantaquidgeon (Tucson: University of Arizona Press, 2000), 3. I attend closely to settler deracination of Indigenous persons as dogs in my book, *The Rich Earth between Us: The Intimate Grounds of Race and Sexuality in the Atlantic World* (Chapel Hill: University of North Carolina Press, 2024).

65. Joanna Brooks, "'This Indian World': An Introduction to the Writings of Samson Occom," in *The Collected Writings of Samson Occom* (Oxford: Oxford University Press, 2006), 3–43 (15).

66. On the Brothertowners' move to Wisconsin, see Silverman, *Red Brethren*, 184–190.

67. For Indigenous and Black sovereignty and land rights in the nineteenth century, see Kathryn Walkiewicz, *Reading Territory: Indigenous and Black Freedom, Removal, and the Nineteenth-Century State* (Chapel Hill: University of North Carolina Press, 2023).

CHAPTER 3

Refashioning Masculinity in Regency England

FEMALE FASHIONS INSPIRED BY THE PERSIAN ENVOY MIRZA ABUL HASSAN KHAN AND HIS CIRCASSIAN WIFE

Humberto Garcia

On April 30, 1819, the Anglo-Irish author Maria Edgeworth wrote to her stepmother, Frances Anne Edgeworth (née Beaufort), to gossip about the most famous visitor to England at the time:

> What do you think of her [Frances Maria Edgeworth; Fanny] having been taken notice of by the Persian Ambassador yesterday as she was riding in the park with Mr. S. Whitbread—True upon my veracity! I have Mr. Whitbreads word for it not contradicted by her own very modest suggestion that it was the poney which his Persian Highness noticed... She has a new brown habit which fits to admiration. Seriously as she was cantering in the park they saw approaching the Persian embassador in his black turban and scarlet flowing robes and with a very long bushy black beard mounted on a beautiful horse, attended by two Persians and a great number of English gentlemen—of the first distinction no doubt. The embassador was walking his horse quite slowly and all others did the same. Fanny and Mr. Whitbread pulled up their canterers and walked them slowly to have a full view of men and turbans. His Persian Excellency then did himself the honor to point to Fanny with his stick saying at the same time some words with emphasis to the gentlemen with him. These words have been interpreted... that she is far fairer than his far famed Circassian—whom by the way his Excellency it is said is willing to give to whoever will have her, since she has been seen by the eyes of men and consequently has lost all value in his eyes![1]

Edgeworth's letter takes up Mirza Abul Hassan Khan Shirazi Ilchi Kabir (1776–1846), envoy extraordinary and minister plenipotentiary from the Qajar ruler Fath 'Ali Shah (r. 1797–1834) to King George III from 1809 to 1810 and again from 1819

55

to 1820. The envoy or "Ilchi" became a fashion trendsetter before and during his second mission to London to rekindle the Anglo-Persian alliance against Tsarist Russia (ratified during his first trip in 1809). Englishwomen were obsessed with his sumptuous clothing, equestrian athleticism, and his "very long bushy black beard," a signifier for virile political power in Qajar culture. Five days before Edgeworth wrote her letter, the envoy's new wife, Delarom, a Circassian concubine from Istanbul, landed at Dover amid gawking fans and tabloid journalists. Delarom was often portrayed in the British media as both an enslaved captive and an object of intense sartorial interest, and this representation tethered racialized masculinity to clothing and visual presentation in complex ways. This chapter argues that the fanfare surrounding the couple and the "great number of English gentlemen" gathered around them index underexamined sartorial archives useful for historizing a genteel British masculinity in flux during the reign of King George III, until the ascension of King George IV in 1820. The masculine gallantry on display in Edgeworth's letter was mediated by Persian-stylized fashions for Englishwomen. Described in the letter as elegantly attired in "a new brown habit" on horseback, Frances's unwed twenty-year-old daughter, Fanny, allegedly had an erotic rendezvous in Hyde Park with the forty-three-year-old Abul Hassan. Coveted items such as Fanny's brown habit and Abul Hassan's "black turban" rendered female-to-male attraction in public socially acceptable yet questionable in relation to male-to-male intimacies.

Anglo-Persian diplomacy unsettled Regency Britain's equestrian-based heteronormative identities, reversing standard roles wherein Englishmen on horseback were expected to woo their passive female companions. Such a blurring of what was perceived as normal versus abnormal courtship behavior pertains to Abul Hassan's eroticized horse-riding excursions into London parks with throngs of Englishwomen and men in tow, eager to emulate his dress and demeanor. Similarly, in Jane Austen's *Mansfield Park* (1814), the chic London coquette Mary Crawford actively pursues the young gentleman Edmund Bertram, "both on horseback, riding side by side," as his future wife Fanny Price half-imagines, half-perceives the couple's intimacy from afar.[2] But unlike the prudish Edmund, the envoy was celebrated for his ostensible sexual prowess among female admirers who saw him as a more exemplary man than those native to Britain. Edgeworth's letter suggests that gentlemen wooers such as Mr. Whitbread were less attractive and less masculine than the Persian celebrity. At stake here was a cultural shift in the term "gentleman," from the chivalrous knight-errant who performs a chaste heterosexual love for "madame Britannia" to the fops, macaronis, and dandies who had previously appeared too foreign and feminine in their sartorial styles to count as men. Englishwomen were not passive recipients of male chivalric love but rather played active roles, as writers, in shaping British gentlemen's malleable gender.[3]

Abul Hassan's iconic masculinity encapsulates this dynamic. His homosocial repartees with dandyish gentlemen were a cause célèbre during a time when his female fans saw public interactions between the sexes as potentially scandalous yet desirable. For twenty-first-century readers, the love "between men" that takes centerstage in the letter might appear "queer," which Eve Kosofsky Sedgwick has influentially defined as an in-betweenness that transgresses sexual and gender norms.[4] Yet, men engaging in homosocial relationships who treated women's bodies as vehicles for expressing forbidden same-sex desires—a phenomena that Sedgwick considers germane to nineteenth-century Britain's imperial expansion—birthed new ways for how opposite-sex lovers should publicly conduct themselves.

If "something about queer is inextinguishable," then that something is a scholarly fetish for treating gender fluidity as inherently transgressive.[5] I instead argue that aberrant sexual behaviors can harbor their own norms: to prepare unruly young women for monogamous heterosexual marriage. Anglo-Persian sociability entailed a normative pull from within the fashionable circles that Edgeworth moved in and wrote about.[6] Abul Hassan's racy interaction with fashionables like Fanny indirectly served to differentiate impotent suitors from marriageable gallants, as the "desire for heterosociality" was becoming customary in Regency England before Iran underwent a similar reorientation a century later.[7] Afsaneh Najmabadi has traced this desire to the impact that European modernity had on late nineteenth-century Iran as the Qajar dynasty was giving way to a republican-constitutional order. But this history has a backstory elided in scholarship that prioritizes European systems of gender and sexuality in isolation from other cultures. As such, I contribute to "Islamicate sexuality studies" by decolonizing Eurocentric frameworks that privilege queerness as a destabilizing ahistorical category rather than as a norm-stabilizing force in a specific place and time.[8] For Britons spellbound by a Persian fashionable in Hyde Park, Qajar clothing and visual presentation (including his beard) offered a viable alternative to the equestrian gentlemanliness held suspect by female observers unimpressed by insipid Englishmen like Edmund Bertram.

To demonstrate how Islamicate sexualities spurred the normalization of heterosocial relations in Regency England, this chapter focuses on how gentlemanly virtues were confounded with dandyish vices in an array of verbal and visual mediums between 1810 and 1820. Although representations of Abul Hassan as the dandy-in-the-gentleman appear transgressive in these mediums when studied separately, they conjointly generate gendered refractions that are disorienting as well as reorienting. The Persian male physique helped Britons translate Regency dandyism's perceived effeminacy into a negative foil used for determining which gentlemen are masculine enough to head up an empire. The first part of this chapter focuses on the craze for cashmere shawls and Qajar headgear among Englishwomen who fetishized the bearded manliness that the Persian envoy performed in polite company. British men and women performed risqué behaviors that the metropolitan media attributed to the cross-dressed dandy figure in exotic flair; these behaviors became a means to normalize the aspiration of upward social mobility. The second part examines how the liminal figure of the envoy was Orientalized as an impotent eunuch in connection to his wife Delarom, the trendiest shawled fashionable in British ladies' magazines like *La Belle Assemblée*. The "Fair Circassian," as Delarom was often referred to, modeled Oriental fashions that stirred public controversy in a series of anti-dandy satires, mainly the 1820 pantomime *Harlequin and Cinderella; or, the Little Glass Slipper*. Such representations, I argue, heteronormalized the social (and potential sexual) deviancy associated with the body politic to create new criteria for distinguishing norms of masculinity, femininity, and romantic courtship by midcentury.

A Persian Celebrity's Female Fans

Born in 1776 to a noble Shi'ite family in Shiraz, Iran, Abul Hassan helped stabilize his country's patriarchal monarchy during the tumultuous transition from the Zand to the Qajar dynasty (1789–1925). Having exiled himself to Hyderabad after he and his family lost Fath 'Ali Shah's favor, he returned to Iran with immunity in 1800, after which the shah officiated him envoy to Britain on the recommendation of British ambassador Sir Harford Jones (1764–1847). He was to convince Qajar officials that the British were better allies than the French, who were planning to invade British India. Jones promised to assist the shah militarily in recapturing Tiflis in Georgia, as well as other Caucasian territories taken by the Russians, if the shah would agree to halt any eastward advances by Napoleon. This treaty was finalized in Tehran by Jones, who led the delegation to obtain King George III's formal approval. Upon disembarking at Plymouth on November 25, 1809, Abul Hassan was disheartened not to receive in London the ceremonial *istikbal*, a stately reception customarily held for foreign dignitaries in Iran. To make matters worse, his meeting with the king was delayed for several weeks. To set him at ease, British officials indulged him in countless entertainments held in his honor at dinner parties, playhouses, masquerades, and breakfast gatherings, mostly presided over by aristocratic ladies "curious to look upon the visage and beard of a native of Iran."[9] Their attention compensated for his hosts' improprieties. Napoleon's defeat by Britain and its allies in 1815 prompted Abul Hassan's final 1819–1820 visit to England in a failed bid to salvage the Anglo-Persian alliance.[10] In the intervening years, he had become the "fashion everywhere," even as European gentlemen disparaged "this diplomatic barbarian."[11]

Images of Abul Hassan in dashing attire were conducive to Englishwomen's spectatorial identification with what Joseph Roach calls the "It-effect" peculiar to "abnormally interesting people."[12] Sites for fostering this identification included Hyde Park and St. James's Park. Fashionables rode horses in these parks to see and be seen, with women and men sporting nearly identical riding hoods, military-style colors and fabrics, and decorative bridles and saddles.[13] In this "Garden of Eden," Abul Hassan was shocked to see "pretty girls and handsome youths" playing polo together, besides "some 100,000 men and women parading themselves on foot and on horseback,"[14] This scene recalls the Qur'an's verses on a sensual afterlife populated by pretty boys and female virgins eager to please pious Muslim adults. Yet, this scene presented the envoy with a gender-nonconforming spectacle: Englishwomen playing *torktazi*, a javelin-throwing game that he and his servants played regularly during their stay. He also used another term in his diary to describe the games the women were participating in: *jaridbazi*, referring to a sport played predominantly by male warriors and hunters honing their skills.[15]

Abul Hassan's sportsmanship among men presented equestrian Englishwomen with an occasion for asserting their public agency in upper-class, masculine-coded spaces. Beholding horsewomen such as Fanny behaving and dressing like their male counterparts, while galloping on Arabian horses (identified as *Asban-e Tazi* in his diary), was as strange for Abul Hassan as for his Persophilic fans.[16] Prized by Europeans, Arabs, Persians, Ottomans, Mughals, and Central Asians, these horses symbolized Britain's imperial sovereignty insofar as the accoutrements and activities associated with them invoked a stylization unique to ancient aristocratic manhood in Eurasia.[17] Englishwomen's manly "riding" oriented the envoy toward an illicit desire for heterosociality: "I thought to myself how wonderful it would be if the men—and indeed the ladies—of the Iranian Court could be in that meadow to learn how to ride and gallop."[18]

However, such encounters were problematic for the foreigner. For example, an article in *The Morning Post* reported that while "the PERSIAN AM[b]ASSADOR was on horseback with his attendants . . . two Ladies, dressed in Persian costume," attracted his notice.[19] He was outraged by this report, for those women resembled dressy high-class Iranian courtesans on horses in silver and golden tack.[20] This news coverage accounts for the depictions of Abul Hassan in equestrian gear, a "portraitive mode" that encouraged viewers to identify with his appearance.[21] A prime example is the sketch of him "in his riding dress" by Scottish miniature painter and caricaturist John Kay, printed with a biography extolling the bearded celebrity's courteousness toward "gentlemen" (Figure 3.1).[22] What appeared as an indecorous affront to elite Persian masculinity in Abul Hassan's park jaunts came to signify what was decorous and genteel for his British spectators. In other words, the publicity he elicited for cavorting among men and women in the very newspapers that he decried for printing lies about his excessive libido made public heterosocialization appear normal.

This reorientation from homosociality to heterosociality is ironic given that the clean-shaven face was then the norm for Englishmen, with male beardedness coming out of vogue after the 1500s and not making a comeback until after 1850. In the interim, no British men would have dared to appear bearded, except for political radicals, Irishmen, criminals, and bohemian artists infamous for their perceived vulgarity and effeminacy.[23] Yet, some Regency ladies saw beards differently. Their views hearkened to early modern representations of Muslim men with copious beards that communicated their "fertility and virility, despite the associated carnivalesque implication" that these men were lechers.[24] As Eleanor Rycroft has argued, British men who styled their facial hair after Muslims rendered the fantasy of a cohesive national identity for Britain farcical. But for women like Fanny and Maria Edgeworth, the "long bushy black beard" recalled the valor, vigor, and self-confidence of a bygone Tudor era, a primal manhood that became the symbolic crux for yoking Victorian patriarchalism and sportsmanship to beardedness.

Figure 3.1. A sketch of Mirza Aboul Hassan Khan, by John Kay. *A Series of Original Portraits and Caricature Etchings* (1838), RB 272237, The Huntington Library, San Marino, California.

Though seemingly out of fashion, Abul Hassan inspired his female fans through his public appearances to reboot outdated masculinities.

For example, in 1810, Lady Elizabeth Fielding (née Fox-Strangways) fell instantly in love with the envoy at an aristocratic assembly, drawn to his "long curly *clean* beard."[25] However, he was too preoccupied with Lady Elizabeth Villiers (the fourth earl of Jersey's daughter), who flirtatiously "reclined by him on an ottoman while he fanned himself."[26] This luxury sitting piece was modeled after those in the Ottoman Empire. Its symbolic association with Muslim lechery sets the scene for what happened next.[27] When Lady Fielding asked him if he felt exhausted by his ambassadorial engagements, he replied, "'No, not tired—very long evening (and putting his hands on his embroidered breast)—patience, patience!' This answer, which he meant to be very civil, conveyed quite another idea to the company, who were all much diverted."[28] Ascribing an entertaining eroticism to a foreigner near an English woman lying on an eroticized Oriental-style piece of furniture reflects the racy undertones of England's polite culture, in which libidinous desires were invoked through innuendo, humor, and half-concealment.[29] Crucial to this affective register was the bushy, clean, and black beard, which has an ambivalent significance in early modern humoral theory as a phallic symbol for semen and procreation signifying barbarity, adultery, and licentiousness, as well as martial fortitude, unpretentious refinement, and innate talent. This semiotic slipperiness tended to destabilize gender and racial differentiations, given that penal-shaped beards were especially fetishized by most Englishwomen.[30]

The parenthetical reference to "his embroidered breast" is also significant. Abul Hassan's modish wear enhanced the sense of rarity and novelty of Eastern-styled embroideries in upper-class Englishwomen's wardrobes. Britain's military campaigns in Mysore (1797–1798) and Egypt (1798–1801) inspired metropolitan civilians to adapt Turkish turbans and silken fabrics to convey bodily elegance.[31] For example, an article from the *Morning Post* reported that ladies of fashion with Eastern hairdos were donning "Mirza turban[s]" with a "large pearl crescent in front" (symbolizing the Islamic faith), flaunting cloaks embroidered in "pink Persian," and dancing in balls to "Persian dance ... in compliment to Mirza Abul Hassan."[32] The trendiest headgear for women in March and April 1810 was the "Mirza turban of frosted satin," an anglicized version of the black astrakhan (with tiny crescent) shown in Kay's sketch.[33] *The Lady's Magazine* recommended the "Persian turban cap of white satin" as appropriate for women's "riding dress."[34] In 1819, decorative shawls from "the valley of Cachemire" (Kashmir) were in high demand among spectators who "beheld these rich envelopes composing the clothing of the Persian Ambassador."[35] Produced in Iran and Central Asia, cashmere shawls (*chal* or *shaal* in Persian) were signature accessories for elite Englishwomen's dress repertoire in imitation of Greek nude statuary, a style called *robe á la grecque*.[36] This fabric's transcultural currency symbolized "class, money, and the ability to keep a woman," as it often does today.[37]

Abul Hassan–style clothing brands were a marketing ploy for naturalizing neoclassical garb: light vibrant drapes pressed up against the female figure to showcase corporeal transparency and authenticity, with flowing, high-waisted muslin gowns to heighten the effect of whiteness, making the women wearing them like naked animate statues.[38] Consider the fashion plate of Englishwomen modeling the Mirza turban in Rudolph Ackermann's periodicals. His *Repository of Arts, Literatures, Commerce, Manufactures, Fashions and Politics*, along with *La Belle Assemblée: or Court and Fashionable Magazine*, functioned as "paper shops," a virtual storeroom "allowing shoppers to fantasize their own refashioning and . . . providing ongoing cultural schooling for their readers."[39] Whetting consumer appetite for desirable images of the Iranian's clothed body, ladies' magazines were mediums through which Englishwomen could normalize an eccentric femininity.[40] Paradoxically, the more that they dressed like the macho other, the more they authenticated their classy feminine selves in domestic terms.

Turning the self-in-clothes into a spectacle for the opposite sex to imitate had the potential to unsettle the status quo. I have examined elsewhere how metropolitan media cast the gentlemanly Abul Hassan as a buffoonish effeminate in that his showy exterior recalled the dandy's arbitration of aristocratic masculine taste.[41] Minimalist speech, upright posture, and an air of social pretentiousness imbued the dandy with a narcissistic theatricality whereby spectators were his co-participants in producing homosocial norms. Dandies such as Beau Brummell—a man from a humble background who inspired the Prince of Wales and his coterie to wear sleek Hussar uniforms—were infamous precisely because they imitated their social superiors with precision. But, once this performance became cliché, dandies were tainted with the ascription of an alien hybridity unassimilable to the male-female binary.[42] Abul Hassan was thus reluctantly drawn into the cult of dandyism. Although an antiquated yet potent English masculinity is conveyed through his black beard, its talismanic ability to attract women away from beardless suitors would have recalled the way that Brummell dominated the social scene through unconventional fashions.

The gender nonconformity that the beau monde attributed to Abul Hassan is evident in Edgeworth's representation of Fanny, who coyly claims that "his Persian Highness" is interested only in her "poney" rather than her person in "a new brown habit which fits to admiration." The insinuation is that the superstar is too self-consumed among "English gentlemen . . . of the first distinction" to flirt with a well-dressed fan (from the rural gentry) feigning feminine modesty. Her performative ruse has delirious effects on polite masculinity, as if heterosexual attraction must be routed through the male gaze (Mr. Whitbread's testimony to the contrary) to disavow what might otherwise appear as a dandyish confusion of sexual orientation. In other words, this dalliance implies that gentlemanly homosocial norms are aberrant, symbolized in Abul Hassan's pointing with his riding "stick" to signal "to the gentlemen with him" (as "interpreted" by them) his lust for a fashionable youth superior to his Circassian wife.

The equestrian subtext is crucial. Female equestrians redefined ideologies of race and empire in Britain well into the twentieth century, and the equestrian sport likewise compelled Abul Hassan to rethink Qajar protocols for how the sexes should interact in public.[43] Moreover, Hyde Park was where dandies displayed their tastes in clothing and horses, as male gallants dressed in Brummell-like, tight blue coats with brass buttons, stiff white cravats, leather breaches, and high boots while strutting on horseback alongside elegant damsels.[44] One of the earliest usages of the term "dandy" dates to the 1760s, when the wealthy British landowner Coke of Norfolk arrived in London wearing riding clothes to petition King George III—a fashion emulated by dandies.[45] Abul Hassan's *torktazi* performances among his bearded Persian servants prompted spectators to situate him in the "dandy's border world," a "deeply cosmopolitan" world of constant movement, crossovers, and dislocations.[46]

A Circassian Celebrity's Dandy Fans

The media fascination with the Persian ambassador's marriage to Delarom also raised questions about the dandies who reportedly courted her in London as a fashionista worthy of female emulation. Edgeworth's insinuation that Fanny and the Fair Circassian are sex objects exchangeable between men seems to confirm Gayle Rubin's theory that the "exchange of women is a profound perception of a system in which women do not have full rights to themselves," wherein female social agency is denied by domineering patriarchs—a point that is similarly taken up in chapter 9 by Jeremy Chow and Riley DeBaecke in their critique of the heterodomestic marriage plot.[47] Yet the bizarre fanfare following April 25, 1819, illustrates how Delarom is caught in homosocial discourses and debates over women's fashions, in which her veils and scarves could evidence either patriarchal control or her dissent to becoming a fetishized object under the gaze of British crowds and the press.[48] On that date, crowds thronged to behold Delarom's landing at Dover via Paris, where she was the rage among the fashion paparazzi. British newspapers reported that she was in "a hood, which covered the upper part of her head, and a large silk shawl screened the lower part of her face, across the nose, from observation." Only her "truly beautiful" eyes and "forehead" were visible. Two days later, she arrived at her husband's London residency in Charles Street Berkeley Square; she stayed "in one of the back apartments, the door of which is guarded all day by two black eunuchs with swords, who . . . dress and undress her."[49] The fantastical notion that only these castrated men had access to her nude body and wardrobe—fantastical because her attendants were in fact two Persian servants—was spread by the tabloid news circuit, which linked racialized sexual impotency to her dandy aficionados. As reported in *The Times*, the envoy and his new wife rode in a carriage through London under the protection of "ten or a dozen persons habited in silks and turbans, with daggers and long beards," and two Black eunuchs who kept her hidden from "the inquiring eyes of the hundreds of loungers and dandies."[50] In this reportage, trafficking an enslaved woman was coded as a dandyish affront to British national virility. Her fashionable look was nonetheless lucrative for businesswomen who marketed Oriental-style clothing brands, mainly the Circassian corset that was satirized in anti-dandy visual prints and theatrical farces.

Delarom's full biography and portrait first appeared in *La Belle Assemblée*, owned by the bookseller John Bell and published by the fashion entrepreneur and innovator Mary Ann Bell, his daughter-in-law. For John, the magazine was meant for "the education of young ladies in the way of modesty,"[51] but for Mary, the magazine had a commercial end potentially at odds with its didactic tone. She held monthly fashion shows catering to the nobility at her shop on London's Upper King Street and advertised them in the magazine's plates, which were designed so that ladies could craft their unique sartorial personalities by freely adapting the featured dresses according to their tastes and economic means.[52] The tension between moral prescription and consumer autonomy subtends Delarom's biographical sketch. "Delarom" (meaning "Heart's Ease") is described as a "barred and bolted female" inaccessible to "the male sex." She is "dressed in the more becoming potency of loveliness" rather than in the hard armor formerly worn by the masculine women who descended from ancient Amazonian warriors.[53] The sketch rehashes racial stereotypes about the celebrated beauty and bravery of women from Circassia in the Caucasus, a region extending from the Black Sea to the Caspian Sea. Many of them became concubines to Ottoman elites.[54] Their fabled connection to the Amazons, a Scythian tribe famous for their skilled horse-riding and military prowess, was a common trope since Robert Shirley's Circassian wife, Teresa Sampsonia, traveled with him to Tudor England on his embassy from the Safavid ruler Shah Abbas I.[55] Keen on tracing their European ancestry to Caucasians, readers are to identify with Delarom's off-whiteness; her "complexion is brown" but with a "soft and very clear" skin, even as her "face is very far from Grecian."[56] Having lost her Amazonian ferocity, she was sold by her poor shepherd parents to "Turkish slave merchants" bound for Istanbul, where she was purchased by Abul Hassan, falsely rumored to have four wives and twenty concubines in Iran (in truth he had one wife). Despite her humble upbringing, she possesses "a sweet and native politeness, which evinces itself in a genteel address, and in a manner perfectly graceful," as relayed by the Englishwomen who had the privilege to meet her.[57]

Magazines' biographical sketches were usually printed with head portraits like the one of Delarom taken by "a female artist of superior eminence."[58] These portraits "tended to reify gender roles," translating bodily features into prescriptive knowledge.[59] While the Circassian's life story is supposedly unmediated (coming "chiefly from her own lips"), her portrait is said to be a "faithful" copy. This piece of information was conveyed to the artist by someone in Abul Hassan's suite. Delarom is shown in "the dress of London and Paris," with a pendant of precious stones, as customarily worn by Circassian concubines to enhance their commercial value.[60] Her head reflects Englishwomen's neoclassical tastes in two regards: the hair bundled into ringlets on the back side recalls Greek or Roman statues, and the white-complexioned oval face with large eyes, soft pouting lips, small mouth, and rosy cheeks reflected a typical portraiture style for fashionable ladies, as in Figure 3.2. These ladies were keen on imitating the "Oriental" look of beautiful women from Circassia and Georgia.[61] Most notably, an ornate shawl drapes Delarom's shoulders. Her face was an imaginary mirror through which fashion-savvy viewers could

Figure 3.2. "Ladies Evening or Opera Dress," plate 25, by Samuel Howitt (1756–1823). Rudolph Ackermann, *The Repository*, vol. 3, April 1810. Photographic reproduction courtesy of The Los Angeles Public Library.

appropriate, or rather domesticate, foreign ideals of feminine beauty. Thus, although the portrait "is neither the work of imagination or hearsay," a footnote by the magazine's "distinguished female correspondent" contradicts this claim: Delarom has told her that the "imagined *costume*" appeared to her "like a bundle of rags," unlike the "thick yellow veil" she had worn on her arrival to London, and that she had "no white satin with gold fringe; no diamond on my hair."[62] Her sartorial resistance induces the viewer to imagine in realistic portraiture's artifice the enslaved celebrity's willful subjectivity. In this sketch-portrait pairing, biographical intimacy functions as an invitation for female consumers to reject, refashion, and revalue what they see on display.[63]

Verbal and visual satires about Delarom's salacious rumored threesome with the Persian envoy and the prince regent cast her as a "fictional non-person," a pornographic object trafficked between vulgar dandies.[64] These representations set out to address two sets of anxieties: first, her biography reminded women resistant to patriarchal control that they were fortunate to have been born in "a land of freedom . . . where civil and moral law is a protection and safeguard to the weak and defenceless."[65] Second, Delarom's confinement in Britain was controversial due to the outlawing of the transatlantic slave trade in 1807. After the alderman of London led a campaign to liberate her through "a writ of Habeas Corpus," which she reportedly declined, her fans were lampooned in print.[66] Reports about her "oppressed" life on returning to Persia vilified the fashionables who, on September 30, 1819, gathered at Gravesend to witness her departure.[67] Most conspicuous was her "Anglo Cashmire shawl, (from Mr. Everington's fashionable depôt in Ludgate-street), placed over her head, which nearly covered her figure."[68]

Such accounts convey the impression that metropolitan outfitters profited from the Fair Circassian fiasco, given that Abul Hassan gave expensive cashmere fabrics and shawls to Empress Josephine (Napoleon's wife and a fashion trendsetter) and the prince regent—a gift-giving ritual crucial to Qajar diplomacy.[69] To learn how to reproduce these coveted gifts cheaply, "twenty ladies of fashionable distinction" met with Delarom at the ambassador's home; while some did not consider her "a model of female beauty" as the newspapers had claimed, all praised "the costume of her country," her quaint "manners," and slim waistline.[70] The latter detail is emphasized in *La Belle Assemblée* and other fashion periodicals, informing readers that Circassian women's "slender waist" was achieved soon after birth by "a corset, or broad belt of undressed leather, [that] is sowed from below the breasts to the hips, and, among more distinguished persons, it is fixed with silver clasps."[71] The girdle was a cultural norm for displaying an aesthetic symmetry between the stomach and breasts by tight vesting as shown in Figure 3.3, and was cut by the husband with a dagger on the wedding night.[72] Conforming to "Circassian, and . . . Turkish ideas of beauty," this look, though not "pleasing to the eye of a European," was marketed for Englishwomen after Mary Ann Bell had invented the "Circassian corset."[73] Unlike European corsets, hardened with whalebone that were painful and unhealthy, her invention after that worn by the envoy's wife was advertised in *La Belle Assemblée* and elsewhere as a concealer of "deformities . . .

Figure 3.3. A portrait of Delarom. Stipple with engraving, after a painting. *La Belle Assemblée* (July 1819), RB 337850, The Huntington Library, San Marino, California.

in females" and an "antidote to Cancer."[74] "Conducive to health and comfort," Circassian corsets for shaping "the bosom to the greatest possible advantage" among "those who are inclined to corpulency" normalizes female ableism insofar as fatness is a disability to be concealed by whiteness—a racialized capacity for pristine European beauty coextensive with Delarom-inspired fashions in Paris.[75]

Satires attributed this latest commodity to dandies. For example, the printmaker and etcher Charles Williams caricatured three corpulent ladies in feathered hats corseting Delarom, the famed beauty (Figure 3.4).[76] In the image, she screams, "Ah! Ah! me no bear dat; too tight; nasty tiff ting Me no eat no drink no do noting at all in dat." The nearest lady assures her that "Poh Child You will soon be used to

Figure 3.4. "British Graces, Attireing the Circassian Venus in the English Costume," handcolored engraving by Charles Williams, 1819. Courtesy of The Lewis Walpole Library, Yale University.

them," while the one on the left, holding an embroidered collar, quips, "And then she'll like the nasty tiff ting, as well as we do they keep us in shape! pray what would the Dandys do without them." Two presumed eunuchs with long beards gaze approvingly, one touching the Circassian's corset (his hand near her genitalia) and telling his companion: "Very good ting Muley No want us guarde now!" The latter replies, "Ah! den we go drink de brown tout Hamet!" The woman holding a gown behind them exclaims, "Aye and you must drink a rare quantity before it will make men of ye!!" Viewers are to infer that Delarom's female admirers were against British liberty in being greater enslavers of their own kind than emasculated Persians feigning masculinity were, with dandies held accountable for this national debasement. In this period, tight corsets and stays were most popular among upwardly mobile Englishwomen,[77] but dandies were also changing their appearance through tight lacing, wearing corsets underneath their costumes.[78] The satirical cartoon implies that dandyism is what happens between xenophilic women behind closed doors.

Similarly, the dandy's corseted body was the butt of the joke in *Harlequin and Cinderella; or, the Little Glass Slipper*, arranged by Charles Farley and first staged in Covent Garden theater on April 3, 1820. Pantomime's fashionable décor, Eastern scenery, and Persian costumery (including turbans and shawls) had been major crowd-pleasers since the 1790s.[79] This "new pantomime" featured painted panels depicting "the Persian Ambassador's House" and "the Grand Boudoir of the Fair Circassian," a private space for staging sexual seductions on a par with Oriental harems dominated by female coquettes.[80] The farce was received "with shouts of laughter & applause" and to be "repeated every evening," as the actors who played the exotic couple "assisted not a little to the amusement of the spectators," besides the "new scenery, machinery, dresses, and decorations."[81] Most astonishing to the audience was when a raggedy Cinderella, having been confined to the kitchen by her mother and two sisters, rode to the ballroom in the prince's palace on a "gourd" with "rats and mice" transformed into horse-drawn "magnificent equipage" by her fairy benefactress's magic. In the distance appeared London landmarks: the Haymarket Opera House, Regent's Park, Southwark Bridge, and the home in which Abul Hassan and his wife were residing.[82] No surprise, then, that the pantomime was advertised in *La Belle Assemblée* and *Bell's Weekly Messenger* to appeal indirectly to the beau monde's eccentric consumerism.

Fashion displays are central to *Harlequin and Cinderella* and its antecedent, a pantomime performed at Drury Lane in 1804 and based on Charles Perrault's 1697 fairy tale "Cendrillon."[83] An afterpiece to five-act comedies, the first version's dumbshow, dance, recitative, and song carried over into the 1820 adaptation. Starring in both versions was the famous clown Joseph Grimaldi, who in the remake played Baroness Pomposini (Cinderella's mother) before morphing into Clown. Accordingly, the first half of the pantomime follows the fairy tale's familiar storyline, with the second half introducing the harlequinade's stock characters: Cinderella morphs into Columbine, her lover Prince Celidoze into Harlequin, her father Baron Pomposini into Pantaloon, and the "servant [named Pedro], violently enamoured of Cinderella, . . . into a Dandy."[84] The fairy dooms the lovers to "wandering and persecution" until they find the magic slippers that accompanied Cinderella's neoclassical dress, which she found floating midair in the kitchen.[85] The dress is decked "in transparent drapery, dazzling with silk and silver." Donning it made Cinderella "naked as a woman of fashion should be."[86] The fairy's spell is broken once "Venus's golden doves bears the long-sought slipper, and drops it on Harlequin's head." Cinderella and the prince afterward return to their normal form to be married "in bliss." The grand finale has the three female actors performing, as if in a fashion show, "their beautiful shawl dance."[87] Cinderella pantomimes popularized and thereby normalized crossdressing fashions in masquerade ballrooms.[88] Spectators were cued to see in these unruly performances the same normative ideals of able-bodied femininity inculcated in periodicals for fashionable ladies, with their desires for the opposite sex ultimately sanctioned by marriage—points that Shelby Johnson similarly discusses in the preceding chapter.

Regency-era pantomimes regularly satirized dandyism, as inferable from Grimaldi's antics in *Harlequin and Cinderella*. His son, Joseph Samuel William Grimaldi, played Pedro, the "poor enamour'd loon [who] changes to Dandinee."[89] The name "Pedro," a blackface role, conjures France's West Indies slave plantations.[90] Joseph had played this role before his son, in the 1804 pantomime after the prince's valet—named Dandini—in Gioachino Rossini's 1817 opera *La Cenerentola* (first performed at Covent Garden in 1820). "Dandinee" was part of the elder Grimaldi's repertoire as "Dandy Lover," known as "the foolish, vain, and insipid young man personifying the deservedly spurned suitor."[91] Modeled after Brummell, this character appeared as an exquisite imitating French fashions. He was Pantaloon's dim-witted servant or lackey, eager to marry Pantaloon's daughter, Columbine, yet incapable of charming her or copulating. His corseted body was usually misshaped to inhuman proportions, self-fetishized in its sartorial excesses.[92] *Harlequin and Cinderella* not only racially others the Dandy Lover but also uses him as a satiric figure aimed against the gentlemen whom he uncannily resembles. In one scene, "*Dandy* . . . is made to exchange cards with the *Clown*; and in a subsequent meeting, these two well-matched Gentlemen at first run away, and when compelled by their seconds to fire, shoot each his second."[93] The duel between look-alikes, both fatally wounding one another in this spoof against gentlemanly bravado, deflates patriarchal authority for an audience aware that the dandified Pedro was a role invented by the father and now played by the son. What was to be a play promoting novel female fashions turns out to be a comical interrogation of who, if anyone, embodies an authentic genteel masculinity.

More titillating for the spectators would have been the dead Clown's return as the dandy's female double, "Dandizetta," whom the elder Grimaldi performed in other pantomimes to great acclaim.[94] In that role, he cross-dressed as the Fair Circassian in her boudoir, a bawdy scene that garnered the greatest applause. The blending of Clown, Pedro, Dandy, and Dandizetta into one amorphous body in a harem-like setting received the audience's implicit approval, in contrast to their unanimous hissing of Grimaldi's other cross-dressing satire: as the Baroness in a "toilet scene," he had "exhibited the mysteries of her dress rather plainly [corset or stays]," a bawdiness that "certainly ventured too far."[95] Besides concerns for maintaining sexual propriety, what was perhaps so unacceptable about this scene was the unveiling of white feminine embodiment as an ableist performance, a normative whiteness exposed as artifice. Hence, dandyism's gender-sex-race fluidity—symbolized in the corset—is the mechanism for distinguishing male from female and British from Oriental.

REGENCY ENGLAND'S ISLAMICATE SEXUALITIES

Enmeshed in an anti-dandy mediascape, *Harlequin and Cinderella* suggests that the question of who counts as a gentleman is for the audience to decide. What appears transgressive about the Persian envoy and his wife helped British spectators heteronormalize themselves: the same type of sociality seen in the "love between men" became the medium for Abul Hassan's female fans to perform sexual agency in public with and for male non-kin. Heterosocial bonding thereby became acceptable for Regency Britons around the same time that gentlemen's homosocial bonding was undergoing heightened public scrutiny for its possible effeminacy across various mediums. Furthermore, these mediations recalibrated British gender norms remarkably receptive to the Persian-Islamic masculinity transmitted via Abul Hassan's mediatized beardedness. From its protean assimilation of eccentricities in fashion and appearance emerged new standards for modernizing Western courtship rituals and heterosexual marital conventions.

Ultimately, extending Islamicate sexualities to Regency England helps connect gender and sexual formations that are usually studied apart within siloed academic disciplines. The upshot to working across imperial archives is to show that the consolidation of a sex-gender binarism in late Qajar Iran was underway earlier in Regency-era newspapers, visual prints, and theatrical performances. Before European gender ideals became a catalyst for Iranian modernization, they had to become normal. This historical reorientation dates to the Regency dandies and dandizettes in love with all things Persian. My goal is to present an interdisciplinary lens for interpreting Anglo-Persian transculturation in the long nineteenth century as a multidirectional exchange. Such an approach allows us to see that the sexual deviant is not the bearded Abul Hassan or the habited Fanny but the beardless suitor who failed to secure Fanny's hand in matrimony: Mr. Whitbread.[96] "Fanny's gentleman in waiting"—the Member of Parliament of Middlesex in 1820—was spurned by her, who would "not run after" Whitbread despite his persistent pursuit of her to go horse riding with him.[97] Edgeworth described him in terms fit for an impotent Dandy Lover: a "good but too meek looking a youth."[98] His marriage prospect might have improved had he been as virile and venerable as the Persian horse rider who stole the spotlight on that memorable day in Hyde Park.

NOTES

1. Maria Edgeworth, *Letters from England, 1813–1844*, ed. Christina Colvin (Oxford: Clarendon Press, 1971), 202–203.

2. Jane Austen, *Mansfield Park*, ed. James Kinsley (Oxford: Oxford University Press, 2008), 79.

3. Mary Beth Harris, *A Genealogy of the Gentleman: Women Writers and Masculinity in the Eighteenth Century* (Newark, DE: University of Delaware Press, 2024); Rory Muir, *Gentlemen of Uncertain Fortune: How Younger Sons Made Their Way in Jane Austen's England* (New Haven, CT: Yale University Press, 2019); and Philip Mason, *The English Gentleman: The Rise and Fall of an Ideal* (New York: William Morrow, 1982). On scholarship linking fear of effeminacy in this period to concurrent imperialist and xenophobic discourses, see Peter McNeil, *Pretty Gentlemen: Macaroni Men and the Eighteenth-Century Fashion World* (New Haven, CT: Yale University Press, 2018); Julia Banister, *Masculinity, Militarism, and Eighteenth-Century Culture, 1689–1815* (Cambridge: Cambridge University Press, 2018), 14–43; and Declan Kavanagh, *Effeminate Years: Literature, Politics, and Aesthetics in Mid-Eighteenth-Century Britain* (Lewisburg, PA: Bucknell University Press, 2017).

4. Eve Kosofsky Sedgwick, *Between Men: English Literature and Male Homosocial Desire* (New York: Columbia University Press, 2015).

5. Eve Kosofsky Sedgwick, *Tendencies* (Durham, NC: Duke University Press, 1993), xii. On the problematic fetishization of queerness, see Brad Epps, "The Fetish of Fluidity," in *Homosexuality and Psychoanalysis*, ed. Tim Dean and Christopher Lane (Chicago: University of Chicago Press, 2001), 412–431.

6. On fashion as nationally debasing yet socially enabling in Edgeworth's 1809–1812 *Tales of Fashionable Life*, see Andrew McInnes, "Amazonian Fashions: Lady Delacour's (Re)Dress in Maria Edgeworth's *Belinda*," in *Picturing Women's Health*, ed. Francesca Scott, Kate Scarth, and Ji Won Chung (London: Pickering & Chatto, 2014), 29–44; and Heidi Thomson, "'The Fashion Not to Be an Absentee': Fashion and Moral Authority in Edgeworth's Tales," in *An Uncomfortable Authority: Maria Edgeworth and Her Contexts*, ed. Heidi Kaufman and

Chris Fauske (Newark: University of Delaware Press, 2004), 165–191. On the feminization of British nationhood in the eighteenth century, see Emma Major, *Madam Britannia: Women, Church, and Nation, 1712–1812* (Oxford: Oxford University Press, 2012).

7. Afsaneh Najmabadi, *Women with Mustaches and Men without Beards: Gender and Sexual Anxieties of Iranian Modernity* (Berkeley: University of California Press, 2005), 48.

8. See Kathryn Babayan and Afsaneh Najmabadi, eds., *Islamicate Sexualities: Translations across Temporal Geographies of Desire* (Cambridge, MA: Harvard University Press, 2008), especially Valerie Traub, "The Past Is a Foreign Country? The Times and Spaces of Islamicate Sexuality Studies," 1–40.

9. Abdul Hassan Khan, *A Persian at the Court of King George, 1809–10: The Journal of Mirza Abul Hassan Khan*, trans. and ed. Margaret Morris Cloake (London: Barrie and Jenkins, 1988), 28.

10. On Abul Hassan's life, see Denis Wright, *The Persians amongst the English: Episodes in Anglo-Persian History* (London: I. B. Tauris, 1985), 54; Henry McKenzie Johnston, *Ottoman and Persian Odysseys: James Morier, Creator of Hajji Baba of Ispahan, and His Brothers* (London: British Academic Press, 1998), 120–122; and H. Javadi, "Abu'l-Ḥasan Khan Īlčī," *Encyclopædia Iranica*, I/3, 308–10, accessed May 13, 2020, https://www.iranicaonline.org/articles/abul-hasan-khan-ilci-mirza-persian-diplomat-b.

11. Louis Simond, *Journal of a Tour and Residence in Great Britain, during the Years 1810 and 1811*, vol. 1 (London: A. Constable and Company, 1815), 160.

12. Joseph Roach, *It* (Ann Arbor: University of Michigan Press, 2007), 1.

13. Erica Munkwitz, *Women, Horse Sports, and Liberation: Equestrianism and Britain from the 18th to the 20th Centuries* (New York: Routledge, 2021), 52–53, 105–108.

14. Khan, *A Persian*, 78.

15. Willem Floor, *Games Persians Play: A History of Games and Pastimes in Iran from Hide-and-Seek to Hunting* (Washington, DC: Mage Publishers, 2011), 125–130.

16. Mirza Abul Hassan Khan-e Ilchi, *Heyratnameh: Safarnameh-ye Mirza Abul Hassan Khan-e Ilchi be London*, ed. Hassan Morsalvand (Tehran: Rasa, 1986), 215–216.

17. Donna Landry, *Noble Brutes: How Eastern Horses Transformed English Culture* (Baltimore, MD: Johns Hopkins University Press, 2009), 3, 137.

18. Khan, *A Persian*, 164–165.

19. "Grand Review," *Morning Post* (April 17, 1810), 4.

20. Naghmeh Sohrabi, *Taken for Wonder: Nineteenth-Century Travel Accounts from Iran to Europe* (Oxford: Oxford University Press, 2012), 40. On Iranian courtesans' equestrian dress, see Willem Floor, *A Social History of Sexual Relations in Iran* (Washington, DC: Mage Publishers, 2008), 211.

21. On fashionable portraiture as a medium for viewers to adopt new identities in sociable settings, see Elizabeth A. Fay, *Fashioning Faces: The Portraitive Mode in British Romanticism* (Hanover, NH: University Press of New England, 2010), 6–11, 13.

22. Hugh Paton, *A Series of Original Portraits and Caricature Etchings, by the Late John Kay*, vol. 2, part 2 (Edinburgh: Hugh Paton, Carver, and Gilder, 1838), 308.

23. See Christopher Oldstone-Moore, "The Beard Movement in Victorian Britain," *Victorian Studies* 48, no. 1 (Autumn 2005): 7–34, especially 10; Jennifer Evans and Alun Withey, "Introduction," in *New Perspectives on the History of Facial Hair: Framing the Face*, ed. Jennifer Evans and Alun Withey (Cham, Switzerland: Palgrave, 2018), 1–11; Susan Walton, "From Squalid Impropriety to Manly Respectability: The Revival of Beards, Moustaches and Martial Values in the 1850s in England," *Nineteenth-Century Contexts* 3, no. 3 (Fall 2008): 229–245, especially 229; and Kathryn Hughes, *Victorians Undone: Tales of the Flesh in the Age of Decorum* (Baltimore, MD: Johns Hopkins University Press, 2018), 73–150.

24. Eleanor Rycroft, "Hair, Beards and the Fashioning of English Manhood in Early Modern Travel Texts," in *New Perspectives on the History of Facial Hair*, 69–89 (74).

25. Elizabeth Fielding to Harriot Frampton, February 3, 1810. See Mary Frampton, *The Journal of Mary Frampton* (London: S. Low, Marston, Searle & Rivington, 1885), 140.

REFASHIONING MASCULINITY IN REGENCY ENGLAND 73

26. Fielding to Frampton, February 3, 1810, 141.

27. On the European incorporation of the ottoman and its association with Orientalism and libertinism, see Madeleine Dobie, "Orientalism, Colonialism, and Furniture in Eighteenth-Century France," in *Furnishing the Eighteenth Century: What Furniture Can Tell Us about the American and European Past*, ed. Dena Goodman and Kathryn Norberg (New York: Routledge, 2006), 13–36.

28. Fielding to Frampton, February 3, 1810, 141.

29. See Karen Harvey, *Reading Sex in the Eighteenth Century: Bodies and Gender in English Erotic Culture* (Cambridge: Cambridge University Press, 2004).

30. Mark Albert Johnston, *Beard Fetish in Early Modern England: Sex, Gender, and Registers of Value* (Farnham, UK: Ashgate, 2011), 43–46, 70–72, and 90–92; Will Fisher, *Materializing Gender in Early Modern English Literature and Culture* (Cambridge: Cambridge University Press, 2006), 102–103, 107–108; and Evans and Withey, "Introduction," 3.

31. Hilary Davidson, *Dress in the Age of Jane Austen: Regency Fashion* (New Haven, CT: Yale University Press, 2019), 38, 234–235.

32. "Female Fashions," *Morning Post* (April 3, 1810), 3.

33. The following newspaper articles on the "Mirza turban" were culled from Rudolph Ackermann, *The Repository of Arts, Literatures, Commerce, Manufactures, Fashions and Politics*, vol. 3 (London: Rudolph Ackermann, 1810), 262. See also "Mouse of Commons," *Chester Chronicle* (March 30, 1810), 2; "Friday, Saturday, Sunday, and Monday's Posts," *Trewman's Exeter Flying Post or, Plymouth and Cornish Advertiser* (March 29, 1810), 1; "Fashions for April," *Jackson's Oxford Journal* (April 7, 1810), 4; and "Fashions for Ladies and Gentlemen, for April," *Lancaster Gazette and General Advertiser* (March 31, 1810), 4.

34. "Fashionable Costume for July," *The Lady's Magazine; or Entertaining Companion for the Fair Sex* (July 1817), 281.

35. "Cashemire Shawls," *La Belle Assemblée: or Court and Fashionable Magazine* (June 1819), 233.

36. Amelia Rauser, *The Age of Undress: Art, Fashion and the Classical Ideal in the 1790s* (New Haven, CT: Yale University Press, 2020), 7; Adam Geczy, *Fashion and Orientalism: Dress, Textiles and Culture from the 17th to the 21st Century* (London: Bloomsbury, 2013), 100–105; and Aileen Ribeiro, *Facing Beauty: Painted Women & Cosmetic Art* (New Haven, CT: Yale University Press, 2011), 208.

37. Geczy, *Fashion*, 104.

38. Rauser, *The Age*, 9, 18, 22.

39. Fay, *Fashioning Faces*, 95.

40. On magazine fashion images as normalizing eccentric attitudes and regulating sexual identities for viewers, see Davidson, *Dress in the Age of Austen*, 48–51; and Diana Fuss, "Fashion and the Homospectatorial Look," *Critical Inquiry* 18, no. 4 (Summer 1992): 713–737.

41. Humberto Garcia, "Queering Fashion in Hajji Baba: James Morier, Mirza Abul Hassan Khan, and the Crisis of Imperial Masculinity," *Eighteenth-Century Fiction* 34, no. 1 (Winter 2021): 1–31.

42. See Laura George, "The Emergence of the Dandy," *Literature Compass* 1, no. 1 (Spring 2003–2004): 1–13; Jane Rendell, *The Pursuit of Pleasure: Gender, Space, and Architecture in Regency London* (New Brunswick, NJ: Rutgers University Press, 2002), 49–54; James Eli Adams, *Dandies and Desert Saints: Styles of Victorian Masculinity* (Ithaca, NY: Cornell University Press, 2018); and Elizabeth Amann, *Dandyism in the Age of Revolution* (Chicago: University of Chicago Press, 2015).

43. Munkwitz, *Women*.

44. Ellen Moers, *The Dandy: Brummell to Beerbohm* (Lincoln: University of Nebraska Press, 1960), 64–66.

45. James Laver, *Dandies* (London: Weidenfeld and Nicolson, 1968), 12.

46. Susan Fillin-Yeh, "Introduction: New Strategies for a Theory of Dandies," in *Dandies: Fashion and Finesse in Art and Culture*, ed. Susan Fillin-Yeh (New York: New York University Press, 2001), 1–34 (5).

47. Gayle Rubin, "The Traffic in Women: Notes on the Political Economy of Sex," in *Toward an Anthropology of Women*, ed. Rayna R. Reiter (New York: Monthly Review Press, 1975), 157–210 (177).

48. We might recall Saba Mahmood's reformulation of gender and agency in relationship to the hijab in *Politics of Piety: The Islamic Revival and the Feminist Subject* (Princeton, NJ: Princeton University Press, 2005): "If we think of 'agency' not simply as a synonym for resistance to social norms but as a modality of action, then this conversation raises some interesting questions about the kind of relationship established between the subject and the norm, between performative behavior and inward disposition" (157).

49. "Court and Fashionables," *The Examiner* (May 2, 1819), 280–281. See also "April," *The Edinburgh Annual Register* (January 1819), 303; "Epitome of Public Affairs for May, 1819," *The Lady's Monthly Museum, or Polite Repository of Amusement and Instruction* (June 1819), 340; and "Mirror of Fashion for June, 1819," *The New British Lady's Magazine; or Monthly Mirror of Literature and Fashion* (June 1819), 274.

50. "Arrival of the Persian Ambassador and the Fair Circassian. Dover, April 25," *The Times* (April 27, 1819), 3; and "The Persian Ambassador and the Circassian," *The Times* (April 30, 1819), 3.

51. Quoted in Stanley Morison, *John Bell, 1745–1831: Bookseller, Printer, Publisher, Type-founder, Journalist* (Cambridge: Cambridge University Press, 1930), 65.

52. Fay, *Fashioning Faces*, 24; and Neil McKendrick, J. H. Plumb, and John Brewer, *The Birth of Consumer Society: The Commercialization of Eighteenth-Century England* (London: Europa, 1982), 190.

53. "Biographical Sketches of Illustrious and Distinguished Characters. Delarom, the Fair Circassian," *La Belle Assemblée: Being Bell's Court and Fashionable Magazine* (July 1819), 6, 4.

54. On Circassian women celebrated for their heroism and gallantry since biblical times, and their trafficking as concubines in the Ottoman Empire, see Amjad Jaimoukha, *The Circassians: A Handbook* (New York: Palgrave Macmillan, 2011), 12, 169.

55. Manoutchehr Eskandari-Qajar, "Persian Ambassadors, Their Circassians, and the Politics of Elizabethan and Regency England," *Iranian Studies* 44, no. 2 (Summer 2011): 251–271; Munkwitz, *Women*, 1; and Bernadette Andrea, *The Lives of Girls and Women from the Islamic World in Early Modern British Literature and Culture* (Toronto: University of Toronto Press, 2017), 29–35.

56. "Biographical Sketches," 5.

57. "Biographical Sketches," 5.

58. "Biographical Sketches," 5.

59. Fay, *Fashioning Faces*, 43.

60. "Biographical Sketches," 4. On Circassian concubines' traditional dress and jewelry, see Jaimoukha, *The Circassians*, 195–196.

61. On the ideal female face in eighteenth-century portraiture, see Ribeiro, *Facing Beauty*, 152–56, 170. On female hairstyles in early nineteenth-century Britain, see Phyllis G. Tortora and Keith Eubank, *Survey of Historic Costume: A History of Western Dress*, 5th ed. (New York: Fairchild, 2010), 317.

62. "Biographical Sketches," 5.

63. For a discussion of this periodical genre's consumerist logic, see Fay, *Fashioning Faces*, 40–43, 70.

64. Eskandari-Qajar, "Persian Ambassadors," 257.

65. "Biographical Sketches," 3. The sketch concludes with a poem "giving advice for the treatment of an English wife:" "Be to her faults a little blind, / Be to her virtues very kind, / Let all her ways be unconfin'd, / And clap your *padlock* on her *mind*" (6).

66. "Court and Fashionables," 280. See also "Miscellaneous: Chiefly Domestic," *The Observer* (May 5, 1819), 4; "Epitome," 341; "The Fair Circassion [sic]," *Shadgett's Weekly Review of Cobbett, Wooler, Sherwin and Other Democratic and Infidel Writers* (1818–1819), 168; and "The Fair Circassian," *The Observer* (May 5, 1819), 2.

REFASHIONING MASCULINITY IN REGENCY ENGLAND   75

67. See, for example, "The Fair Circassian," *The Northern Whig: A Political, Commercial, and Literary Miscellany* (1824), 419; and "Execution," *The Observer* (May 27, 1822), 4.

68. "The Fair Circassian," *The European Magazine, and London Review* (September 1819), 224.

69. Abul Hassan traveled with an extensive collection of cashmere tapestries and shawls as diplomatic gifts for European royals in Vienna, St. Petersburg, Paris, and London. See Marie-Anne Adélaide Le Normand, *Historical and Secret Memoirs of the Empress Josephine, First Wife of Napoleon Bonaparte*, vol. 2, trans. Jacob M. Howard (Philadelphia: Carey and Hart, 1848), 82; "Oriental Presents and Style," *The Literary Gazette: A Weekly Journal of Literature, Science, and the Fine Arts* (April 1, 1820), 221; and "Persian Customs," *The Kaleidoscope: or, Literary and Scientific Mirror* (May 16, 1819), 134. In 1819, he reportedly gave the Prince of Wales sixteen fine Arabian horses, jewelry, "carpets of Cashmere Shawls," and "ten magnificent shawls, of various sizes and denominations" ("Persian Customs," 274). On the projection of Qajar power through diplomatic gifts, including shawls, see Assef Ashraf, "The Politics of Gift Exchange in Early Qajar Iran, 1785–1834," *Comparative Studies in Society and History* 58, no. 2 (April 2016): 550–576, especially 570–575.

70. Paton, *A Series*, 304; "Epitome," 341.

71. "The Fair Circassian," *Fitzhenry: The Literary Chronicle and Weekly Review* (June 5, 1819), 39. Also see "Biographical Sketches," 4; "The Fair Circassian," *Observator*, 221; and "Court and Fashionables," 315–316.

72. On the tight vests used to slim Circassian girls' waists, see Jaimoukha, *The Circassians*, 196.

73. "The Fair Circassian," *Fitzhenry*, 39; and "The Fair Circassian," *Observator*, 221.

74. See "Mrs. Bell's 'Circassian Corsets,'" *The Morning Chronicle* (May 4, 1819), 1; and "Mrs. Bell's Circassian Corsets," *New Times* (May 4, 1819), 1. On European corsets and the contemporary negative commentary on their use, see Rauser, *The Age*, 10–12; and Ribeiro, *Dress*, 96, 129, 134–135.

75. Morison, *John*, 69–70. "Circassian pelisses, without sleeves" and "turbans of Cachemire and pearls, and other Oriental turbans" were marketed for "Parisian ladies" during Delarom's stay in Paris, as described in "Cabinet of Taste: A Parisian Correspondent," *La Belle Assemblée: Being Bell's Court and Fashionable Magazine* (May 1819), 184–185.

76. For a description of this print, see Mary Dorothy George, *Catalogue of Political and Personal Satires Preserved in the Department of Prints and Drawings in the British Museum*, vol. 9, 1811–1819 (London: British Museum Trustees, 1949), 974–975.

77. Elizabeth Wilson, *Adorned in Dreams: Fashion and Modernity*, 2nd ed. (London: Virago, 2003), 97, 99.

78. Ribeiro, *Dress*, 124.

79. David Mayer, *Harlequin in His Element: The English Pantomime, 1806–1836* (Cambridge: Cambridge University Press, 1969), 156–161.

80. See "Harlequin and Cinderella," *A Collection of Playbills from Covent Garden Theatre, 1819–1820. MS British Playbills, British Library*. Nineteenth Century Collections Online; and Gülen Çevik, "Boudoirs and Harems: The Seductive Power of *Sophas*," *Journal of Interior Design* 43, no. 3 (September 2018): 24–41, especially 27–29.

81. See "Harlequin and Cinderella"; "Covent-Garden," *La Belle Assemblée: or Court and Fashionable Magazine* (May 20, 1820), 184; *Bell's Weekly Messenger* (April 9, 1820), 5; and "Covent-Garden," *New Times* (April 4, 1820), 3.

82. See "Theatricals," *Public Ledger and Daily Advertiser* (April 4, 1820), 3; and "Covent-Garden," *New Times*, 3.

83. Jennifer Schacker, *Staging Fairyland: Folklore, Children's Entertainment, and Nineteenth-Century Pantomime* (Detroit, MI: Wayne State University Press, 2018), 64; and *Cinderella; or, The Little Glass Slipper*, in *The Routledge Pantomime Reader: 1800–1900*, ed. Jennifer Schacker and Daniel O'Quinn (New York: Routledge, 2022), 37–56.

84. "Covent-Garden Theatre," *Globe* (April 4, 1820), 3; "Theatricals," 3.

85. "Covent-Garden Theatre," 3.

86. "Covent-Garden," *New Times*, 3.

87. "Covent-Garden Theatre," 3.

88. Schacker, *Staging*, 43.

89. *Harlequin and Cinderella; or, the Little Glass Slipper. A New Pantomime*, Theatre Royal Covent Garden (March 22, 1820), LA2144, John Larpent Plays, The Huntington Library, San Marino, California; and Mayer, *Harlequin*, 176.

90. *Cinderella*, 38–39.

91. Mayer, *Harlequin*, 169.

92. Jonathan Buckmaster, *Dickens's Clowns: Charles Dickens, Joseph Grimaldi and the Pantomime of Life* (Edinburgh: Edinburgh University Press, 2019), 193–194.

93. "Covent-Garden Theatre," *Globe*, 3.

94. Mayer, *Harlequin*, 166, 184. On Grimaldi's cross-dressing performances as sartorial satires, see Jane Moody, *Illegitimate Theatre in London, 1770–1840* (Cambridge: Cambridge University Press, 2000), 217, 224.

95. "Covent-Garden," *New Times*, 3.

96. J. M. Walker and W. S. Pike, "Pen Portraits of Presidents: Samuel Charles Whitbread, FRS," *Weather* 52, no. 12 (1997): 396–399.

97. Edgeworth, *Letters*, 203.

98. Edgeworth, *Letters*, 180.

PART II

Novel Intimacies

CHAPTER 4

"My sister, my friend, my ever beloved"

QUEER FRIENDSHIP AND ASEXUALITY IN *THE MEMOIRS OF MISS SIDNEY BIDULPH*

Ziona Kocher

Intimate female friendships are a mainstay of the eighteenth-century novel, serving as a crucial entry point for queer readings of the period. From the epistolary relationship between Clarissa Harlowe and Anna Howe in Samuel Richardson's *Clarissa* (1748) to the femicentric utopian community of Sarah Scott's *Millenium Hall* (1762) to the bond between Belinda and Lady Delacour in Maria Edgeworth's *Belinda* (1801), female friendships are central to the genre. Examinations of such relationships through a queer lens often seek to unpack desires that are embedded in bonds between women, shining an important light on the eroticism expressed through their interactions.[1] In seeking the possibility of queerness rooted in sexual desires, however, other forms of queer intimacy, such as asexuality or queer friendship, can be ignored. In *Queer Friendship*, George Haggerty notes that "we often want to assume that the love between friends is different from the love between lovers. As I hope to show, that is rarely an easy distinction."[2] My goal here is not to draw boundaries around these different types of love but rather to illustrate how reading these messy webs of affection with asexuality in mind can reinvigorate understandings of queerness in the eighteenth century.

Frances Sheridan's epistolary novel, *The Memoirs of Miss Sidney Bidulph* (1761) illustrates these webs, as the novel represents Sidney's struggles to navigate marriage when her suitor, Orlando Faulkland, is revealed to have fathered a child with an unmarried woman. These events are narrated in Sidney's agonized letters to her friend and closest confidante, Cecilia. By reading Sheridan's *Sidney Bidulph* through an asexual lens, the heroine's passivity regarding marriage and her longing to return to a time when she and Cecilia were inseparable suggest that, while her romantic feelings for Faulkland persevere, she would be happier existing in a world free of the pressures of marriage. Though marriage serves as both an outlet for romantic feelings and a means of maintaining familial wealth and status, it is also a tool that reinforces compulsory sexuality and limits access to other forms of intimacy. *Sidney Bidulph* read through an asexual lens critiques compulsory sexuality to locate a queer, asexual potential that Sidney expresses in her writings to Cecilia.

Friendship, particularly between women, holds a tense position in queer scholarship of the eighteenth century. Eve Kosofsky Sedgwick evolves Adrienne Rich's construction of the lesbian continuum to suggest that "the adjective 'homosocial' as applied to women's bonds . . . need not be pointedly dichotomized as against 'homosexual'; it can intelligibly denominate the entire continuum."[3] While such a continuum is undeniably useful for understanding these relationships, it simultaneously holds the potential to flatten the various forms of desire and intimacy that exist between women. Documenting an astonishing array of representations of women's relationships in literature, Lillian Faderman's *Surpassing the Love of Men* attempts to untangle the distinctions between lesbianism and "romantic friendships," a concept that has met criticism for its potential to distance these relationships from their eroticism. Susan Lanser, for example, describes the term as "obfuscating . . . with its odd blend of discrediting (eighteenth-century) and desexualizing (twentieth-century) baggage."[4] The relationship between Sidney and Cecilia could easily be read as a romantic friendship, as described by Faderman, or as sapphic, as Lanser argues in *The Sexuality of History*. By introducing asexuality as a means of understanding Sidney's longing for Cecilia, I aim to sidestep "a tendency in the reception of queer scholarship to demand incontrovertible evidence of homoerotic desires or acts" while exploring the heroine's queerness through and beyond her relationship with Cecilia.[5] These women's bond is undeniably queer, but Sidney's asexual tendencies expand far beyond their longing for one another.

Rooted in feminist and queer theory, asexual approaches to reading are not simply invested in labeling characters as asexual.[6] Rather, as Ela Przybylo and Danielle Cooper explain, "Through a queerly asexual reading strategy and an attention to the touches, instances, moments, and resonances, we begin to assemble an asexual archive that can accommodate the ephemeral and elusive fragments of asexuality."[7] By assembling such an archive, "asexuality encourages us to rethink the centrality of sex to feminist and queer politics, and to consider critically what has been at stake in the neglect of asexual articulations and perspectives."[8] This approach to queerness is not an attempt to erase sex or eroticism, or to hide it behind euphemism, but, instead, encourages the exploration of alternate forms of queer relationality. Though many assume that asexuality equates to a lack of feeling, asexuality studies remain closely tied to queer affect theory.[9] Ann Cvetkovich describes the production of "'an archive of feelings,' an exploration of cultural texts as repositories of feelings and emotions, which are encoded not only in the content of the texts themselves but in the practices that surround their production and reception," and *Sidney Bidulph*, both in form and content, acts as a fictionalized version of such a repository.[10] Despite her many attempts to repress her emotions, Sidney's narrative overflows with deep, queer feeling, and it is through those feelings—and her own reactions to them—that her asexual potential becomes legible.

Sheridan published the novel during the age of sensibility and the rise of companionate marriage, so there is little surprise that Sidney's troubled and troubling feelings are so central to the text, as she struggles to negotiate her passions and discomfort when faced with marriage and the possibility of love. Paul Kelleher argues that "eighteenth-century literature and philosophy fundamentally rewrote the ethical relationship between self and other as heterosexual fiction, as the sentimental story in which the desire, pleasure, and love shared by man and woman become synonymous with the affective virtues of moral goodness."[11] Texts like Samuel Richardson's *Pamela* highlight the positive potential of such dynamics, as Kelleher suggests that "in Richardson's hands the travails of seduction become a particularly effective means of provoking forms of reflection that expand and expound upon virtues that, if narratively entangled with the question of female chastity, do not simply mirror its gendered, irreversible, either-or logic of 'honest' versus 'ruined.'"[12] Though Sidney, like Pamela, is deeply invested in propriety and virtue, hers does not match that heroine's happy fate.

Instead, her narrative is far more similar to that of Richardson's Clarissa, whose story illustrates "how the union of sexuality and moral feeling can be tragically betrayed."[13] Rather than trusting their intense feelings, both Sidney and Clarissa attempt to suppress them as a form of self-protection, but this suppression repeatedly backfires. In describing Clarissa, Wendy Anne Lee explains that, in the eyes of other characters, her "hard-heartedness offends not because it reflects an inability to love but because it betrays an absolute unwillingness to do so. The hardhearted person is not just unfeeling, affectless, and inhuman . . . but she refuses to feel, to express affect, to be human."[14] Such a description mirrors the reactions Sidney faces to her denial of romantic feeling as well as the harmful assumptions that circulate around asexuality, which, rather than viewing it as a legitimate embodiment of queerness, instead frame it as a dehumanizing defect. Analyzing Sidney's narrative with an asexual lens rejects this impulse in favor of highlighting how her tragedy critiques the period's linkage of sensibility, morality, and (hetero)sexuality.

Sheridan's novel illustrates the trauma caused by compulsory sexuality, primarily represented by the unceasing pain and hardship that accompany Sidney's multiple attempts at marriage. Kristina Gupta explains that through the recognition of its existence within our social structures, the critique of compulsory sexuality "seeks to emphasize that [it] is a system that regulates the behavior of all people, not just those who identify as asexual."[15] The eighteenth-century novel often emphasizes the importance of marriage, reinforcing compulsory sexuality to maintain social hierarchies. The suggestion that marriage leads to positive outcomes is thus in tension with the misery it may cause. Sheridan's critique of compulsory sexuality extends far beyond its connection to marriage and reproduction: while Sidney's discomfort with marriage and love are central to an asexual reading of the text, it must be noted that an adherence to compulsory sexuality is what repeatedly destroys relationships. Both Orlando Faulkland and Mr. Arnold are shown incapable of controlling their sexual desires, and it is *their* actions that lead to conflict rather than Sidney's rejection of sexual and romantic feelings. By embracing the assumptions produced by a society that promotes compulsory sexuality, these men induce problems that Sidney is then held accountable for, further complicating her understanding of herself and her own desires. While they meet tragic ends themselves, Sidney is the one left to pick up the pieces of her doomed attempts at adhering to a system that she would rather reject, and it is her deep-rooted relationship with Cecilia that provides her with comfort as she navigates these events.

Asexual tensions arise in both form and content. Reading with critiques of compulsory sexuality in mind can expose a "logic of asexuality" that organizes a text. As Elizabeth Hanna Hanson explains, "An asexually structured narrative frustrates both the teleological movement towards closure *and* the aimless desire that may also characterize those narratives that resist closure."[16] Looking for such tensions within *Sidney Bidulph* reveals the influence of asexual potential: viewing asexuality as both a tool that allows us to better understand the construction of oppressive social structures *and* a way to better understand desires and behaviors opens up new opportunities to examine modes of queerness that have otherwise been ignored. By reading *Sidney Bidulph* as an archive of asexuality, I reinterpret the possibilities that are embedded within Sheridan's novel as they relate to the queer friendship between Sidney and Cecilia and its view of marriage as a tool of compulsory sexuality. If we focus on the ways Sheridan's novel refuses to reproduce the assumed rewards of marriage, the novel points to an alternative understanding of desire that is often ignored in favor of an emphasis on romantic love or sex. Christina Lupton describes *Sidney Bidulph* as "a series of 'what ifs.' [It] is presented as a journal of a young woman who writes to a friend of a marriage that might have been but wasn't, another that might have worked but didn't, and another contracted on the basis of a death which might have occurred but didn't."[17] The novel actively encourages readers to pursue those "what ifs" and learn from them: Sidney's epistolary narrative emphasizes her continual reconsideration of the decisions she has made and their varied potential outcomes, feeding into the novel's refusal of closure.

In seeking asexual possibilities, *Sidney Bidulph*'s "what ifs" expand even further, no longer limited by the constraints of compulsory sexuality, which, for Sidney at least, is primarily represented by her need to marry. Sidney regularly reflects on her life before marriage, with a particular focus on her youth with Cecilia, making it clear that she longs to return to that period of her life. While many of the "what ifs" in the novel focus on Sidney's relationships with men, reading asexually allows us to ask what might have happened if she and Cecilia were able to remain in that premarital state, free from the pressures of a system that uses women as tools for maintaining and producing capital through the reproduction of family structures—questions that other essays in this collection, including those by M. A. Miller, Jeremy Chow, and Riley DeBaecke, take up explicitly. Examining *Sidney Bidulph* through an asexual lens makes it clear that Sidney's passivity regarding marriage, her longing for Cecilia, and the narrative's refusal of closure reflect an important critique of compulsory sexuality while encouraging readers to consider asexual alternatives that, within the world of the novel, can only exist in Sidney's imagination. Though an emphasis on the rise of companionate marriage often attempts to mask the economic function of marriage in favor of an emphasis on romantic love and attachment, the continued belief that women must be pure and chaste to ensure the protection of the family line suggests that an asexual heroine would be an eighteenth-century ideal, even as an adherence to such an embodiment endangers the reproduction of these structures. While Sidney is unable to find permanent happiness through her asexual impulses and desires, her story reveals both the dangers of compulsory sexuality and the potential pleasures of asexual existence and queer friendship.

"If you find no disinclination, it is enough": The Perils of Compulsory Sexuality

Sidney Bidulph is commonly read as a commentary on the sentimental novel; in particular, scholars frame Sidney's misery, rooted in her obedience to her mother, as a critique of female passivity and over-adherence to the norms presented in popular conduct books.[18] Though readings of asexuality are scant if not absent, critiques of Sidney's attempts at marriage illustrate a concern about the heroine's position as a marriageable object and provide a groundwork for extending this critique to compulsory sexuality more broadly. Written as a series of journal entries addressed to Cecilia, *Sidney Bidulph* follows the trials the eponymous heroine faces as she attempts to find happiness in marriage and, following her failure to do so, attempts to provide a stable life for herself and her daughters. After her rejection of Orlando Faulkland, Sidney marries Mr. Arnold, a man for whom she feels little. Following the revelation of Mr. Arnold's unfaithfulness, he falsely accuses Sidney of infidelity and abandons her, taking their children and leaving her destitute. Though the pair eventually reconciles, their happiness is short-lived as they face financial ruin and Mr. Arnold's death. Sidney, estranged from her brother due to her refusal of Faulkland's proposals, is left poor and virtually friendless until a forgotten cousin appears, providing her with a large fortune as a reward for her generosity. Sidney's happiness is again temporary, as Faulkland returns once more and finally convinces her to marry him, this time under the threat of suicide after he kills his wife. Once the pair have finally married, it is revealed that Faulkland's wife lives, and he takes his own life. The cycle of trauma perpetuated by the pressure for Sidney to marry combined with repeated sexual betrayal by the men she is meant to love reveals the perils of compulsory and coercive sexuality, while Sidney's representation of the events of her life suggests a longing for an asexual existence free of such imperatives.

The tensions among virtue, desire, emotion, and trauma are constantly present in the novel, and the interpretation of Sidney's suffering guides an asexual, affective reading of the text. Sidney's first experience of trauma is the direct aftermath of her engagement to Faulkland: she and her mother learn that before he came to London, he had an affair that impregnated a woman. At the recommendation of her mother, Sidney immediately ends their engagement, much to her brother's disappointment, and though Sidney reveals her feelings about Faulkland in a state of feverish delusion, she convinces herself that she must fully abandon them.[19] Patricia Meyer Spacks frames this decision as Sidney making herself "invulnerable" to Faulkland through her "proclaimed *lack* of feeling, although her account makes it clear that the 'lack' signifies refusal rather than absence."[20] Sidney's decision to reject feeling marks an important critique of compulsory sexuality: rather than being persuaded by her feelings of love and attraction, Sidney acknowledges that these emotions are not sufficient grounds for marriage, recognizing how they can easily lead to destructive outcomes. This choice highlights her desire for an asexual existence, wherein her attraction toward Faulkland (or any other man) cannot impact her behavior and she can instead rely on her reason rather than her emotions. Though Sidney repeatedly discusses her lack of feelings for Faulkland as something that she has chosen, it is crucial to recognize that her agency does not undermine the asexual impulse: the decision to simply stop feeling rather than acknowledge this loss more fully reinforces the discomfort with romantic emotions threaded through her narrative.

While the end of Sidney's engagement to Faulkland serves as a flashpoint of asexual expression, this is far from the only moment—or even the first—when she embodies asexual potential. From the novel's opening, Sidney's journal reveals a discomfort with romantic feelings, even as she admits her interest in the man her brother intends her to marry. Writing about her concern that Faulkland may not like her, she explains, "I have a heart not very susceptible of what we young women call love; and in all likelihood I shall be as indifferent towards him, as he may be towards me—Indeed I think I ought to resolve on not liking him."[21] While there is a certain playfulness in Sidney's declaration, her claim to be "not very susceptible" to love is proven by her own behavior after meeting her husband-to-be. Sidney spends far more time relating how others react to Faulkland than detailing her own opinions. This attention to other people's feelings proves to be the driving force in Sidney's relationships with men, even if her own feelings draw her in a specific direction. Carol Stewart points out that Sheridan's novel acknowledges "that marriage is necessary primarily as a means of ensuring the legitimate inheritance of property. Women, and women's sexuality, are linked to sums of money, or are equated with money."[22] By focusing on the opinions of her mother and brother, Sidney illustrates an understanding that her marriage is less about her feelings than it is about what will be best for the family and its economic situation, itself a useful critique of the intertwined nature of compulsory sexuality and compulsory marriage. This critique becomes even more obvious as the novel progresses and Sidney is encouraged to marry Mr. Arnold.

Sidney's willingness to follow familial guidance is compounded by her obvious anxiety concerning vulnerability and love. Even in the moments where Sidney expresses her feelings, they are couched in the interpretation of others, and she is quick to guard her heart by sharing her fears. As Stewart observes, compared to the plot of *Clarissa*, "as Anna Howe . . . tells the heroine that she is attracted to Lovelace, so Sidney's friend Cecilia tells her that she is in love with Faulkland."[23] This passage comes less than two months after their initial meeting, and Sidney's journal is filled with italicized phrases emphasizing her surprise: "You are unkind, Cecilia, and do not do justice to my sincerity, when you say, *you are sure I am in love with Mr. Faulkland*. If I were, can you conceive it possible that I would want to deny it to you? Ah! My sister, must I suspect *you* of wanting candour by your making a charge of disingenuity against your friend? Indeed, Cecilia, if I *am* in love with him, I do not *yet* know it myself."[24] Though Sidney expresses her fondness for Faulkland, and that she would "certainly give him preference . . . over all the rest of his sex," she writes that "I still endeavour to keep a sort of guard over my wishes, and will not give my heart leave to center *all* its happiness in him."[25] While Sidney occasionally shows her hand, revealing deeper feelings for Faulkland, her anxiety over doing so is undeniable, illustrating a desire for a path forward that is not determined by romantic feelings.

Sheridan continues to emphasize Sidney's investment in fulfilling her duty as a daughter while distancing herself from her own emotions. Her refusal to show her feelings about Faulkland is reflected in the interactions she records, particularly those involving her brother. While Lady Bidulph approves of this control over her emotions, Sir George finds it frustrating: "Well, Sidney, you are either very affected, or the greatest stoic in the world; why, any other girl would be in raptures at such proof of the honest tenderness of that heart which she knows she possesses entirely, and on which the whole of her future happiness depends."[26] Sir George remains annoyed at his sister's refusal to admit that they are destined to be married, illustrating his own investment (and return) in compulsory sexuality: he believes that, because Faulkland has expressed interest in Sidney, she must return those feelings in kind. Additionally, her marriage to his friend would secure their own homosocial relationship, serving as the third point of the triangulation Sedgwick describes in *Between Men*. When Faulkland eventually proposes, Sidney agrees, but is quick to place the bulk of the responsibility on her mother and brother, suggesting her understanding that the marriage is of greater concern for the members of her family who control money and property. Sheridan, by continually highlighting Sidney's understanding of the purpose of marriage as she struggles to process her own feelings of love and attraction—many of which, based on what she writes in her journal, are confusing and potentially unwelcome—indexes the hypocritical nature of compulsory sexuality and the ways in which cultural structures utilize a faulty emphasis on love in marriage to reproduce patriarchal hierarchies.

Sidney's story repeatedly illustrates that love is not enough to save a woman, and for this reason she relies on her "proclaimed *lack* of feeling" for protection.[27] Having left her desire for Faulkland in the past (at least in theory), she soon deigns to marry Mr. Arnold. Sidney's practiced pattern of indifference is heightened during their courtship when Cecilia once again lays claim to an understanding of her friend's true feelings. Sidney responds to her accusations, "You say, you are *sure*

Mr. Arnold is, or will be my lover; and insist on my being more particular in my description of him."[28] This description, however, is far from complimentary, ending with an insistence that "I have told you already, he plays divinely on several instruments; this is the only circumstance about him that pleases me."[29] This judgement proves to be immaterial: describing a conversation with her mother, Sidney writes, "I did not find in myself any great inclination towards Mr. Arnold. Oh, my dear, said she, if you find no disinclination, it is enough."[30] Sidney convinces herself to marry Mr. Arnold, and following their wedding, she determines that "it is not necessary to be passionately in love with the man we marry."[31] Sidney makes a distinct effort to train herself to love Mr. Arnold in order to align with the ideals she has been taught about how to be a proper wife, but her attempts prove insufficient when faced with assumptions about compulsory sexuality that threaten the stability of marriage.

Marriage serves as Sidney's primary means of adhering to cultural expectations regarding love and sex despite her own distaste for these feelings, but Sheridan's novel illustrates that compulsory sexuality can destroy matrimony as easily as it can produce it. Faulkland's premarital affair with another woman ends their engagement, but his ongoing connection to Sidney and their assumed desire for one another proves to be the undoing of the marriage between the heroine and Mr. Arnold. Having caught her husband having an affair with the manipulative Mrs. Gerrarde, Sidney "resolved not to interrupt them; nor if possible, ever let Mr. Arnold know that I had made a discovery so fatal to my own peace, and so disadvantageous to him and his friend."[32] Such efforts are unsuccessful when her rival executes a plan for Mr. Arnold to find Sidney and Faulkland together. Assuming the worst—that an adherence to the norms of compulsory sexuality means that she too must have been unfaithful—Mr. Arnold abandons his wife, declaring, "You have broke your faith with me, in seeing the man whom I forbad you to see, and whom you so solemnly promised to avoid. As you have betrayed my confidence in this particular, I can no longer rely on your prudence or your fidelity."[33] Having embraced a form of compulsory sexuality that implies an inability to resist sexual desires, Mr. Arnold is incapable of trusting his wife, instead relying on the hypocrisy of marriage as a patriarchal system to turn Sidney out for the *appearance* of having behaved like him. While the truth eventually surfaces, their relationship ends in disaster: they are reunited and grasp at happiness but Mr. Arnold's early death leaves Sidney destitute. Despite her best efforts to be a perfect wife, the system of compulsory sexuality irreparably disrupts her marriage, even though the two structures are expected to support and reproduce one another.

While it may be tempting to read Sidney as "hopelessly naïve in her understanding of the realities of female sexuality," reading asexually, with attention to the structures of compulsory sexuality, suggests that Sidney's decision to repress her feelings and adhere to the norms presented by her mother stems from an awareness of the trap that she is caught in by virtue of being a woman who possesses enough of a fortune to be considered worth marrying.[34] The novel highlights how Sidney replaces her own feelings with those of the people around her to clarify that she is not simply following their instructions out of pure obedience; rather, she attempts to protect herself from the harsh realities of marriage by distancing herself from her own emotions. Combined with the discomfort Sidney expresses to Cecilia about her own romantic feelings, Sheridan presents her heroine in such a way that challenges notions about love, romance, and sexuality circulating in mid-eighteenth-century conduct books and novels. Reading asexually allows the reader to explore a new "what if" within the novel: rather than asking "what if Sidney had followed her brother's advice and married Faulkland?," we can ask, "what if Sidney was able to reject the burdens of compulsory sexuality, primarily represented in the pressure to marry, and embody the asexual potential she longs for in her journal?"

"You, my dear Cecilia, mix yourself in all my thoughts": Imagining Asexual Alternatives

Though Sidney's various trials relating to marriage drive the plot, her queer friendship with Cecilia—physically embodied in the journals that make up its text—serves as the grounding force. Many scholars have attended to the impact of *Sidney Bidulph*'s epistolary form and its resistance to closure: these formal features have been read as a way of "subvert[ing] reader expectations," a means of calling "attention to the issue of narrative privacy," and a challenge to "fixed rules for behavior, and didactic fiction."[35] Reading the form of the novel asexually, however, introduces another understanding of its various resisting moves. Hanson explains that "the logic of asexuality dissolves the meaningful relationship between narrative middles and ends, dragging narrative's forward movement not just off course but to a screeching halt, shutting down the possibility of meaning and closure."[36] In the eighteenth-century novel, narrative closure is often found through the promise or ascertainment of marriage, and Sidney's failures in this realm resist such a horizon. Her relationship with Cecilia, however, presents a hopeful alternative for the novel's heroine, even as she repeatedly acknowledges the impossibility of their future happiness together. Lupton suggests that "Sidney is resilient . . . in her consciousness of alternative realities," and I argue that the most important of these alternative realities is the potential of Sidney and Cecilia building a life together.[37] The novel's resistant, asexual form successfully critiques marriage while pointing toward the power of queer friendship, as Sidney allows herself to imagine an alternate world where the pair can exist together, in a state that pre-dates the conjugal pressures of compulsory sexuality.

Sidney's intimacy with Cecilia is most clearly articulated by the fact that the novel is written as a journal addressed to her, opening with the heroine mourning Cecilia's recent departure: "My dear and ever-beloved Cecilia is now on her way to Harwich. How insipid will this task of recording all the little incidents of the day appear to me, when you, my sister, friend of my heart, are no longer near me? How many tedious months will it be before I again embrace you? How many days of impatience must I suffer before I can even hear from you, or communicate to you the actions, the words, the thoughts of your Sidney?"[38] The longing expressed in this opening passage remains consistent through the novel, a sharp contrast to the way Sidney obscures her feelings for Faulkland and performs the love she claims to feel for Mr. Arnold. Doubt can be cast upon her feelings for men, but her love for Cecilia is never questioned, as the language she uses when addressing Cecilia is far more passionate than that used when talking to or about the men she marries. Lanser argues that the novel "is built upon blatant trade-offs in the object of desire: just as Cecilia leaves to *go* abroad, Sidney's brother returns *from* abroad to introduce Faulkland."[39] This trade-off is best illustrated directly following Sidney's marriage to Faulkland, when she writes, "I would it were possible for my Cecilia to arrive in England before my departure for Holland. Indeed, my dear, I shall not be sorry if I am detained from Mr. Faulkland, till I have the happiness of first embracing you."[40] By prioritizing Cecilia over her new husband, Sidney further emphasizes the importance of companionate friendship. Sidney's longing to see Cecilia, paired with her repeated reminiscence of their time growing up together, positions their relationship as a powerful example of queer friendship, a relationship that does not compete with Sidney's asexual potential but rather thrives because of it.

Though Sidney's reflections on her relationship with Cecilia illustrate her longing to be reunited with her friend, they are often mournful in tone. Sidney Castle, where the pair grew up together, serves as a touchstone for their relationship, and Sidney alternately longs for and avoids the comfort her home may provide. Upon her broken engagement with Faulkland, Sidney writes, "Sidney Castle is too long a journey for me at present to think of undertaking, and [my mother] talks of going into Essex . . . I shall like this better than going down to Wiltshire, where the want of my Cecilia would make my old abode a melancholy place."[41] Cecilia's absence from the neighborhood haunts Sidney, turning a space of comfort into one of melancholy. She repeatedly rejects the idea of returning to Sidney Castle, explaining that it "is a prospect which loses much of its charm, by the reflection that my dear Cecilia is not there."[42] Sidney's desire for her home wanes in moments of happiness (either feigned or genuine) while increasing in moments of misery or tragedy. It thus appears that Sidney fears her sadness regarding the absence of her dearest friend will distort the positive feelings that she is trying desperately to perform—positive feelings that are meant to be implicit when a woman marries or reunites with her husband after a conflict but that Sidney must actively work to produce.

This theory, that Sidney's sadness over Cecilia has the power to undermine any other happiness, is proven true when she returns to Sidney Castle with Mr. Arnold following their reconciliation. Though Sidney's journal entry opens with a declaration of joy, her attention is quickly overwhelmed by thoughts of the past.

> You, my dear Cecilia, mix yourself in all my thoughts; every spot almost brings
> you fresh into my memory . . . From what trifles do minds of such a turn derive

both joy and grief! Our names, our virgin names, I find cut out on several of the old elm trees: this conjures up a thousand pleasing ideas, and brings back those days when we were inseparable. But you are no longer Rivers, nor I Bidulph. Then I think what I have suffered since I have lost that name, and at how remote a distance you are from me; and I weep like a child.[43]

A common symbol of love, the detail of their "virgin names" carved together on numerous trees signals the intense affection shared by these women.[44] Sidney's emphasis on the change of their names following marriage highlights their inability to return to this idyllic past, while also illustrating a desire for a time *before* sex and romantic love was forced on their identities. Though they may still harbor these deep feelings of love for one another, they cannot access their relationship as it once was; instead, Sidney must return to the role of faithful wife. She attempts to convince Cecilia—and herself—that her future with Mr. Arnold has the potential to bring her a greater form of joy, writing, "I am now happier, beyond comparison happier, I think, than I was before my afflictions overtook me."[45] The implication that her happiness now exceeds that of the earlier part of her marriage, however, illustrates an unspoken comparison to the past she has recently described with Cecilia. Sidney's careful language emphasizes that nothing can compare to the happiness she once felt with her dearest friend, even as it appears that her marriage may be improving.

Cecilia is not only prioritized above the male love interests in Sidney's story but is shown to be preferable to all other women too. Throughout *Sidney Bidulph*, the heroine longs for a companion who can fill the gap left by Cecilia's departure. As such, she often dedicates more space on the page to her potential women friends than to possible suitors. Some of these women prove to be valued companions, such as Lady V—and Sidney's maid, Patty, but others, like Mrs. Vere, are valued only when they are actively present, suggesting that their connection is a matter of convenience. Despite numerous attempts to replace Cecilia, the women Sidney finds are never sufficient. As she writes, "We can have but *one friend* to share our heart, to whom we have no reserve, and whose loss is irreparable; but I perceive the absence of a pleasing acquaintance . . . is a loss easily supplied; this I find by experience. There are Mrs. Veres every where; but alas! there is but *one* Cecilia!"[46] That Sidney expresses such an unbreakable bond with a friend while illustrating, not only through her actions but in her own writing, that one's relationship with a husband need not be grounded in undying love, proves that her relationship with Cecilia is, and always will be, the most important. This longing for queer friendship and asexual existence without the pressure to marry suggests that Sidney might thrive in a femicentric utopia like the one described in *Millenium Hall*, published a year after Sheridan's novel. What is clear from Sidney's tragedy, however, is that such a freedom cannot exist in a world that is so singularly dedicated to reproducing compulsory sexuality through marriage: she may imagine the possibility through her memories of Cecilia, but they will never attain an uninterrupted future together.

"I WAS NOT MISTRESS OF MYSELF AT THE SIGHT OF HER":
NARRATIVE AS QUEER UNION

Though Sidney and Cecilia are unable to return to the romanticized world of their youth, where they could be together beyond the bounds of compulsory sexuality, the narrative form of the novel binds them together eternally. Sheridan makes it clear that Cecilia is more than the passive recipient of these letters; rather, she is the one who compiles and copies the journals before providing them to the fictitious editor who arranges their publication. Throughout the novel, Cecilia provides brief editorial notes where she has removed passages to move the plot forward and she breaks in at the end to complete the story, following Sidney's shock at the news that Faulkland's wife is still alive. Lanser argues that Cecilia's involvement in the production of Sidney's story represents an "exchange of narration and story [in which] heterosexual marriage dies off to be replaced by a kind of female textual union."[47] This ending, wherein Cecilia takes over narration from Sidney to close the novel, simultaneously exposes and forecloses the potential for their queer, asexual future together: because she is married, Cecilia cannot remain with Sidney forever, but the published journal remains a testament to their love.

Cecilia's position within the novel, as both the intended recipient of Sidney's narrative and its first editor, provides her with complex power over her friend's story. Kaley Kramer explains that "*Sidney Bidulph . . .* reveals the authorial impulse towards control and ownership of history. Told only through Sidney's voice and letters, *Memoirs* condenses various interpretations and experiences into one individual's history."[48] Sidney's production of her own history, however, is influenced by what Cecilia has chosen to include or exclude from her friend's journal. As the only character who "exists outside of Sidney's memoirs," Cecilia asserts her ownership over the story, not as an act of control but as an act of affection and admiration.[49] By completing Sidney's narrative, Cecilia attempts to interpret the events of her later life rather than simply describe them, before her narrative, too, ends abruptly. The repetition of these interrupted endings allows, as Spacks explains, "other interpretations, including the theological one suggested by Cecilia: God works in mysterious ways; human beings cannot fathom them. This deliberate ambiguity functions as a courtesy to the reader, a refusal to impose."[50] Cecilia's understanding of the greater meaning of Sidney's life can either be accepted or rejected by the reader. Such ambiguity, however, does not undermine Cecilia's greater control over the final form of Sidney's story.

Cecilia's involvement in shaping Sidney's narrative proves to encourage an asexual reading of the novel, as Sheridan uses her position as editor to "remove" lengthy passages to progress the plot and distance Sidney from the sexual realities of married life. Sidney gives birth to two daughters, yet descriptions of her pregnancy are absent from the narrative, marked with editorial notes that explain, "*though the Journal was regularly continued, nothing material to her story occurred by the birth of a daughter; after which she proceeds.*"[51] Sue Chaplin suggests that "Sidney's loss of textual authority at the moment that she becomes a mother may be seen to reflect the absence of legal authority that Sidney suffers as a mother."[52] This loss of agency, however, also serves to erase her experiences of both sex and birth. Ironically, Sheridan's novel is not particularly shy about sex: the novel is punctuated with allusions to numerous sexual indiscretions. But Cecilia's interference with the narrative obscures the reality that Sidney and her husband are sexually involved. Cecilia's desire to create an illusion of Sidney as both maternal and virginal signals her own discomfort with her friend's marriage. Similarly, the decision to name Sidney's second daughter Cecilia hints at the women's desire for one another: Cecilia cannot be a physical presence in Sidney's life, so the daughter becomes a stand-in for the absent friend and an imagined result of their love. Mr. Arnold's lack of interest in the young Cecilia bothers Sidney, further distancing her from him and emphasizing the unhappiness caused by compulsory sexuality.

As the novel reaches its final climax, Cecilia again inserts herself into the narrative, this time re-centering her importance in Sidney's life. Cecilia removes thirteen months from the journal, explaining briefly that her friend continued using her fortune for charitable acts, before resuming on June 28, 1708, the day before Sidney receives the letter from Faulkland that leads to the tragic events that conclude the novel. By resuming the journal the day *before* this letter arrives, Cecilia preserves the passage wherein Sidney writes of the news that she will soon be reunited with her dearest friend: "And shall I really be so blessed, my ever beloved Cecilia, as to see you at the time you mention? Oh, my dear, after an absence of five long years, how my heart bounds with joy at your approach! . . . Let me but live to embrace my Cecilia, and then, providence, thy will be done!"[53] Comfortably situated with a large fortune and waiting for the return of her dear friend, it appears that Sidney might have attained the happy ending she was repeatedly denied and that her queer friendship with Cecilia may be allowed to grow beyond the bounds of her journal. With Faulkland's return, however, the cycle of compulsory sexuality resumes, driven by Sidney's brother and cousin, who finally convince Sidney to acquiesce to Faulkland. Cecilia takes over the narrative to provide a brief description of the remainder of her friend's life, and though Sidney finds comfort in her children, Cecilia's married state prevents the pair from finding happiness together. Through the novel's form, however, they are united permanently, as their joint production of the journal serves as a material representation.

Sidney Bidulph read through an asexual lens not only accounts for Sidney's complex relationship with marriage and love but also illustrates how an asexual narrative form, which continually refuses closure, can disrupt the conventions of the eighteenth-century novel. Sheridan plays with audience expectations, providing the reader with numerous moments of potential closure yet refusing to follow any of them to a predictable end. The novel's marriages repeatedly end in disaster, and even Sidney's queer friendship with Cecilia cannot reach a fully satisfying conclusion because she too is bound by compulsory sexuality in the form of matrimony. Though genre conventions and the novel's characters continually remind the audience and Sidney both that these systems are meant to bring about happiness,

Sheridan's repeated disruption of tropes forces the reader to reconsider understandings of marriage, sexuality, and desire. The novel discloses how compulsory sexuality has the potential to traumatize those who willingly embrace it and those who resist it simultaneously when it serves as an inflexible structure of control.

An asexual approach similarly informs the queer friendship between Sidney and Cecilia: the groundwork on which the novel is built and even as Sidney navigates her complicated feelings about love, sex, and marriage. Their commitment to one another extends far past marriage: as Sidney tells Cecilia on multiple occasions, one can learn to love a husband, but a true, close friend can never be replaced. *Sidney Bidulph*'s pessimistic outlook on compulsory sexuality, marriage, and obedience provides a flicker of hope in the form of the heroine's queer friendship with her best friend.

NOTES

1. For more about women's queer intimacy in the eighteenth-century novel, see Lisa L. Moore, *Dangerous Intimacies: Toward a Sapphic History of the British Novel* (Durham, NC: Duke University Press, 1997); George Haggerty, *Unnatural Affections: Women and Fiction in the Later 18th Century* (Bloomington: Indiana University Press, 1998); Elizabeth Susan Wahl, *Invisible Relations: Representations of Female Intimacy in the Age of Enlightenment* (Stanford, CA: Stanford University Press, 1999); Susan S. Lanser, *The Sexuality of History: Modernity and the Sapphic, 1565–1830* (Chicago: University of Chicago Press, 2014); and Ula Lukszo Klein, *Sapphic Crossings: Cross-Dressing Women in Eighteenth-Century British Literature* (Charlottesville: University of Virginia Press, 2021).

2. George Haggerty, *Queer Friendship: Male Intimacy in the English Literary Tradition* (Cambridge: Cambridge University Press, 2018), 2.

3. Eve Kosofsky Sedgwick, *Between Men: English Literature and Male Homosocial Desire* (New York: Columbia University Press, 1985, 2015), 3.

4. Lanser, *The Sexuality of History*, 17.

5. Lanser, *The Sexuality of History*, 16.

6. Danielle Cooper, Kristina Gupta, Elizabeth Hanna Hanson, and Ela Przybylo (as cited below) point to the work of Judith Butler, Ann Cvetkovich, Jack Halberstam, Heather Love, José Esteban Muñoz, and Adrienne Rich, among others, to ground their understanding of asexual identity, desire, and eroticism and to build a critique of compulsory sexuality.

7. Ela Przybylo and Danielle Cooper, "Asexual Resonances: Tracing a Queerly Asexual Archive," *GLQ: A Journal of Lesbian and Gay Studies* 20, no. 3 (June 2014): 297–318 (298).

8. Przybylo and Cooper, "Asexual Resonances," 298.

9. For more about assumptions made about asexuality and related queer identities, see Angela Chen, *Ace: What Asexuality Reveals about Desire, Society, and the Meaning of Sex* (Boston, MA: Beacon Press, 2020).

10. Ann Cvetkovich, *An Archive of Feelings: Trauma, Sexuality, and Lesbian Public Cultures* (Durham, NC: Duke University Press, 2003), 7.

11. Paul Kelleher, *Making Love: Sentiment and Sexuality in Eighteenth-Century British Literature* (Lewisburg, PA: Bucknell University Press, 2015), 8.

12. Kelleher, *Making Love*, 132.

13. Kelleher, *Making Love*, 199.

14. Wendy Anne Lee, *Failures of Feeling: Insensibility and the Novel* (Stanford, CA: Stanford University Press, 2018), 59.

15. Kristina Gupta, "Compulsory Sexuality: Evaluating an Emerging Concept," *Signs: Journal of Women in Culture and Society* 41, no. 1 (Autumn 2015): 131–154 (135).

16. Elizabeth Hanna Hanson, "Toward an Asexual Narrative Structure," in *Asexualities: Feminist and Queer Perspectives*, ed. KJ Cerankowski and Megan Milks (New York: Routledge, 2014), 344, 347.

"MY SISTER, MY FRIEND, MY EVER BELOVED"

17. Christina Lupton, *Reading and the Making of Time in the Eighteenth Century* (Baltimore, MD: Johns Hopkins University Press, 2018), 110–111.

18. For more about *Sidney Bidulph* as a commentary on female passivity and adherence to conduct book norms, see Margaret Anne Doody, "Frances Sheridan: Morality and Annihilated Time," in *Fetter'd or Free? British Women Novelists, 1670–1815*, ed. Mary Anne Schofield and Cecilia Macheski (Athens: Ohio University Press, 1986), 324–358; Patricia Meyer Spacks, "Oscillations of Sensibility," *New Literary History* 25, no. 3 (Summer 1994): 505–520; John Richetti, *The English Novel in History 1700–1780* (London: Taylor and Francis, 1998); Candace Ward, "'Cruel Disorder': Female Bodies, Eighteenth-Century Fever Narratives, and the Sentimental Novel," *Studies in Eighteenth-Century Culture* 32 (2003): 93–121; Sue Chaplin, *Law, Sensibility, and the Sublime in Eighteenth-Century Women's Fiction: Speaking of Dread*, (Aldershot, UK: Ashgate, 2004); John C. Traver, "The Inconclusive Memoirs of Miss Sidney Bidulph: Problems of Poetic Justice, Closure, and Gender," *Eighteenth-Century Fiction* 20, no. 1 (Fall 2007): 35–60; Carol Stewart, *The Eighteenth-Century Novel and the Secularization of Ethics* (London: Taylor and Francis, 2010); Kaley Kramer, "The Limits of Genre: Women and 'History' in Frances Sheridan's *The Memoirs of Miss Sidney Bidulph* and Elizabeth Griffith's *The History of Lady Barton*," *ABO: Interactive Journal for Women in the Arts, 1640–1830* 2, no. 1 (March 2012): 1–15; and Karen Lipsedge, *Domestic Space in Eighteenth-Century British Novels* (London: Palgrave Macmillan, 2012).

19. For an explanation of how the Marriage Act of 1753 may have influenced the reception of Faulkland's infidelity, see Eve Tavor Bannet, "The Marriage Act of 1753: 'A Most Cruel Law for the Fair Sex,'" *Eighteenth Century Studies* 30, no. 3 (Spring 1997): 233–254.

20. Spacks, "Oscillations of Sensibility," 509–510.

21. Frances Sheridan, *The Memoirs of Miss Sidney Bidulph*, eds. Heidi Hutner and Nicole Garret (Peterborough, ON: Broadview Press, 2011), 54. All citations are to this edition.

22. Stewart, *The Eighteenth-Century Novel*, 127.

23. Stewart, *The Eighteenth-Century Novel*, 123.

24. Sheridan, *Sidney Bidulph*, 64.

25. Sheridan, *Sidney Bidulph*, 64.

26. Sheridan, *Sidney Bidulph*, 67.

27. Spacks, "Oscillations of Sensibility," 510.

28. Sheridan, *Sidney Bidulph*, 111.

29. Sheridan, *Sidney Bidulph*, 112.

30. Sheridan, *Sidney Bidulph*, 114.

31. Sheridan, *Sidney Bidulph*, 136.

32. Sheridan, *Sidney Bidulph*, 162.

33. Sheridan, *Sidney Bidulph*, 171.

34. Richetti, *The English Novel*, 207.

35. Traver, "The Inconclusive Memoirs," 45; Patricia Meyer Spacks, *Privacy: Concealing the Eighteenth-Century Self* (Chicago: University of Chicago Press, 2014), 105; and Stewart, *The Eighteenth-Century Novel*, 129.

36. Hanson, "Toward an Asexual Narrative Structure," 353.

37. Lupton, *Reading and the Making of Time*, 113.

38. Sheridan, *Sidney Bidulph*, 49.

39. Lanser, *The Sexuality of History*, 178–179.

40. Sheridan, *Sidney Bidulph*, 457.

41. Sheridan, *Sidney Bidulph*, 89.

42. Sheridan, *Sidney Bidulph*, 125.

43. Sheridan, *Sidney Bidulph*, 283.

44. For more about the importance of naming in *Sidney Bidulph*, see Kramer, "The Limits of Genre," 1–15; and Kathleen M. Oliver, "Frances Sheridan's Faulkland, the Silenced, Emasculated, Ideal Male," *SEL: Studies in English Literature 1500–1900* 43, no. 3 (Summer 2003): 683–700.

45. Sheridan, *Sidney Bidulph*, 283.

46. Sheridan, *Sidney Bidulph*, 150.

47. Lanser, *The Sexuality of History*, 178–179.
48. Kramer, "The Limits of Genre," 7.
49. Kramer, "The Limits of Genre," 7.
50. Spacks, *Privacy*, 108.
51. Sheridan, *Sidney Bidulph*, 145.
52. Chaplin, *Law, Sensibility, and the Sublime*, 97.
53. Sheridan, *Sidney Bidulph*, 425.

CHAPTER 5

Redefining the Archive in Queer Historical Romance Novels

Cailey Hall

To fix sexuality within such archival vernaculars of loss (while politically exigent) is to elide alternative historiographical models, to bypass imaginative histories of sexuality, full of intrepid archives and acts of invention.
—Anjali Arondekar, "There Is Always More"[1]

To them, I think, this is history:
breathing air into a previously unfelt opening.
—Jordy Rosenberg, Confessions of the Fox[2]

In 1816, Catherine St. Day, the widow of celebrated English astronomer George St. Day, was in search of a translator for M. Oléron's pathbreaking treatise on celestial mechanics. She learned that Lucy Mulcheney, the daughter of one of her late husband's collaborators, had in fact been doing most of the astronomical calculations for her father in the final years of his life. Against the wishes of her husband's colleagues, St. Day made the choice to financially support Mulcheney's translation of Oléron's work and its notoriously complicated calculations. Over the course of the months that Mulcheney spent with her patroness working on the translation, the two women fell in love. Although their commitment to each other was not documented in a parish register, it is known that Mulcheney and St. Day lived together for the remainder of their lives. They also, fascinatingly, undertook a self-funded project of publishing natural science writing by women who had been denied entry to the androcentric scientific societies that had begun to proliferate in early nineteenth-century Britain.

How do historians know this much about a queer romance that occurred over two hundred years ago? They don't. None of this actually happened. I have just

95

related the plot of Olivia Waite's 2019 romance novel, *The Lady's Guide to Celestial Mechanics*.[3] What I hope to argue in this chapter is that, even though Waite's novel is not based on a true story, so to speak, it is nevertheless telling a story that *could* be true. Or, to put this in slightly different terms that are significant to what follows: while the novel is not drawn from extant archives, it narrates a love story that might not be out of place in the archives of queer history.

The first female/female historical romance released by romance publishing powerhouse Avon books,[4] *The Lady's Guide to Celestial Mechanics* is still one of relatively few queer historical romances published in an industry that represents roughly one-third of all fiction sold in America and generates over $1 billion in sales annually.[5] As I see it, Waite and a small cohort of recent queer historical romance novelists—including Alyssa Cole, Courtney Milan, Cat Sebastian, and Alexis Hall—conceive of their relationship to long-eighteenth-century history as both reparative and revolutionary, offering a counternarrative to the assumption that queer historical love stories are inevitably tragic. By drawing on archival resources and innovating within archival lacunae, these queer historical romance writers are engaged with questions of historical accuracy while also challenging who dictates the terms of historical accuracy. *The Lady's Guide to Celestial Mechanics* intriguingly challenges the limits of the archive on two levels: it tells the story of queer women in Regency England and makes a diegetic engagement with archival practice central to the queer romance at the heart of the novel.

POPULAR CULTURE AND THE VERY LONG EIGHTEENTH CENTURY

One of my goals in this chapter is to argue that long-eighteenth-century scholars must consider how the period we study becomes depicted in current popular culture—and in turn, consider how this media informs and shapes people's sense of the history and the period's legacy. It is tempting for scholars to think that, as "experts" in long-eighteenth-century literary and cultural history, we hold the reins, so to speak. We do not; we should not. At the same time, I want to shed light on popular culture that is helping to challenge dominant narratives, both within and outside of academia, about the long eighteenth century.

In recent decades, the dominant eighteenth-century pop cultural narrative has been shaped by the Austen industrial complex. There are distinct limitations to viewing the eighteenth century through this lens, especially when it comes to topics of race, gender, and sexuality. Attempts to open up Austen's worlds are often met with disbelief and hostility from a certain subset of Austen devotees, who tend to levy accusations at such adaptations of historical inaccuracy that too often reinforce hegemonic and supremacist projections and value systems. Take, for example, the backlash to the 2019 ITV adaptation of Austen's unfinished final novel, *Sanditon*. The show substantially developed the character of Georgiana Lambe, the Black West Indian heiress who is only passingly referenced in Austen's manuscript. In an article detailing the racist backlash to *Sanditon*, Amanda

Rae-Prescott cites a fan lamenting the possibility that the second season of the show will replace the main love interest of the first season (played by the white actor Theo James) with "'a coloured hero. An insult to historical reality.'"[6] This irate fan does not acknowledge—or probably even recognize—the extent to which their perception of "historical reality" has likely been shaped by popular culture indebted to Austen and her legacy. Gretchen Gerzina has demonstrated that, by the later eighteenth century, a "thriving and structured black community" of at least fifteen thousand existed in London.[7] Yet, representations of the eighteenth century in recent popular culture have done very little to expose Austen fans like the one quoted above with reasons to question the limitations of their view of "historical reality."[8] Indeed, the extensive "longing" of and for the eighteenth century is at the heart of Eugenia Zuroski's coda, which concludes this collection.

Despite the fact that Austen herself remained unwed, her novels—and numerous adaptations of them—have also helped entrench ideas about the centrality of heteronormative companionate marriage in eighteenth-century Britain. As D. A. Miller observes, "the realism of [Austen's] works allows no one like Jane Austen to appear in them. Amid the happy wives and pathetic old maids, there is no successfully unmarried woman."[9] The creators behind the relatively recent Austen "biopics" *Becoming Jane* and *Miss Austen Regrets*, which both explore the possibility that Austen experienced (straight) romantic love, seem to have missed this memo. (Suggestions that Austen might have had any queer inclinations have not been given any screen time and have been met with considerable derision.)[10] Perhaps this is because the genre conventions of romance that Austen helped to create still dominate today, especially in the form of romance novels.

It is not a coincidence that present-day romance publishing has its origins in historical romance novels, and particularly in romance novels set in Regency England. Fantastical tales of rich men reformed and poor women elevated by companionate marriage—stories that have their origins in long-eighteenth-century novels like *Pamela* and *Pride and Prejudice*—have helped to shape how Anglophone readers think about the structure of romantic stories.[11] And, indeed, one can find many best-selling historical romances published in the last five or so decades that seem indebted, consciously or not, to the narrative beats and expectations shaped by writers like Samuel Richardson and Austen, and reinforced by the surge of Austen adaptations that began in the 1990s. Romance publishing is not, of course, comprised solely of Regency romances; these days, especially with the advent of Kindle Universe, one can find countless romance subgenres that cater to every imaginable interest, and some that reveal the previous limitations of one's imagination.

Yet, the Regency romance remains a stalwart subgenre in romance publishing. Take, for example, the supremely popular Netflix series *Bridgerton*, which was adapted from a bestselling Regency romance series by Julia Quinn. *Bridgerton* rewrites both history and Quinn's series in order to include Black aristocrats in early nineteenth-century British society. Detractors of *Bridgerton* note that while the show has been celebrated for its diverse cast, its plot requires a radical rewriting of history to integrate Black people into Regency aristocracy.[12] Yet the series remains silent on the source of these aristocrats' wealth. As Mira Assaf Kafantaris et al. point out, "The pleasures that the series promises . . . rest on the materiality of Regency Britain, the lavish and inordinate wealth of which came directly from its colonized territories, primarily via enslaved people's labour and the looting of India."[13]

Unlike *Bridgerton*, which reimagines the inclusion of Black characters without actually grappling with issues of race, empire, or class (or, thus far, much queerness), Waite's novel offers a more plausible if nonetheless idealistic view of what long-eighteenth-century queer lives and loves might have looked like. Along with other writers of queer historical romance, she is dealing with the same questions that have vexed fiction writers from the start: how do you tell stories about people who might not have actually existed but who could have existed? Who controls the terms of what is a plausible story to tell?

Romance, (Un)reality, and Anachronism

Even though Waite was contracted, as is often the case in romance publishing, to write a trilogy within the same fictional world, *The Lady's Guide to Celestial Mechanics* reads in some ways like it was written by an author who feared she might not get another chance to write queer historical romance. The novel luxuriates in the possibilities for world remaking that are opened up by the embracing of queerness. Writing as what Henry Jenkins terms an "aca-fan," I find it difficult to balance my genuine affection for Waite's novel with the adoption of some kind of critical distance—a challenge that is further complicated by the stigma romance novels still face within academia. Waite's novel is not subtle in much of the work it is doing. In this sense, I would argue that it shares something in common with eighteenth-century proto-feminist novels like Sarah Scott's *Millenium Hall* (1762) and Mary Wollstonecraft's *Maria; or, The Wrongs of Woman* (1798), which use the novel form for an explicitly didactic purpose. Waite, of course, is writing from a very different time and place, and within a genre (the romance novel) that prioritizes pleasure above didacticism—though we should not assume that they are mutually exclusive.

In the world of *The Lady's Guide to Celestial Mechanics*, queer romance—and especially one set in a time when people understood gender and sexuality in different ways than they do today—looks subtly but fundamentally different from a straight one. At the same time, Waite is also attentive to the privilege that protects her characters from the threats faced by other queer people of the time. Lucy is middle class; Catherine is wealthy and titled; both are white cis-women.[14] Lucy, it is clear, has long understood her sexuality, although the novel is careful to communicate that queerness in early nineteenth-century Britain was not discussed or understood in the terms used now. For Catherine, however, discovering her queerness is a revelation, both about herself and her understanding of the world: "A lady-love could assert no authority over Catherine's finances, or claim any rights in legal matters. Should desire wear itself out, separation could be done privately and discreetly, requiring no Act of Parliament to make it official . . . It was shocking how perfect a solution it was. She wondered everyone didn't think of it. Then again . . . maybe quite a few of them did, and Catherine just hadn't noticed."[15] Catherine's late husband, we learn, was emotionally abusive and married her in large part for her fortune. Queer love—which offers the possibility of a relationship without either the legal strictures of marriage or the patriarchal confines of a heterosexual union—is therefore especially liberating for her. This passage also resonates with José Esteban Muñoz's articulation of queer utopianism—a concept that is threaded throughout this larger collection. Here, Waite emphasizes Catherine's dawning awareness that queerness might be all around and simply overlooked by those who do not know what to look for.

This sense of the possible simultaneous prevalence and invisibility of queerness also shapes recent work in historically oriented queer studies. As historian Jen Manion argues in *Female Husbands: A Trans History*: "Histories of earlier periods are less legible as explicitly 'queer' histories," both because "our contemporary belief that gender and sexuality are identities that individuals articulate has dramatically skewed our view of the long-ago past" and because, "until relatively recently," most legal cases did not explicitly address queer relationships, "diarists and letter-writers self-censored and wrote in euphemisms and analogies," and "family guardians and archivists would further purge evidence that might scandalize a reputation when offering papers to a historical society."[16] Such silences, euphemisms, and expurgations mean that "historians continue to argue that the absence of such evidence constitutes its nonexistence," which Manion compellingly argues "reveals the limits of historical method and the lie of objectivity."[17] Yet, even Manion acknowledges that the history they have wrested from the archives is not one that "tell[s] a 'feel-good story.'"[18] While Manion's focus is specifically on the figure of the "female husband" in eighteenth- and nineteenth-century Anglo-American culture, the attention to narrating "a very painful past" resonates with much of the work done on queer melancholia and in pop cultural representations of queer love stories ranging from accounts of Oscar Wilde's 1895 trial for gross indecency to Radclyffe Hall's 1928 novel, *The Well of Loneliness*, to Céline Sciamma's 2019 film, *Portrait of a Lady on Fire*. Stories about queer love do not have a great track record for ending happily, and to the extent that one can find such stories in the archive, the evidence seems to reinforce that.

The Lady's Guide to Celestial Mechanics is not, however, just a story about queer love. It is also a romance novel—and, as such, it has particular generic responsibilities that seem potentially at odds with the limits of the archive. While the romance reading community—and romance Twitter in particular—is notoriously given to any number of disagreements, almost all romance readers will agree that a romance novel requires an HEA (happily ever after) in order to be considered a romance novel.[19] While an HEA no longer requires marriage, it does require the romantic protagonists to be alive and together at the novel's close.

In her author's note to *That Could Be Enough*, a 2017 novella about two Black women falling in love in 1820s New York City, Alyssa Cole (who is herself Black and queer) turns to the archive as a place to bolster her story's happy ending. She explains that her characters joyfully committing to each other at the end of the novella "is not anachronism in the name of happily ever after: queer people have always existed, and though society has generally excelled at making their lives difficult and dangerous, there were people who lived as openly as they could and were accepted within their communities."[20] What particularly interests me in this author's note is Cole's defense that she is *not* being anachronistic. Cole in fact ends her note by citing the academic books she consulted to strengthen her case.

In discussing anachronism, Jacques Rancière examines how historians who represented anachronism as a "sin" drew—in a partial and misleading way—on the techniques of literary modernism to produce a kind of "homogeneous time that leaves its mark in the same way on all individuals, situations, perceptions, and thoughts" and thus "tried to rule out the possibility that anybody could escape his or her own time."[21] Yet, Rancière cautions against those who would reclaim anachronism "in terms of a return of the repressed or the anticipation of a future to come" as such approaches "are containing discontinuity within a plot of continuity."[22] For Rancière, anachronism cannot have a telos or be seen "as the fulfillment of a collective subject's destiny." Instead, the kind of anachronism that Rancière embraces is part of an "emancipat[ory]" project that centers on "changing one's manner of inhabiting time."[23]

Rancière's interpretation of the emancipatory potential of anachronism thus troubles the issue of anachronism as it relates to historical romance novels. On the one hand, I am interested in how the authors of queer historical romance are putting important pressure on what readers of historical romance (and academics) often think is possible in the past, especially when it comes to stories about queer people and people of color. On the other hand, as Rancière elucidates, anachronism has a liberatory potential that resonates with queer temporalities. As Jack Halberstam argues: "Queer uses of time and space develop, at least in part, in opposition to the institutions of family, heterosexuality, and reproduction . . . what has made queerness compelling as a form of self-description in the past decade or so has to do with the way it has the potential to open up new life narratives and alternative relations to time and space."[24] How does such an approach—an understanding that queer ways of being defy linear, progressive time—relate to the generic expectations of the romance novel and the demands of the "happy ending"? The phrase "romance novel" itself is a potential oxymoron, uniting two forms of fictional prose narration that scholars—especially eighteenth-century scholars— have for so long set in opposition to each other. Despite their roots in what is often referred to as the realist novel, romance novels have been viewed by detractors as encouraging unrealistic expectations in readers.[25] In contrast with these critics, I mean to suggest that the seeming unreality of queer historical romance novels can be understood as anachronistic in Rancière's sense—that is, in a potentially emancipatory way. To make this claim, I want to turn briefly to how romance novels more broadly have been discussed by scholars.

To the extent that academics have engaged with romance novels, they have tended to do so in derogatory terms. As Northrop Frye so succinctly puts it: "Romance [is] always a despised form of writing."[26] Almost forty years after its publication, Janice Radway's *Reading the Romance* (1984) remains perhaps the most famous—and generally respected—academic work on romance novels. In the book, which is shaped by reader-response scholarship, Radway concludes that romance novels give "the reader a strategy for making her present situation more comfortable without substantive reordering of its structure rather than a comprehensive program for reorganizing her life in such a way that all needs might be met."[27] Romance novels, in other words, give women—Radway's focus is solely on heterosexual, cis-women readers[28]—just enough escapist pleasure to avoid having to make changes to lives that she perceives as unhappy and unfulfilling. Such moral panic over the subject of feminized reading practices is nothing new, of course. It is part of a long tradition that arguably can be traced back (in British literary history at least) to eighteenth-century Britain; depending on the interpretation, a novel like Charlotte Lennox's *The Female Quixote* (1752) either subverts or upholds the perspective that women cannot be trusted to read fiction safely, a debate Austen herself takes up in *Northanger Abbey* (1817). In response to criticisms of the unreality of romance novels, bell hooks—an avowed romance reader—was described in a *Washington Post* article as "bristl[ing] at the notion that the books set women up for disappointment and promote unrealistic fantasies about being rescued."[29] If defenders of the genre typically argue that readers of course understand the distinctions between the fantastical elements of romance novels and the reality of life, hooks goes further than most in her defense, implying that readers of romance are in fact more than usually attuned to their own pleasure, needs, and desires; hooks embraces the fantasy that romance offers, declaring: "'Only a crazy person doesn't want to be rescued.'"[30]

Romance novels are also censured for what is, understandably, seen as their conservative embrace of a monogamous courtship narrative that has traditionally culminated in marriage. Tracing the longer history of the romance novel back to eighteenth-century works like *Pamela* and *Pride and Prejudice*, Pamela Regis explains how these novels emerge "as a dominant form of the English novel just as the expectations surrounding the choice of a husband shifted. Affective individualism added to the choice a desire for liberty, and the shift from older forms of union to companionate marriage added a requirement that the wife- and husband-to-be love each other. The woman's search for liberty and love in marriage, a lifelong commitment that resulted in her loss of property rights, made courtship a time of conflicting goals."[31] Novels ending in marriage—or, as is more common these days, a committed pairing off—are often read as foreclosing possibilities for their women protagonists, a point that Jeremy Chow and Riley DeBaecke return to later in this collection.[32] Indeed, Radway argues that the "ending of the romance undercuts the realism of its novelistic rendering of an individual woman's story" and thus "reaffirms its founding culture's belief that women are valuable not for their unique personal qualities but for their biological sameness and their ability to perform that essential role of maintaining and reconstituting others."[33] While I do not think all such novels merit this cynical take, I am particularly interested in how *The Lady's Guide to Celestial Mechanics* relies on the genre beats of romance, even as it subverts them. While the novel is both indebted to the Regency romance and set in the period associated most closely with the triumph of the heterosexual marriage plot, it also shows how placing queerness at the center of the story necessitates a different relationship to romance novels' generic conventions.

Undoing the Marriage Plot, Archiving Queerness

The Lady's Guide to Celestial Mechanics is an exemplary case of what I have found holds true in the still small subgenre of queer historical romance more broadly: when queerness is made central to historical romance, the foundations of the marriage plot—bourgeois culture and property consolidation—also recede. That is to say, even when queer historical romances are indebted to the marriage plot and follow some of its key beats, they resist the sense of narrowing possibility that is often associated with romantic closure. Instead, and without devolving into the counterfactual or the radically ahistorical, these novels almost always find ways to open up new possibilities of love, of companionship, and of being in relation to others.

For both Lucy and Catherine, committing to each other also involves an explicit rejection of marriage and a desire to find "something better" that reimagines the possibilities of partnership.[34] Although Catherine never wants to remarry, she also wants "to offer Lucy something that would last for the rest of their lives."[35] Catherine becomes inspired by an archival project Lucy begins after the success of her translation and adaptation of the fictional astronomer Oléron's treatise. (In a significant reveal late in the novel, Lucy meets Oléron, who turns out to be a Black woman.) Working her way through old issues of science society publications in Catherine's late husband's library, Lucy is astonished to learn that, as a woman in science, she is far from an anomaly. Her investigations seem inspired in part by evidence about noted long-eighteenth-century women scientists in Europe, such as Laura Bassi and Caroline Herschel. But the novel goes further, pointing out both the limits of archival evidence that tends to erase women from the record and the necessity of a different kind of archival reading practice. As Lucy explains: "'There's more, so many more, once you know to look for them. Hiding behind initials and their husbands' names.'"[36] In this sense, she can be seen as advocating for an approach to archival inquiry elucidated by a historian like Manion, for whom the seeming "absence of . . . evidence" does not "constitute its nonexistence" but rather constitutes an invitation to reconsider historical methodologies.[37]

At the same time, the novel acknowledges a sense of inevitable archival loss: "'Every generation had women stand up and ask to be counted—and every generation of brilliant, insightful, educated men has raised a hand and wiped those women's names from the greater historical record.'"[38] For Lucy, her project begins as a way of forging a queer community, even if it's one she will never meet—her desire, she makes explicit, is to recognize her peers and not feel so "alone" as a woman in the sciences.[39] But Catherine comes up with the idea of actualizing this queer community and integrating it with the romantic commitment she and Lucy want to make to each other. Their happily ever after is not just that they end up together, but that Catherine proposes—not with an offer of marriage, but instead with an offer of a partnership committed to an archival reclaiming of women in science:[40]

> "A rather substantial fund, administered by you and me, for the purposes of publishing women's writing on the natural sciences. We would . . . solicit women of science to be authors, and arrange to have them checked thoroughly for accuracy before offering them to the public."
>
> "That . . ." Lucy had to swallow against a dry throat. "That sounds like an immense amount of work."
>
> "Oh, it will be, I assure you. It will tie us together legally, and financially, and probably take us the rest of our lives to accomplish . . . I am asking you to stay with me for the rest of our lives. I am asking you to join me in making this world a better place, insofar as we are able. We cannot stand up in a church and make vows—but we can stand up, publicly, and declare that we are important."[41]

I am captivated by this ending. It both honors and plays with the conventions of romance novels' required HEA in order to revise narrow ideas about what romance and the marriage plot can look like. While the shared publishing mission replaces marriage and, perhaps, any reproductive futurity, it also expands the happy ending beyond Lucy and Catherine. Rather than turning to literal procreation as a way to endure beyond death, Lucy and Catherine embark on a publishing project that makes possible a far more capacious queer community—and queer lineage. *The Lady's Guide to Celestial Mechanics* promises a kind of happiness—or at least justice—to the lovers' (fictional) peers, as well as (fictional) future scholars.

At the same time, this restorative fantasy of a lost archive reclaimed, expanded, and underwritten by queer women should not simply be read as a blueprint for scholarly engagement with the archive. (This fact would be obvious to most readers of romance, who are used to hearing that they should be careful not to mistake fiction for reality.) Looking to the archives when studying queer people—and especially queer people of color—is a fraught undertaking, as Stephen Best and Anjali Arondekar have addressed in their work at the intersection of queer studies and, respectively, Black studies and postcolonial studies. Discussing the "recovery imperative" that has dominated Black studies for at least a century, Best writes: "It is not hard to see in the recovery imperative a powerful and compelling theory of how history works—not simply the theory that the past persists in the present, or the proposition that the past has to be made relevant to the present, but the idea that history is at its core a fundamentally redemptive enterprise" that will yield distinct subjects and be "fundamentally recuperative in its orientation."[42] Arondekar also warns against the desire to find subjects in the archive, arguing instead for "an archival turn . . . that moves away not from the nature of the object, but from the notion of an object that would somehow lead to a formulation of subjectivity: the presumption that if a body is found, then a subject can be recovered."[43] More recently, Arondekar has added, "To fix sexuality within such archival vernaculars of loss (while politically exigent) is to elide alternative historiographical models, to bypass imaginative histories of sexuality, full of intrepid archives and acts of invention."[44] Best and Arondekar both explore a relationship to archives as one explicitly involving—and embracing—loss and failure.

But Best and Arondekar are discussing a relationship to material archives, while Waite's fantasy of archival restoration is, of course, fictional. In this sense, a novel like *The Lady's Guide to Celestial Mechanics* shows its indebtedness to the eighteenth century not only in its setting and reworking of the marriage plot but also in its relationship to fictionality. As Catherine Gallagher has persuasively argued, a hallmark of eighteenth-century fiction is the rise of "nobody's story," featuring characters whom readers knew were *not* based on real people.[45] That Waite's story is fiction alters the terms of any discussion surrounding the relationship between queer histories and the archival turn. In imagining the fictionality of Lucy and Catherine's undertaking of a project of recuperating and expanding a fictional archive of fictional women scientists, Waite does not degrade the importance or reality of accepting the limitations of extant archives. Indeed, the turn to fiction is a way of submitting to the limits of the archives. The novel does not recover particular lives; it instead undertakes a fictional worldbuilding project that offers possible new ways for thinking about the eighteenth century within the space of popular culture.[46]

What is notable about *The Lady's Guide to Celestial Mechanics*—and a small cohort of similar historical romance novels—is not just that it offers up a fictional yet plausible story about queer people in the long eighteenth century, but that it is telling one with an HEA. Muñoz explains that he thinks of "queerness as a temporal arrangement in which the past is a field of possibility in which subjects can act in the present in the service of a new futurity."[47] While I recognize that he's not thinking about queer historical romance here, I think the claim nevertheless applies to how queer historical romance writers are working to counter the still overwhelming narratives of tragedy attached to queerness.[48] Recent work in Black studies on the politics of pleasure echoes these interests. Badia Ahad-Legardy, for example, offers "Afro-Nostalgia" to study a range of texts that help "contextualize the desires of the African-descended to discern and devise romantic recollections of the past in the service of complicating the traumatic as a singular black historical through line."[49] If the only narratives from the past are traumatic ones, it becomes that much more difficult to envision happiness in the present or the future—and that much easier to accept less in the name of some kind of gradualist Whig notion of progress. If such utopian-inflected approaches seem too optimistic, let us turn instead to Sara Ahmed: "Looking back is what keeps open the possibility of going astray . . . This backward glance also means an openness to the future, as the imperfect translation of what is behind us . . . We have hope because what is behind us is also what allows other ways of gathering in time and space, of making lines that do not reproduce what we follow, but instead create new textures on the ground."[50] While I am aware that Ahmed might classify queer romance as veering into the world of "'homonormativity,'"[51] her attention to the "backward glance" captures what I see as a strong desire within *The Lady's Guide to Celestial Mechanics* and other queer historical romance—a desire to figure out new ways of "going astray." They are reckoning with both the history and the narratives that have gotten us to where we are today—and they are trying to imagine new possible futures by returning to the past.

When I teach queer historical romance novels, I stress to students that these novels are, of course, telling us as much about our own time as they are about the past. I recently taught *The Lady's Guide to Celestial Mechanics* as part of a Jane Austen afterlives class in which we had Olivia Waite as a special guest on Zoom. During her conversation with the class, Waite introduced the concept of "historical possibility" (rather than "historical probability") which guides how she thinks about writing queer historical romance.[52] I have found that teaching queer historical romance—especially with the idea of "historical possibility" in mind—not only offers undergraduates a different perspective on the eighteenth century but also gives them narrative resources to think in new ways about their own temporally dispersed lives.

NOTES

Acknowledgment: I am thankful to Jeremy Chow and Shelby Johnson for giving me the opportunity to participate in this collection, for their immensely helpful editorial feedback, and for their understanding and patience throughout the process. I am also grateful to Cass Turner for their belief in (and support of) this project—and for many inspiring conversations along the way, as well as for their always insightful feedback. Thank you also to the anonymous reviewers, whose feedback helped to improve this chapter. Finally, this chapter has its origins in a paper I gave at a queer studies roundtable convened by George Haggerty at ASECS 2021. Thank you to George, the rest of the panel (Emily West, Caroline Gonda, and Madeline Reynolds), and the audience for engaging with my nascent ideas, and inspiring me to keep thinking about this project.

1. Anjali Arondekar, "There Is Always More: Sexuality's Archives," *Foam Histories: The Archival Issue* 59 (2021): 91.

2. Jordy Rosenberg, *Confessions of the Fox: A Novel*, Reprint ed. (London: One World, 2019), 267.

3. Olivia Waite, *The Lady's Guide to Celestial Mechanics* (New York: Avon Impulse, 2019).

4. Avon publishes some of the biggest names in romance, including Julia Quinn's *Bridgerton* series. In a larger project I am developing on romance, I am interested in a variety of queer romance novels (not just ones focused on "female/female" or "f/f," as it is usually referred to in online discussions).

5. "Romance Readers By the Numbers," Nielsen, May 26, 2016, https://www.nielsen.com/us /en/insights/article/2016/romance-readers-by-the-numbers/.

6. Amanda Rae-Prescott, "Race and Racism in Austen Spaces: Notes on a Scandal: *Sanditon* Fandom's Ongoing Racism and the Danger of Ignoring Austen Discourse on Social Media," *ABO: Interactive Journal for Women in the Arts, 1640–1830*, 11, no. 2 (Fall 2021): 1–27.

7. Gretchen Gerzina, *Black London: Life before Emancipation* (New Brunswick, NJ: Rutgers University Press, 1995), 6, 5. For more on Black life in, before, and beyond eighteenth-century Britain, see Peter Fryer, *Staying Power: The History of Black People in Britain* (London: Pluto Press, 1984); and Kathleen Chater, *Untold Histories: Black People in England and Wales During the Period of the British Slave Trade, c. 1660–1807* (Manchester: Manchester University Press, 2009).

8. See also Margo Hendricks on the relationships between historical romances and racialization in *Romance and Race: Coloring the Past* (Tempe: Arizona Center for Medieval and Renaissance Studies Press, 2022).

9. D. A. Miller, *Jane Austen, or The Secret of Style* (Princeton, NJ: Princeton University Press, 2003), 28.

10. See, for example, the responses detailed in Danuta Kean, "Jane Austen's Lesbianism Is as Fictional as *Pride and Prejudice*," *The Guardian*, May 31, 2007, https://www.theguardian.com/books/booksblog/2017/may/31/jane-austen-lesbian-fictional-as-pride-and-prejudice.

11. The romance novel in particular troubles the oft-identified (and debated) divide between realism and romance. Scott Black intriguingly argues that "the realism of the past becomes romance for future readers." See Black, *Without the Novel: Romance and the History of Prose Fiction* (Charlottesville: University of Virginia Press, 2019), 13.

12. Within the world of Chris Van Dusen's *Bridgerton* series, Alyssa Goldstein Sepinwall explains, Queen Charlotte, "rather than simply having been rumored to be of mixed racial heritage & passing as white . . . is presented as a Black woman reigning openly as one." Sepinwall, "On Studios and Patterns of Erasure," in "Unsilencing the Past in *Bridgerton* 2020: A Roundtable January 9, 2021, https://kerrysinanan.medium.com/unsilencing-the-past-in-bridgerton-2020-a-roundtable-792ecffd366. As we learn in season 1, episode 4, it is because of George III's love for Charlotte that Black people were given titles and fortunes.

13. Mira Assaf Kafantaris, et al., "Unsilencing the Past in *Bridgerton* 2020: A Roundtable," January 9, 2021, https://kerrysinanan.medium.com/unsilencing-the-past-in-bridgerton-2020-a-roundtable-792ecffd366.

14. At one point, Lucy reflects on the queer men she knows who have "affairs that could get them transported (or worse) under the full force of law," but there is no character in the novel who faces the explicit threat of prosecution and death dictated by anti-sodomy laws. See Waite, *The Lady's Guide*, 41.

15. Waite, *The Lady's Guide*, 79.

16. Jen Manion, *Female Husbands: A Trans History* (Cambridge: Cambridge University Press, 2020), 9–10.

17. Manion, *Female Husbands*, 10.

18. Manion, *Female Husbands*, 14.

19. Romance Writers of America defines romance novels thusly: "Two basic elements comprise every romance novel: a central love story and an emotionally satisfying and optimistic ending." "About the Romance Genre," Romance Writers of America, accessed March 6, 2022, https://www.rwa.org/Online/Romance_Genre/About_Romance_Genre.aspx. This generic expectation has a long history, which can be traced back at least to the distinctions between the endings of early modern comedies and tragedies.

20. Alyssa Cole, *That Could Be Enough* (Self-published: Kindle, 2017), 116.

21. Jacques Rancière, "Anachronism and the Conflict of Times," *Diacritics* 48, no. 2 (Summer 2020): 110–124 (116).

22. Rancière, "Anachronism and the Conflict of Times," 122.

23. Rancière, "Anachronism and the Conflict of Times," 122.

24. Jack Halberstam, *In a Queer Time and Place: Transgender Bodies, Subcultural Lives* (New York: New York University Press, 2005), 1–2.

25. Romance—in the most capacious sense of the term—has long destabilized conceptions of time and invited accusations of anachronism, both formally and in terms of its content. As Black argues in *Without the Novel*, romance is constituted by its self-awareness and recursivity.

26. Northrop Frye, *Northrop Frye's Notebooks on Romance*, Collected Works of Northrop Frye, ed. Alvin A. Lee et al., vol. 15 (Toronto: University of Toronto Press, 1996), 199.

27. Janice Radway, *Reading the Romance: Women, Patriarchy, and Popular Literature*, 2nd ed. (Chapel Hill: University of North Carolina Press, 1991), 215.

28. Romance novels are often described as being primarily written by—and for—women. In celebrating the genre as one celebrating "women's freedom," Regis echoes many romance readers' explicit embrace of romance as a feminist genre. There is a part of me that wholeheartedly agrees with this assessment and affirms the important role romance novels have played—and still play—in exploring the many dimensions of sexual pleasure, which do not always neatly align with politics. There is also a part of me that is reluctant to adopt an overwhelmingly positive attitude toward seemingly all romance novels, especially given the tendency of many of these novels to uphold gender binaries and heterosexuality. I thus also take seriously scholar and romance novelist Mary Bly's opinion that one cannot offer "a defense of the [romance] genre" as a whole, and that while "a specific reader may engage in a subversive reading of a specific book . . . neither books nor readers are interchangeable." See Pamela Regis, *A Natural History of the Romance Novel* (Philadelphia: University of Pennsylvania Press, 2003), xiii; and Mary Bly, "On Popular Romance, J.R. Ward, and the Limits of Genre Study," in *New Approaches to Popular Romance Fiction: Critical Essays*, ed. Eric Murphy Selinger and Sarah S. G. Frantz (Jefferson, NC: McFarland & Company, 2012), 60–72 (62).

29. Lonnae O'Neal Parker, "Fantasy Aisle: Harlequin Romance Novels Steam through 50 Years of Changing Mores," *Washington Post*, February 20, 1999, https://www.washingtonpost.com/archive/lifestyle/1999/02/20/fantasy-aisle-harlequin-romance-novels-steam-through-50-years-of-changing-mores/9310be9a-473b-400c-9293-80172cf16854/.

30. O'Neal Parker, "Fantasy Aisle."

31. Regis, *A Natural History*, 58–59.

32. The relationship between the rise of companionate marriage (and novels narrating such unions) and the rise of capitalism is a topic I cannot address properly in this chapter. In recent work on romance novels and the Kindle universe, Mark McGurl argues that "from *Pamela* to the present, the novel in the English-speaking world has developed alongside and within a capitalist economy increasingly oriented toward consumer enjoyment and, if only implicitly, has been telling the story of that economy the whole time. What we now label the romance novel is the reflexive expression of the novel's original appeal: it is not only written for the satisfaction of the imaginative needs of the reader but it is about that satisfaction in the figure of the heroine and her mate, who always get what they want and who thereby reassure their readers of the legitimacy and continuity of the social order." See Mark McGurl, "Unspeakable Conventionality: The Perversity of the Kindle," *American Literary History* 33, no. 2 (Summer 2021): 394–415 (404).

33. Radway, *Reading the Romance*, 208.

34. Waite, *The Lady's Guide*, 186.

35. Waite, *The Lady's Guide*, 296.

36. Waite, *The Lady's Guide*, 286.

37. Manion, *Female Husbands*, 10. Jack Halberstam also explores how a return to the archive can yield up different ways of understanding the past. Discussing Peter Linebaugh's and Marcus Rediker's work on "the history of opposition to capitalism in the seventeenth and eighteenth century," Halberstam argues that the authors "do not find new routes to resistance built upon *new* archives . . . their point is that dominant history teems with the remnants of alternative possibilities, and the job of the subversive intellectual is to trace the lines of the worlds they conjured and left behind." Although, as Halberstam also points out: "Gender and sexuality are, after all, too often dropped from most large-scale accounts of alternative worlds (including Linebaugh's and Rediker's)." See Jack Halberstam, *The Queer Art of Failure* (Durham, NC: Duke University Press, 2011), 18–19.

38. Waite, *The Lady's Guide*, 286–287.

39. Waite, *The Lady's Guide*, 287.

40. The publishing project is soon expanded to include women artists and diverse kinds of art. (Catherine is a talented embroiderer.) While I have not had space to address it in this

chapter, the novel is also committed to challenging the disciplinary boundaries between what we now know as the humanities and the sciences—professional boundaries that were beginning to develop in the early nineteenth century.

41. Waite, *The Lady's Guide*, 320–321.

42. Stephen Best, *None Like Us: Blackness, Belonging, Aesthetic Life* (Durham, NC: Duke University Press, 2018), 12.

43. Anjali Arondekar, *For the Record: On Sexuality and the Colonial Archive in India* (Durham, NC: Duke University Press, 2009), 3.

44. Arondekar, "There Is Always More," 91.

45. Catherine Gallagher, *Nobody's Story: The Vanishing Acts of Women Writers in the Marketplace, 1670–1920* (Berkeley: University of California Press, 1994).

46. In *Confessions of the Fox*, Jordy Rosenberg theorizes a fantastical, collectively oriented vision of queer archival recovery that feels related to—although also quite different from—the fictional archival project that Waite imagines in *The Lady's Guide to Celestial Mechanics*.

47. José Esteban Muñoz, *Cruising Utopia: The Then and There of Queer Futurity* (New York: New York University Press, 2009), 16.

48. In recognizing this kind of work, I do not mean in any way to discount work by queer scholars like Ann Cvetkovich, who celebrates "ways of thinking about trauma that do not pathologize it, that seize control over it from the medical experts, and that forge creative responses to it that far outstrip even the most utopian of therapeutic and political solutions." See Ann Cvetkovich, *An Archive of Feelings* (Durham, NC: Duke University Press, 2003), 3.

49. Badia Ahad-Legardy, *Afro-Nostalgia: Feeling Good in Contemporary Black Culture* (Urbana: University of Illinois Press, 2021), 3.

50. Sara Ahmed, "Orientations: Toward a Queer Phenomenology," *GLQ: A Journal of Lesbian and Gay Studies* 12, no. 4 (October 2006): 543–574 (559–560).

51. Ahmed, "Orientations," 567.

52. Olivia Waite, "Visit to Honors 3063: Austenland: Jane Austen's Life and Afterlives," Zoom lecture, Oklahoma State University, April 18, 2022.

PART III

Queer Ecologies and Cartographies

CHAPTER 6

Matters of Intimacy

THE SUGAR-CANE'S ASEXUAL ECOLOGIES

M. A. Miller

"ALL DEPENDS ON ALL": INTIMACY AS METHODOLOGY

Up through the mid-nineteenth century, sugarcane, *Saccharum Officinarum* (see Figure 6.1), was treated and cultivated as an asexually produced crop, meaning, the relationship between the "parent-cane" and its progeny is one of clonal re/production rather than one rendered through a process of breeding—of cross-parent sexual reproduction.[1] This form of clonal propagation can be done either by planting cuttings (portions of the stalk) taken from a cane-parent or through the process of ratooning, where most of the aboveground stalk is cut and only the roots remain. Since "cloning increases colonizing ability and persistence because it eliminates seedlings—the stage of growth when the risk of mortality is highest," planters have continued to rely on and exclusively use asexual reproduction for its efficient and productive alignment with the tempos and rhythms of nascent global capitalism.[2]

The ability to sexually re/produce sugarcane through its flowering and seeds, however, was not discovered until the mid-nineteenth century. This discovery led to breeding efforts that would produce cane species resistant to disease, thus encoding eugenicist implications in sexually re/produced sugarcane. Yet, in *A Treatise on Planting* (1790), author and self-described planter Joshua Peterkin obsesses over the apparent and presumed virile heterosexual vitality of sugarcane. To promote the heterosexualization of sugarcane production, Peterkin obfuscates the necessary African enslaved labor involved and ironically reveals the queerness of sugarcane by conflating a rhetoric of desire with a rhetoric of gendered embodiment. Peterkin attempts to assure Caribbean planters of sugarcane's "normal" desires by focusing on the plant's seemingly cisgender genitals: the "stamina"—the pollen-producing reproductive organ—or what Peterkin calls "the husbands of the flower," and the "female parts" or the "stigma," which through "impregnation" apparently reveals "the origin of the vegetable world."[3] Peterkin's allegiance to Carl Linnaeus

111

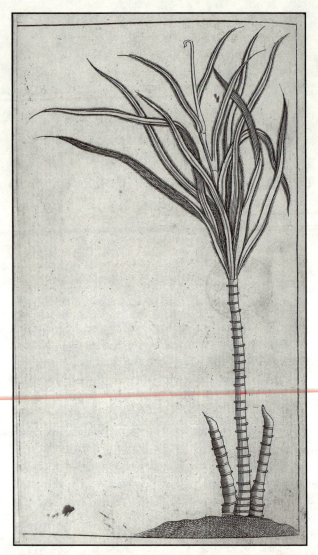

Figure 6.1. An illustration of a sugarcane stalk. Frontispiece to James Grainger's 1766 edition of *The Sugar-Cane*. Used with permission by The British Library.

perpetuates an enforcement of a cisgender and heterosexual framework onto sugarcane's re/productivity within the vegetable kingdom: "The manner in which these species are produced amongst vegetables, greatly resembles the generation of animals: the existence and union of sexes are necessary in the greatest number of plants."[4]

Even in the sexual re/production of sugarcane, which involves two cane-parents, the supposed sex of each parent is arbitrary. As a perennial grass, cane flowerings are, in biological re/productive terms, bisexual or hermaphroditic, which means that cane flowers possess male and female reproductive organs and therefore can be used as *either* parent in cross-fertilization. Scientists have more recently documented an "emasculation" process in which hot water is used to reduce pollen viability, ostensibly producing a sterile male that can then be used as a female parent in breeding programs.[5] Therefore, the further Peterkin, and Caribbean planters more broadly, doubled down on implementing a cisgender and heterosexual rhetoric for describing sugarcane production, the queerer, more non-monogamous, more nonsexual, more erotic, and more biodiverse the process of serving and perpetuating empire actually started to sound.

James Grainger's georgic poem *The Sugar-Cane* (1764) recognizes sugarcane cultivation as a nonsexual form of non/human re/production.[6] Yet, like Peterkin, Grainger infuses his verse with the language of Anglo, cisgender, heterosexual erotic romance. When one refers to the romance of Grainger's georgic, the star-crossed lovers of Theana and Junio, wherein Junio, "the perfect example of Europeanized-Creole manhood" performing gentility and courtship toward Theana, comes to mind.[7] Though Grainger uses this couple as "proof positive that a slavocracy was capable of fostering virtue and steadfastness," thus presenting Anglo, cisgender, heterosexual love in the Caribbean as an ideal form, this chapter considers the *real* romance the poem offers: that between sugarcane and soil.

Throughout the poem, Grainger observes the precarious balance of intimate relations among species and between forms of matter that results in the production of St. Kitts (formerly St. Christopher Island) sugarcane:

An alien mixture meliorates the breed;
Hence Canes, that sickened dwarfish on the plain,
Will shoot with giant-vigour on the hill.
Thus all depends on all.[8]

Grainger's description of healthy and unhealthy cane is framed in terms of phallic virility, wherein a healthy cane "will shoot" vigorously in certain soils over others: "the hill" rather than "the plain" in this verse line. What affords such health, what is healing is "an alien mixture"—soil: the various inorganic matter, organic matter, water, and air that re/produce vegetative life and sustain other species who live and burrow within its pores. It is the messy lack of purity and singularity, an alienness, that drives the soil's fertility, re/productive receptivity, and the healthy production of various species. In ecological terms, "alien" also describes plants or animals that have been "brought to another country or district and subsequently naturalized; not native."[9]

In Grainger's poem, however, the delineation between alien (naturalized) and native is inverted. It is the native soils of St. Kitts that he defines as "alien" matter, suggesting that for Grainger, alienness is that which is foreign to the colonial project and foreign to Anglo whiteness. Such a designation forecasts the failures and violences of colonial expansion at the level of the biosphere because colonial projects forcibly ignore and disregard the unique ecosystems of St. Kitts and the Caribbean more broadly. Native Kittitian species must be "naturalized" to the plantation economy. Those that cannot be effectively naturalized to the plantation, which in the eyes of the colonizer includes translocated fugitive enslaved persons, are abandoned by the colonial project for which they have been stolen. These bodies become spatially conceived of as "outside" the plantation and thus as a proliferating threat that must be contained by the plantation economy through a variety of safeguards, including Kittitian assembly acts.

In a 2010 issue of *Feminist Studies*, KJ Cerankowski and Megan Milks underline asexuality's queerness by suggesting that such an orientation represents a "practice and a politics" that "radically challenges the prevailing sex-normative culture."[10] This chapter, inspired by the asexual turn, as Ziona Kocher's chapter in this collection likewise explores, asks: What would it mean to consider ecological forms of asexual re/production as not only queer but also as the essence of a violently homophobic, heteronormative colonial plantation (mono)culture? Grainger's georgic incidentally reveals sugarcane cultivation as non-monogamous, asexual, cross-racial, cross-species, and dependent on the instrumentalization of a multitude of bodies—human, non/human, animal, organic, and inorganic—to maintain the soil's increased receptivity. This chapter concludes that monocrop production purposefully obfuscates the cross-species and cross-racial erotics integral to sugarcane propagation while simultaneously promoting Anglo, cisgender heterosexuality as natural and naturally produced through and by global agricapitalist expansion. Through the language of love, courtship, and romance readily associated with English pastorals and georgics, *The Sugar-Cane* attempts to enclose and contain the various relationships on which sugarcane propagation depends. Grainger fantasizes that such a system is not only possible but sustainable and able to mitigate the widening gap between sites of production and sites of consumption brought on by plantation exportations.

I situate the poem within the broader historical and (agri)cultural context of St. Kitts, the specific West Indies Island setting for the poem, and the fields of queer ecologies and critical race studies. By using intimacy as a methodology, I argue that asexual re/production for the colonial plantation becomes resolutely hidden behind a framework of heterosexual love and courtship, which is repeatedly mapped onto the sugarcane's relationship to the soil and even to the cane's relationship to the enslaved Black laboring bodies that facilitate the crop's nonsexual propagation. The costs of scalability include the fungible conflation of sugarcane and the enslaved African as compostables. The use of such a "straight" framework is also not rigid enough to refuse the transgressive and resistant queer matters that remain outside of the full control of colonial plantation managers and projects.

I draw from Lisa Lowe's recent reflections on her former work on "intimacy as methodology." Lowe writes that "by emphasizing relation, convergence, contradiction, interdependency, intimacies as method may attend to contacts and conflicts above and below the classifications of national archives, the residual and emergent knowledges that may be elided by the dominant disciplines in which we work."[11] Though I agree with Lowe's depiction of intimate relations and ways of observing types of archival proximities that often shore up coterminous geographic realities, I am equally struck by the voidance of touch, sexuality, desire, love, and the erotic.

To access "convergence, contradiction, and interdependency," and to uncover empire's cooptation and reliance on peculiar manifestations of touch and desire, I look at the ways in which frameworks of sexual re/production crop up in unexpected avenues. I use the concluding phrase of the poem's early line, "all depends on all" then, to develop a methodology of asexual ecologies—a specific method of intimacy in which relations are inevitable and inevitably enmeshed, entangled, and intra-acting. Such a method suggests a fundamental awareness that the discrete separation and containment of environmental bodies is an impossibility. The line also implies Grainger's own awareness and exploitation of sugarcane production as not an inherently closed system, but extremely dependent on its relationship to soil, which is indicative of intimate relationships between and across a diverse spectrum of matter.[12]

The fragility of Grainger's colonial project is not merely based in the fantasy of an enclosed parcel of sugarcane land but also in the fantasy of enclosed sexualities and enclosed intimacies. Brit Rusert argues that "the image of the plantation as an ecologically enclosed, protected space of British cultivation and experimentation is revealed to be a fragile colonial fantasy, always on the verge of being 'infected' or creolized by indigenous plants, animals, and diseases, as well as by Africans both within and outside the plantation."[13] Building on Rusert's exploration of plantation ecologies, I suggest that Grainger knowingly manipulates St. Kitts' open, biodiverse, ecological system in which "all depends on all" toward a singular, teleologically exploitative goal of colonial sugarcane propagation. Through a proliferating ecology of footnotes that textually eclipse the lengthy georgic verse, *The Sugar-Cane* offers a formal symptom of scalability: the attempt to retrofit a material reality of disturbance-based plantation ecologies within specific preexisting discursive frameworks.[14] By reading the *soil/species intimacies* in Grainger's poem—by tracing the porous entanglements between soil and the proliferating scales of life and vitality it registers—this chapter unearths and uncovers what a logics of white Anglo love tries to obfuscate: which matters *matter*.

SURVEYORS OF LOVE: INTIMATIONS OF SUGARCANE CULTIVATION

Early in *The Sugar-Cane*, the speaker muses: "This soil the Cane / With partial fondness loves; and oft surveys its progeny with wonder."[15] The peculiar use of "love" to describe the sugarcane's relationship to the "clay or gravel mix'd" soil of St. Kitts not only gestures toward a non/human romance of sorts between sugarcane and dirt but also to love's attunement with land improvement, particularly the development of monocrop production within the plantation economy. The speaker aligns the sugarcane's "fondness" for the soil with the perspective of the surveyor who must examine and ascertain the value and tenure of one's crop or "progeny" as if the cane itself were a metonymic extension of the colonial planter—as if sugarcane were constitutive of the planter's own offspring, brood, or descendants. Grainger only uses the term "progeny" twice throughout his 2,563-word poem: once in the above reference to sugarcane cultivation and once in describing the enslaved Africans as "Afric's sable progeny."[16] The lines also highlight the specificity of the sugarcane's desire for soil as pointedly heterosexual, given its focus on futural impulses and its result of re/producing offspring.[17]

In "The Future is Kid Stuff," Lee Edelman aligns heterosexuality with reprofuturity through the figure of the Child "who has come to embody for us the telos of the social order and come to be seen as the one for whom that order is held in perpetual trust."[18] Here Edelman aligns the Child with that which is "held in perpetual trust," which ultimately conflates the notion of progeny with property or *as* property. The use of a legal term "perpetual trust" defines a process of indefinite ownership over assets that allows future generations to amass and bequeath wealth without incurring transfer taxes. What if "the image of the Child" could be understood more broadly, to include non/human progeny? To include monocrops, like sugarcane? In reading Edelman's queer sociality thesis more broadly, reprofuturity comes to emphasize the historical logics of colonial plantation management: to control, to contain, and to frame intimacy as inherently white-owned and (hetero) sexual in order to possess, sell, and profit from intimacy's productions.[19]

Grainger's description of how the cane examines its harvest, or progeny, with "wonder" reinforces an earlier connotation of the term "survey" that most aptly reflects the notion that the non/human cane Child is legally owned by the cane parent and by extension, the plantation owner and *not* the enslaved laborer: "To examine and ascertain the condition, situation, or value of, formally or officially, e.g. the boundaries, tenure, value, etc. of an estate, a building or structure, accounts, or the like, more . . . *spec.*, to examine the condition of a property on behalf of its prospective buyer."[20] This definition of "survey" includes a list of objects to be examined and ascertained, but is not exhaustive, ending with a nebulous "or the like" in reference to what can be surveyed for its value, boundaries, and tenure. Such examination is in service of selling, yet another form of strategic and profitable property transfer and one that is completely restricted and regulated, disallowing enslaved Africans any opportunity to sell the literal fruits of their labor. In St. Kitts' *Acts of Assembly (1711–1735)*, a 1711 act fined persons up to twenty pounds if they were to "trade, traffick, or deal with any Negro, or other slaves, for Sugar, Syrrup, Molosses, Indigo, Tobacco, Ginger, Cotton, Brass, Pewter, or any other Goods, Merchandize, or any Stock or Poultry . . . without the Knowledge or Consent of the said Master or Owner of such Negro, or other Slave or Slaves."[21] Though the enslaved African laborers are the ultimate cultivators of sugarcane, their relationship to the monocrop is not perceived to be a direct one or one of direct exchange or trade. Their laboring intimacy with the cane is alienated through this process of global distribution.[22]

"GIVE THE SAP TO RISE": SUGARCANE'S CROSS-RACIAL AND CROSS-SPECIES QUEER EROTICS

Cristobal Silva argues that Grainger "aestheticize[s] sugar as a poetic commodity" for a British literary audience to obfuscate the daily realities of enslaved labor that

MATTERS OF INTIMACY 117

is at the heart of this imperial economy.[23] By inserting a plot of heterosexual romance between sugarcane and soil, Grainger positions the planter's and the enslaved Africans' directed labors as necessary to this poetically constructed non/human procreative relationship. As the obvious hierarchical power dynamic between the planter/owner and the enslaved African becomes overladen with the sugarcane's sweet sap, the relationship between the two becomes increasingly pederastic and homoerotic. Vincent Woodard argues that sites of production offer "an originary framework for the emergence of homoeroticism out of the transatlantic slave trade and plantation culture."[24] As the enslaved Africans hoe the sugarcane, Grainger refers to the planter as "the master-swain [who] reviews their toil."[25] In imagining a pre-enslavement life where the Africans worked "their native land" willingly, he suggests that their lack of effort in St. Kitts stems from being "uninstructed swains."[26] The use of the term "swain" has a significant double meaning, particularly in the context of St. Kitts as a West Indian plantation. "Swain" is predominantly associated with pastoral poetry and can mean both "a country or farm labourer" and "a country gallant or lover."[27] Such a boundary-collapsing term, perhaps most readily signified in a term like "husbandry," prescribes and enforces a specifically *British* heterosexual masculinity onto the process of sugarcane propagation.

Yet, the notion that sugarcane requires the assistance of a British male lover and anglicized laborer also destabilizes the scalability of the term "swain." Rather than maintaining a compulsory heterosexuality, "swain" achieves queer valences in the assumptive pastoral homoerotics associated with a collective of male laborers arousing sugarcane to re/produce.[28] Grainger identifies each part of the power dialectic with a similar term, the planter being the "master-swain" and the enslaved Africans as the "uninstructed swains," which adds a pederastic cross-racial intimacy between and among the white plantation owner and "the Negroe-train"— the line of enslaved Black laborers—as well as a cross-species intimacy between and among the human cultivators, the sugarcane, and the soil. Grainger's georgic obfuscates capitalism's reliance on the integral cross-racial and cross-species erotic intimacies inherent to monocrop production. The notion of an "uninstructed swain" likewise portrays a complex framework of what specific modalities of a culture become colonized. Grainger appears to see the planter's job as one of white instruction, wherein the whiteness is not simply grinded in via enforced style of plantation farming techniques but also through an inculcation into an anglicized male heterosexual role of gallant lover.

The English pastoral poem juxtaposes the enslaved African's role as opposite to the virile Anglo protagonist. The former's role is that of an intimacy coordinator whose own sexuality is predicated upon the colonially produced monocrop sexuality of sugarcane and whose own potential desires are negated or sublimated in service of an objectified and feminized role of arousal labor. Mel Chen argues that animacy works "to blur the tenuous hierarchy of human-animal-vegetable-mineral with which it is associated."[29] Chen's pivot to animacy makes tangible the ways in which sexualities are not containable or separate dynamics; rather, sexualities become contaminated, transformed, encroached on, and altered by constant touches and material proximities between and among forms of matter. The relationship between the enslaved African laborer and the sugarcane becomes erotically charged. Integral to the process of sugarcane cultivation is the necessary "dalliance" or flirtation between "fresh sportive airs" for which the sugarcane joints will "embrace," and thus "give the sap to rise."[30] Once the sugarcane's first blades have lost "their verdure," it is up to the enslaved laborers to strip off these languid, yellowing blades to facilitate—to intimately coordinate—the courtship between the green, virile cane joints and the fresh air.[31] The poem inflects the ratooning process as one that requires the enslaved African laborer to remove the cane's flaccid elements—where they "hang their idle heads"—to facilitate the growth of erect ones.[32] Though the African enslaved laborer occupies the position of "uninstructed" Black male lover in relation to the Anglo white male planter, he also comes to ostensibly occupy the position of a racialized female lover to the sugarcane. With such positioning, the Black laborer's individual desires and sexualities are erased through the process of arousing the virile cane to ejaculative sap completion.[33]

The goal of producing sap invokes a linear erotics of orgasm. Such a framework elucidates the meanings of Grainger's invocation of sap as semen and as productive progeny for commodification and exchange value. Annamarie Jagose suggests that within queer and leftist discourses, (human) orgasm is "figured in the register of normativity" and thus "is always in the service of systems of oppression."[34] For Jagose, the desire to revel in orgasm's incoherence stems from the assertion that orgasm is not inherently teleological. Grainger's poem throws into doubt what counts as incoherent about orgasm. The poem registers the cane's eventual release of sap through a connotative framework of seminal fluid, thus implying the potential for non/human orgasm as a result, not of sexual re/production but of an asexual clonal re/production assisted by the hands of enslaved laborers. Such poetic figurative work reveals and portrays the irony of monocrop production. To contain and enclose the plantation toward a singular production— toward an exclusive monocrop—requires and registers a variety of cross-racial and cross-species intimacies. The drive toward one narrowly defined aim of producing sap for the sugar trade relies on and produces a porous "alien mixture" of soil and species sexualities.

KJ Cerankowski further argues that such enclosure of sexuality is "necessarily tied to the logics of colonization—orgasm, at the right time, in the right way, with the right person [or species]."[35] The enslaved African is crucial to sugarcane propagation through their specifically timed coordination of harvesting techniques, which implies that without them, this particular asexual model of courtship is foreclosed. The assumed need for heterosexually inflected assistance ironically reveals sugarcane production as a much queerer, erotic, asexual, and non-monogamous process. Sugarcane cultivation requires a variety of participants' direct and discretely directed involvement to effectively arouse the sugarcane to mate with the fecund St. Kitts soil. These queer intimacies are also tragically predicated upon a colonial reality of stolen bodies. Hortense Spillers identifies this "theft of the body" as one that severs "the captive body from its motive will, its active desire."[36] Beyond the fruits—sugarcane sap—of enslaved African labor that are stolen by the plantation economy, monocrop sugar production specifically registers the ways in which the plantation system steals from the Black body by sapping it of its own embodiments of desire and of sexuality.

EROTICS OF COMPOSTABILITY: WHOSE MATTER FERTILIZES THE SOIL?

By conflating the enslaved African and the sugarcane through his singular use of the term "progeny," Grainger creates a severing wherein the progeny in the poem are not reflective of heirs *to* property but are the stolen labor and the promised future assets, alongside the sugarcane crop, *of* British heirs to the plantation.[37] Grainger's georgic reveals how monoculture creates a despairing future of land exhaustion that is then narrativized as removed from the very system that has put such a crisis into effect through the language of and attention to composting and re-fertilizing the soil. Abetting such a fantasy of consumption, as Karl Marx asserts, robs "the soil; all progress in increasing the fertility of the soil for a given time is a progress toward ruining the more long-lasting sources of that fertility."[38] Grainger idolizes the soil as that which can be reproductively receptive and seemingly inexhaustible, to imply the plantation's effects are only valuably held in perpetual trust so long as the soil's nutrients can be regularly replenished:

"SCARCE less impregnated, with every power
Of vegetation, is the red-brick mould,
That lies on marly beds.—The renter, this
Can scarce exhaust; how happy for the heir!"[39]

The term "mould," referring to topsoil or surface soil, also specifically names dirt that is extremely friable and fertile due to it being "rich in organic matter": "moulds are loams mixed with animal and vegetable remains, particularly from putrefaction."[40] Grainger insists that the future "heir," that legally promised recipient of this monocrop's productions, can be "happy" now because the "renter," who I understand as the enslaved laborer, "can scarce exhaust" this type of topsoil through repetitive working and ploughing. By being made of composted decaying remains of organic matter that return nutrients to the earth, the mould's fertility and receptivity appear for Grainger cyclical and constant and able to keep up with the tempos of monocrop production. As long as the "rented"—stolen—labor of enslaved Africans to work the sugarcane is available, the sugarcane appears effortlessly and indefinitely fertile, and there is no end to its re/productive capacity. Grainger's poem idealizes and fantasizes the possibility and potential for earthen metabolic balance and harmony.

Grainger's need for and involvement of so many bodies—human, animal, living, non/living, organic and inorganic—in the sugar cultivation process reveals the environmental contradictions produced by colonial monocropping. Simply put, Grainger's georgic exposes the awareness and manipulation of "soil as a living world rather than a mere receptacle and input for crop nutrition" through the plantation system's very insistence to exploit and exhaust the soil solely toward one end.[41] St. Kitts' soil, which becomes exponentially more productive, "likely to make more sugars this year, than since it has been first settled," is often juxtaposed with Nevis' and Antigua's soil, which is often impacted by "dry weather and will make but very small crops this year."[42]

The nineteenth-century cartographer, John Pinkerton, describes St. Kitts' soil as not only especially fertile but also uniquely plowable as if the soil was made *only* for sugarcane propagation: "No part of the West Indies that I have seen, possesses even the same species of soil that is found in St. Christopher's. It is in general a dark grey loam, so light and porous as to be penetrable by the slightest application of the hoe."[43] In an attempt to describe St. Kitts soil as uniquely productive, Pinkerton aligns the soil's porosity with penetrability via a harvesting tool, implying that its porous nature is uniformly geared toward agricultural re/production even though the more porous a soil is, the more species and organisms, including bacteria, can survive and develop there. By relying on the language of speciation to define St. Kitts soil, Pinkerton falsely and discursively encloses soil as a contained or containable entity. A soil's natural receptivity to re/production is broad and broadly distributed among species and organisms.

As St. Kitts' sugarcane production increases, the physical health and bodily constitution of the enslaved African laborers becomes jeopardized: "After the prospect of making the largest crop of sugars that has been known . . . and were their negroes in health to labour, yet the inhabitants would now loose [*sic*] more than half of their expectations."[44] The tension between increased production and decreased labor is that of profit margins for the plantation owners. Samuel Baker's 1753 map of St. Kitts (see Figure 6.2) sketches the overarching topography of the island, including illustrations of the hills, volcanoes, and other more rugged terrain formations, including icons for the various ponds. Baker's map also includes icons for the parishes' various "Windmills for Grounding Sugar Canes," which are multiply located throughout each parish parcel on the island. For Grainger, mills are crucial to sustaining the soil's increased fertility, able to "double thine estate" for the planter.[45] He instructs to "never, ah never, be asham'd to tread/Thy dung-heaps, where the refuse of thy mills,/With all the ashes, all thy coppers yield,/With weeds, mould, dung, and stale, a compost form,/Of force to fertilize the poorest soil."[46] The dung-heaps are made of the refuse of the mills, creating a "compost form" or mixture of weeds, topsoil, excrement, and leftover plant stalks and stems necessary to maintaining the soil's increased fertility. Grainger attends to the ways in which composted decaying organic materials can manage to revitalize even the "poorest soil"; however, such knowledge of composting lends to extractive exhaustion of the soil—only revitalizing the soil for the sake of the sugarcane—and to speculations of further abuse of the enslaved laborer, by begging the question of what counts as refuse?[47] Or, does it matter which matter fertilizes the soil?[48]

MATTERS OF INTIMACY   121

Figure 6.2. Lieutenant Samuel Baker et al. *A new and exact map of the island of St. Christopher in America, according to an actual and accurate survey made in the year 1753. Describing the several parishes, with their respective limits, contents, & churches; also the high ways, the situation of every gentleman's plantation, mills, and houses; with the rivers, and gutts. Likewise the bays, roads, rocks, shoals and soundings that surround the whole.* [London, Printed for Carington Bowles . . . and Robt. Wilkinson . . . ?, 1753] Map. Used with permission by the Library of Congress, Geography and Map Division.

Beyond these obvious forms of fungibility—the enslaved Black body's value being not in monetary pounds simply but in pounds worth of consumptive material of sugar—there is the fungibility of compostability.[49] If Marxists are concerned about the increasing distance between sites of consumption and sites of production, then what about the increasing proximity between the bodies of enslaved Black laborers and the sites of their work? (see Figure 6.3)[50] In Book III, Grainger mentions an "accident" that "will sometimes happen, especially in the night" at the mill: the forcible dismemberment of an enslaved Black laborer's limb.[51] In this same footnote, Grainger speculates on a practice Pere Labat was informed of where if "the English were wont, as a punishment, [. . .] they would] grind their negroes to death." The fact of speculation of the conflation of the enslaved Black body and of sugar in the plantation's social imaginary is fact enough of an erotics of compostability, which is a symptom and consequence of the exponential expansion of

Figure 6.3. "No. [1, 2] of a Series of Views in the West Indies" by Theodore Henry Fielding. Messrs. Underwood: London, 1827. Engraving of the Eastridge Estate, situated on the Northeast or windward side of the island, which was known to possess more fertile soil. Includes the Indigenous-named stratovolcano Liamuiga ("Mount Misery") in the distance. Used with permission by the British Library.

sugarcane exportation. The increasing fungible proximity between the enslaved Black laborers and sugarcane is also registered in the payment of returned fugitives—dead or alive—to the plantation in the amount of "six Pounds current Money of this Island, or the Value thereof in Sugar."[52] The supposed milling accidents of "imprudence or sleepiness" wherein the cane and "the entangled member" become conflated within and by the mill grinder produces a fungibility indicative of the costs of scalability.[53]

The potential for literal "dismembering" was a regularly occurring punishment for enslaved Africans and noted in St. Kitts' *Acts of Assembly* in the case of wounding or maiming a white person while figurative dismemberment was as regularly occurring and registered as a poll tax: "*A duty of eight shillings per poll* [per head] *on all negroes and slaves.*"[54] Further, after the passing of these acts, if an enslaved African was to be condemned for a crime, said individual was to be appraised in "pounds of sugar" and that estimated value could be lessened if said individual suffered a disability, "by having but one Limb."[55] Not only are the enslaved Africans alienated from the crop they labor over so tirelessly but they have become alienated quite literally from their own selves, their own bodily matter having become fodder for the mill. Anna Tsing defines the monocrop as a system of alienation "in which only one standalone asset matters; everything else becomes weeds or waste."[56] They are no longer simply plowing the soil to plant the cane or arousing the cane to cultivation, but rather, they are forced into a haphazard confrontation and misguided reconstitution of their selves as the reproductive waste needed to fertilize the soil and maintain the plantation's monocrop productionist tempos. The cost of scalability is Black flesh.[57]

Transplantation: Moving beyond from within Metes, Bounds, and Provision Grounds

Can the conflation of the Black body and the soil ever produce a form of metabolic harmony that does not reconstitute a white Humanism? If the monocrop plantation is an unsustainable system that anticipates infrastructural collapse while continually promoting anti-Blackness, what, if anything, lies beyond its bounds? Fugitive enslaved persons disrupted the rhythms of monocrop production by disregarding the metes and bounds of the plantation and by resisting the metabolic exhaustion of their own provision grounds through a Black asexual erotics.[58] A land parceling logic of "metes and bounds," a mode of legal containment owned and administered by individual landowners, cannot fully control the everyday uses and means of occupancy by enslaved persons within those bounds.

William McMahon's 1828 survey map of St. Kitts (see Figure 6.4) can be more accurately understood as a cadastral map, or a "metes and bounds" map, which is

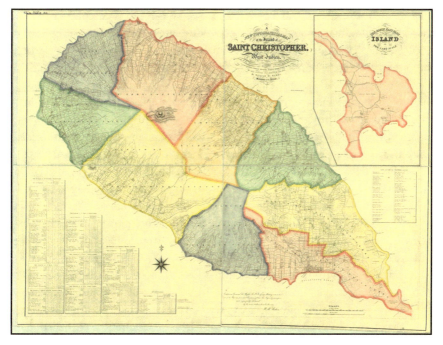

Figure 6.4. *A New Topographical Map of the Island of Saint Christopher* [St. Kitts] *in the West Indies* (1828) by William McMahon, surveyor of the island. Used with permission by the American Geographical Society Library at the University of Wisconsin-Milwaukee Libraries.

a large-scale, comprehensive recording of a country's geography as illustrated through property parcels, boundaries, and subdivisions for the purposes of legal documentation of land ownership. McMahon's map lists the various parish boundaries and provides all the parcel owners for each parish as well. The acreage of land within each parish is then calculated and categorized as either "Cane Land" or miscellaneous: "Works, Negro Huts, Pasture, Mountain, and Uncultivated Land." What counts as cane land, also, unsurprisingly, outmeasures the leftover land, leftover for sustaining human and non/human life directly on the island, which suggests a continued increasing of distance between production and consumption through a dwindling of land parcels for the production of sustenance. This division of land types can be summed up as productive land versus unproductive land, which ultimately implies that the land used for enslaved Black persons' homes as well as for their own food and sustenance is considered wild or uncultivated space despite still being contained by the metes and bounds of parish divisions. In "Novel and History, Plot and Plantation," Sylvia Wynter argues that provision grounds—the plots of land given to enslaved Black persons by enslavers—are indicative of a process of transplantation in which not just African bodies but African customs and traditions become transposed and recultivated, offering forms of "cultural guerilla resistance" to the plantation from within through a return to a system of shared use value against the colonial system of exchange value.[59]

This chapter has argued that to worship at the altar of the monocrop is to promote sugarcane production as a perverse love story as if such a discourse can ever bridge the widening gap between sites of production and sites of consumption. It is not merely that Grainger and other planters hide sugarcane's complex asexual production behind a humanist framework, but more specifically that such a discourse attempts to efface the increasing banality of sex that enslavement and capitalist industry has produced through the language of romance and courtship. Through the process of transplantation, Wynter theologizes: "The land remained the Earth—and the Earth was a goddess; man used the land to feed himself; and to offer fruits to the Earth; his funeral was the mystical reunion with the earth."[60] Transplantation resists the banal—"All forms of de-spiritualized and impersonal human interaction"—by re-introducing a reciprocal, consensual, nurturing relationship between bodies (bodies of land and bodies of flesh).[61] What Wynter identifies through the maintenance of sustenance plots by enslaved Africans is a Black asexual erotics. For Ianna Hawkins Owen, asexuality denotes "the banality of sex or the substitutability of sex with other kinds of pleasure that may lie outside of the bounds of the hegemonic notions of sex and sexual desire."[62] Through this Black asexual ontology, land occupies the role of direct sustenance, a gift given on the condition and expectation of a return offering. Such an exchange of metabolic energy does not require the exploitation and exhaustion of one body at the expense of another.

I do not find it a coincidence that Wynter's conception of transplantation emphasizes a logic of transparency. Here, I am drawing a connection between the use of the prefix trans (meaning across, with, and beyond categorical difference)

MATTERS OF INTIMACY 125

in both "transplantation" and "transparency" and the conceptualization of an anti-capitalist framework that does not attempt to hide, disguise, deny, or obfuscate the porosity, fluidity, and openness of asexual ecologies and multispecies intimacies. The *OED*'s entry examples for "transparency" during the years of 1651–1653, 1705, 1750, and 1860 rely on objects of the biosphere: crystal minerals, streams, stones, and the atmosphere, therefore implying a material meaning to the term, or more simply put: transparency is an environmental concept.[63] By accepting and treating the soil of the biosphere as a living world that is open and porously connected to the Black body, the Black self is reconstituted. As land is recognized as a site of sustenance for the Black body, the Earth still requires metabolic offerings of decay—"his funeral was the mystical reunion"—to regenerate the soil. Within these African precolonial soil intimacies are future-facing salves to the widening gaps between production and consumption. Such soil intimacies reintroduce Black pleasure to projects of sustainability and restoration; they are erotic, nonsexual, and recommit to a pleasure that does not need to be duplicitously bound by and within the language of Anglo romantic love and courtship to prosper.

NOTES

1. For broader frameworks of gender and sexuality in nature, see Joan Roughgarden, *Evolution's Rainbow: Diversity, Gender, and Sexuality in Nature and People* (Berkeley: University of California Press, 2004); and Catriona Mortimer-Sandilands and Bruce Erickson, eds., *Queer Ecologies: Sex, Nature, Politics, Desire* (Bloomington: Indiana University Press, 2010). See also James Grainger, *The Sugar-Cane, Caribbeana: An Anthology of English Literature of the West Indies, 1657–1777*, ed. Thomas Krise (Chicago: University of Chicago Press, 1999), 166–270 (180). All citations are to this edition.

2. Barbara D. Booth, Stephen D. Murphy, and Clarence J. Swanton, *Invasive Plant Ecology in Natural and Agricultural Systems* (Wallingford, UK: CABI, 2010), 68.

3. Joshua Peterkin, *A Treatise on Planting, from the Origin of Semen to Ebullition; with a Correct Mode of Distillation and a Melioration on the Whole Process Progressively. Dedicated to the Planters of the Leeward Charribbee Islands* (St. Christophers, Basseterre: Printed by E. L. Low, 1790), 2–3.

4. Peterkin, *A Treatise on Planting*, 2–3.

5. See also, "The Biology of *Saccharum* spp. (Sugarcane)," Australian Government Department of Health and Ageing Office of the Gene Technology Regulator, version 3 (May 2011); and D. J. Heinz and T. L. Tew, "Hybridization Procedures," in *Sugarcane Improvement through Breeding*, ed. D. J. Heinz (Amsterdam: Elsevier, 1987), 313–342.

6. See Noreen Giffney and Myra J. Hird's defense of the necessary backslash in the term "non/human": the placement of "the slash between as well as" part of "'non' and 'human'" recognizes "the trace of the nonhuman in every figuration of the Human" and "of the exclusive and excluding economy of discourses relating to what it means to be, live, act, or occupy the category of the Human." See Noreen Giffney and Myra J. Hird, eds., "Introduction," in *Queering the Non/Human* (Farnham, UK: Ashgate, 2008), 1–16 (2).

7. Richard Frohock suggests that "the georgic is ultimately a flawed form for celebrating the planter-hero: on the one hand, it allows for the elevation of agriculture to the heroic work of empire in the fashion of Virgil's model. On the other hand, the georgic requires didacticism, and in detailing the planter's modus operandi the abuses and brutalities inherent in the chattel slavery system necessarily appear." See Frohock, *Heroes of Empire: The British Imperial Protagonist in America, 1596–1764* (Newark: University of Delaware Press, 2004), 179; and Keith A. Sandiford, "The Sugared Muse: Or the Case of James Grainger MD (1721–66)," *New West Indian Guide* 61, no. 1/2 (Spring 1987): 48.

8. Grainger, *The Sugar-Cane*, 1:459–1:462.

9. See "alien 1b(b)," *OED Online*, December 2021, Oxford University Press, https://www.oed.com/dictionary/alien_adj?tab=meaning_and_use#7106962.

10. KJ Cerankowski and Megan Milks, "New Orientations: Asexuality and Its Implications for Theory and Practice," *Feminist Studies* 36, no. 3 (Fall 2010): 650–664 (661).

11. Lisa Lowe, "Response: Intimacies as Method," *Eighteenth-Century Fiction* 34, no. 2 (Winter 2022): 207–213 (208).

12. Neel Ahuja notes that "it is necessary to reconfigure notions of intimacy and reproduction across the planet: minerals, mosquitoes, settlers, gases, solar rays, and other bodies share in reproductive metabolisms crossing scales, species, and systems." See Ahuja, "Intimate Atmospheres: Queer Theory in a Time of Extinctions," *GLQ: A Journal of Gay and Lesbian Studies* 21, no. 2–3 (June 2015): 365–385 (367).

13. Brit Rusert, "Plantation Ecologies: The Experimental Plantation in and against James Grainger's *The Sugar Cane*," *Early American Studies* 13, no. 2 (Spring 2015): 341–373 (346).

14. In *Three Essays on the Theory of Sexuality* (1910), Sigmund Freud writes about the development of (hetero)sexuality as one in which the Social drives and encloses the natural and "infantile" desire for the whole body as an erogenous zone into one that focuses solely on genital stimulation and thus becomes geared toward copulative acts and intimacies between differently sexed bodies. Anna Tsing defines "scalability" as the "ability to make projects expand without changing their framing assumptions." See Freud, *Three Essays on the Theory of Sexuality* (New York: Basic Books, 2000); and Anna Lowenhaupt Tsing, *The Mushroom at the End of the World: On the Possibility of Life in Capitalist Ruins* (Princeton, NJ: Princeton University Press, 2015), 38.

15. Grainger, *The Sugar-Cane*, 2:128–130. The poem's use of "survey" in this early line readily aligns with the traditional prospect poem: "To look at from, or as from, a height or commanding position; to take a broad, general, or comprehensive view of; to view or examine in its whole extent," which was still in fashion at the time of the poem's publication. Even so, it is necessary to consider other definitions that further emphasize the term's discrete association with property management, such as: "To determine the form, extent, and situation of the parts of (a tract of ground, or any portion of the earth's surface) by linear and angular measurements, so as to construct a map, plan, or detailed description of it" ("2"). See "survey, v. 4a," and "survey, v. 2," *OED Online*, December 2021, Oxford University Press, https://www.oed.com/dictionary/survey_v?tab=meaning_and_use#19802827.

16. Grainger, *The Sugar-Cane*, 1:4.

17. Lee Edelman, *No Future: Queer Theory and the Death Drive* (Durham, NC: Duke University Press, 2004).

18. Edelman, *No Future*, 11.

19. John Gilmore's biography of Grainger emphasizes how he had married into what "modern historians call the plantocracy, that is, the local elite of European descent whose wealth and position was dependent on the ownership of plantations and of the slaves of African origin or descent who cultivated the land in sugar-cane and processed the cane into sugar for export to Britain." See John Gilmore, *The Poetics of Empire: A Study of James Grainger's "The Sugar Cane"* (London: Athlone Press, 2000), 14.

20. See "survey, 1. *Transitive*," *OED Online*, December 2021, Oxford University Press, https://www.oed.com/dictionary/survey_v?tab=meaning_and_use#19802827.

21. See *Acts of Assembly, Passed in the Island of St. Christopher; from 1711, to 1735, Inclusive* (London: printed by John Baskett, Printer to the King's Most Excellent Majesty, 1739), 9.

22. Walter Johnson points out that it is not just enslaved persons' abstract labor that becomes violently appropriated but also their material knowledge, their "ways of knowing that planters might command or even claim as their own, but that [planters] could never fully understand." See Walter Johnson, *River of Dark Dreams: Slavery and Empire in the Cotton Kingdom* (Cambridge, MA: Harvard University Press, 2013), 165.

23. See Cristobal Silva, "Georgic Fantasies: James Grainger and the Poetry of Colonial Dislocation," *ELH* 83, no. 1 (Spring 2016): 127–156 (138).

24. See Vincent Woodard, *The Delectable Negro: Human Consumption and Homoeroticism within U.S. Slavery Culture* (New York: New York University Press, 2014), 19.

25. Grainger, *The Sugar-Cane*, 1:405.

26. Grainger, *The Sugar-Cane*, 1:229.

27. See "swain, n. 4" and "swain, n. 5," *OED Online*, December 2021, Oxford University Press, https://www.oed.com/dictionary/swain_n?tab=meaning_and_use#19498157.

28. See David Shuttleton, "The Queer Politics of Gay Pastoral," in *De-centering Sexualities: Politics and Representations beyond the Metropolis*, ed. Richard Phillips, Diane Watt, and David Shuttleton (London: Routledge, 2005), 125–146.

29. Mel Chen, *Animacies: Biopolitics, Racial Mattering, and Queer Affect* (Durham, NC: Duke University Press, 2012), 98.

30. Grainger, *The Sugar-Cane*, 1:666–1:667.

31. Grainger, *The Sugar-Cane*, l:664–1:665.

32. Grainger, *The Sugar-Cane*, l:664–1:665.

33. Owen problematizes the mammy figure's rendering as asexual through her racist and white supremacist constitution. Owen argues for "the necessity of disentangling the human as fundamental to notions of asexuality. The historical construction of some figures as not fully human (recall the Three-Fifths Compromise) and as asexual offers additional trouble to the stability not just of sexuality as a human given but also of human as asexuality's emergent given." See Ianna Hawkins Owen, "Still, Nothing: Mammy and Black Asexual Possibility," *The Feminist Review* 120 (2018): 70–84 (72).

34. Annamarie Jagose, *Orgasmology* (Durham, NC: Duke University Press, 2012), 8–9.

35. KJ Cerankowski, "The 'End' of Orgasm: The Erotics of Durational Pleasure," *Studies in Gender and Sexuality* 22, no. 3 (September 2021): 132–146 (136).

36. See Hortense J. Spillers, "Mama's Baby, Papa's Maybe: An American Grammar Book," *Diacritics* 17, no. 2 (Summer 1987): 64–81 (67).

37. Christopher Allan Black describes *The Sugar-Cane* as promoting stewardship rather than exploitation. However, Black concludes, even Grainger's model only further "equalizes commodity producers and commodities in ways that induces forms of anthropomorphism and dehumanization simultaneously." Benevolent treatment of Black enslaved laborers only in service of yielding healthy and abundant sugarcane crops merely maintained and perpetuated violent abuse of the Black body and over-exhaustion of the land. There is no sustainable stewardship under global agricapital. See Christopher Allan Black, "Slavery and Plantation Stewardship: The Eighteenth-Century Caribbean Georgics of James Grainger and Philip Freneau," in *Eighteenth-Century Environmental Humanities*, ed. Jeremy Chow (Lewisburg, PA: Bucknell University Press, 2023), 189–204 (191).

38. See Karl Marx, *Capital: Volume 1*, trans. Ben Fowkes (New York: Vintage, 1976), 638. See also John Bellamy Foster, Brett Clark, and Richard York, *The Ecological Rift: Capitalism's War on Earth* (New York: Monthly Review Press, 2010).

39. Grainger, *The Sugar-Cane*, l:84–1:87.

40. See "mould, 1b," *OED Online*, December 2021, Oxford University Press, https://www.oed.com/dictionary/mould_n3?tab=meaning_and_use#35712937. See also Richard Kirwan, *Elements of Mineralogy*, 1794–1796, 2nd ed., 2 vols. (London: Printed by J. Nichols, for P. Elmsly, in the Strand, 1794).

41. María Puig de la Bellacasa, *Matters of Care: Speculative Ethics in More than Human Worlds* (Minneapolis: University of Minnesota Press, 2017), 172.

42. See Governor Hart, *The Calendar of State Papers, Colonial: North America and the West Indies 1574–1739*, vol. 33, Jan. 20, 1723; and Governor Hart, *The Calendar of State Papers, Colonial: North America and the West Indies 1574–1739*, vol. 35, February 15, 1727.

43. See John Pinkerton, *Modern Geography, A Description of the Empires, Kingdoms, States, and Colonies with the Oceans, Seas and Isles in All Parts of the World . . . Digested on a New Plan* (London: Cadell, 1807), 463.

44. See Governor Hart, *The Calendar of State Papers, Colonial: North America and the West Indies 1574–1739*, vol. 33, January 20, 1723.

45. Grainger, *The Sugar-Cane*, 1:222.

46. Grainger, *The Sugar-Cane*, 1:223–1:227.

47. See Saidiya Hartman, "Venus in Two Acts," *Small Axe* 12, no. 2 (June 2008): 1–14.

48. Jennifer Mae Hamilton and Astrida Neimanis rework Donna Haraway's ethics of compost, writing: "In our paraphrase it matters what compostables make compost and it matters if and how those nutrients are acknowledged." See Jennifer Mae Hamilton and Astrida Neimanis, "Composting Feminisms and Environmental Humanities," *Environmental Humanities* 10, no. 2 (November 2018): 501–527 (502).

49. In a letter to the Council of Trade and Plantations, Governor Hart refers to the British practice of selling enslaved Africans for "money or sugar: . . . if they sell for money they generally resort to these islands [St. Eustacia and Martinique] to purchase sugars for Great Britain: But if they dispose for sugars, then they carry them for Ireland directly." See Hart, February 15, 1727.

50. See Jordy Rosenberg, "Afterword," in *Transgender Marxism*, ed. Jules Joanne Gleeson and Elle O'Rourke (London: Pluto Press, 2021); and Kathryn Yusoff, "White Utopia/Black Inferno: Life on a Geologic Spike," *e-flux journal*, no. 97 (February 2019): 1–13.

51. Grainger, *The Sugar-Cane*, 221.

52. Grainger, *The Sugar-Cane*, 70.

53. Grainger, *The Sugar-Cane*, 221.

54. See *Petition of Wavell Smith and Savile Cust, to the Council of Trade and Plantations*, in *The Calendar of State Papers, Colonial: North America and the West Indies (1574–1739)*, vol. 42, (May 28, 1736), 9. Edward Bancroft, John Gabriel Stedman, and Bartolomé de las Casas' travel narratives also include references to the regular practices of enslaved persons' dismemberments as punishment.

55. *Petition*, 11. See also Monique Allewaert's discussion of fragmented personhood in *Ariel's Ecology: Plantations, Personhood, and Colonialism in the American Tropics* (Minneapolis: University of Minnesota Press, 2013), 85–114.

56. Tsing, *Mushroom*, 6.

57. Sophie Gee contends that "waste is always *made* not found—created by political and social processes, and, most importantly, by language itself." See Sophie Gee, *Making Waste: Leftovers and the Eighteenth-Century Imagination* (Princeton, NJ: Princeton University Press, 2010), 9.

58. Audre Lorde emphasizes that a Black feminist erotics differentiates between "the power of each other's feelings" and "using another's feelings as we would use a Kleenex." She argues that when "we use rather than share the feelings of those others who participate in the experience with us" we turn away from reciprocated consent and turn toward abuse. See Audre Lorde, "Uses of the Erotic: The Erotic as Power," in *Sister Outsider: Essays and Speeches* (New York: Crossing Press, 2007), 58.

59. See Sylvia Wynter, "Novel and History, Plot and Plantation," *Savacou* 5 (June 1971): 95–102 (100). In a recent issue of *ABO* on teaching Mary Prince, Nicole Carr describes how classroom visual analyses of Caribbean sugar iconography affords student engagement with "the myriad and mundane ways enslaved Black people asserted their humanity," which included resilient practices of home and family within the metes and bounds of the plantation. See Nicole Carr, "The Black Wanderer: Reading the Black Diaspora, Resistance, and Becoming in *The History of Mary Prince* in the Classroom," *ABO: Interactive Journal for Women in the Arts, 1640–1830*, 13, no. 1 (Summer 2023): 1–14 (9).

60. Wynter, "Novel and History," 99.

61. See Stefan Sullivan, "Banality," in *Marx for a Post-Communist Era: On Poverty, Corruption, and Banality* (New York: Routledge, 2002), 135–160 (136).

62. See Ianna Hawkins Owen, "Ordinary Failures: Toward a Diasporan Ethics" (PhD Dissertation, University of California, Berkeley, 2016), 74.

63. See "transparency n., 1a," *OED Online*, June 2020, Oxford University Press, https://www.oed.com/dictionary/transparency_n?tab=meaning_and_use#17971238.

CHAPTER 7

Fantasy Maps and Projective Fictions

Tess J. Given

ON THE MAP

This map is a fantasy of a circumscribed world (see Figure 7.1). A dotted line to "Crusoe's" island off the northern coast of South America traces a fictional itinerary across neatly bisected hemispheres, "skipping" in the middle over the divide between not-quite-aligned halves of the cartograph. This map bifurcates the globe through the Atlantic Ocean into eastern and western hemispheres, "old" and "new" world. The latitude lines are given equal parity with what political borders exist on the map, neither form of projection taking precedence in their visual overlap. Place names occasionally interrupt the other lines in the image, but there is no obvious visual hierarchy declaring which names take precedence over the navigational lines and which names do not. Most important is the juxtaposition of completeness and incompleteness: though the map seems at first to be neatly contained within the binary opposition of hemispheres, a closer look reveals a world fraying at its edges. North America and other regions dissolve into open-ended space. In one way, this reflects a commitment to empiricism, the openness a means of reflecting the "truth" of the continents' constitutive but as-yet unknown borders. In another more literal way, this openness reveals a world imperiled by the colonial knowledge of what already exists.

This world is brought into relation with what has not (yet) been mapped, perceived, anticipated, or speculated about—a world actively but not unselfconsciously being made in the image of what Tiffany Lethabo King calls the "conquistador eye," which predicates its visualizing power on eliding and overlooking Indigenous, Black, and noncolonial space.[1] It produces a map tenuously held together through imaginary navigational lines, but the very material edges of land mass that cannot be made to appear threaten to unwrite and unmap the entire document at any moment. The aporias in the map gesture to the frailty of cartography as a whole: the literal mapmaker would not have seen a fraction of what they depicted—thus, the entire exercise in mapping might be read as simply a maker's fantasy or

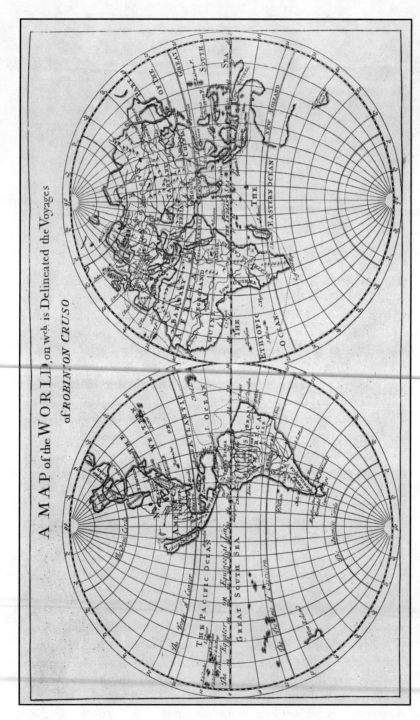

Figure 7.1. "A Map of the world, on wch is delineated the voyages of Robinson Cruso [sic]" (1719). Used with permission by the Beinecke Rare Book and Manuscript Library.

projection.[2] Even as Crusoe's little island is perfectly plotted near the shores of South America, the world around the island recedes. The imaginary lines that produced the material infrastructures of early modern global trade—the equator, the Tropics of Cancer and Capricorn—are as real here as Crusoe's island. However, the radically open-ended and unbounded spaces that had yet to be assimilated into the meaning-making systems of global trade and domination throw these "real" lines into sharp relief, casting doubt on the generative truth of the colonial gaze. The map necessarily bears a truthful resemblance, a verisimilitude, to the world "out there," but at the same time, there are strange occlusions that threaten to undo the fundamental conceit of mapmaking.

In tracing this fissure, what becomes apparent and strange about this map is how it serves two functions at once—or rather, how it fails two functions at once. Even as it pledges to tell a spatial truth to help orient one's view(s) of the world, it also breaks apart, or performs a "queer" action in the sense that Sara Ahmed discusses in *Queer Phenomenology* (2006). She notes that "queer" denotation is a particular way of *dis*orienting forces, objects, and subjects—of turning these things obliquely against and sometimes integrating them into the smooth functioning of systems like heterosexuality or whiteness.[3] For Ahmed, queer mo(ve)ments are visible when these smooth orienting infrastructures that pattern the world are occluded or otherwise "fail to keep things in their place."[4] This map both offers its world to whiteness and colonial systems of sex-sexuality-gender-race-etc.[5] by placing it "within reach" and collapses in on itself so that it can only display its own imaginative failures as truth.[6]

The roiling relationship between what is given and what is lost to the viewer of this map encodes an emergent form of scopophilic erotics imbricated within the larger matrix of power, fantasy, and desire at play in Daniel Defoe's novel *Robinson Crusoe* (1719). Although the novel is most famous for its portrayal of Crusoe's decades-long residence on an uninhabited island, other incidents in the text—including his enslavement as a Barbery captive, his organization of a sugar plantation in Brazil, and his movements as a sailor—locate Crusoe within the complex geographies of British colonial and imperial expansion. Crusoe's relationships, notably with the "Moor" Xury and the Indigenous captive Friday, illustrate power dynamics that are not only intensely entwined within British economies but also intensely eroticized. As Melissa K. Downes notes in her exploration of *Crusoe* as ostensibly a "famously sexless text" and its BDSM-like dynamics, this interpretation requires a slightly different understanding of "the erotic."[7] She abstracts the colloquial usage of "the erotic" as a force driving sexual relations between people, and instead employs it in a more diffuse and psychoanalytically tinged sense. By presenting the erotic as a key relational force at play in *Crusoe*, I follow Downes's claim that "to understand Robinson Crusoe as erotic is to understand the erotic as tied to relationships, but not always necessarily to relationships between and among people."[8] This chapter is interested in how the map, as infrastructure, channels and (re)directs that relational force. Moreover, it explores how queer spaces on the map catalyze a paradoxical and characteristically colonial mode of erotic nonrelation, creating a map that *unqueers* the things it presents.

My goal here is not to offer a "queer" reading of *Crusoe* that will allow me to produce a proper queer subject in whom erotics can appear as nonnormative desires or anxieties; relatedly, I do not seek to redefine erotics as something a map can feel or enact, queerly or otherwise. Rather, I investigate the map's dual failure—an apparent/initial queerness of the map that is then unqueered—and the effects of that dual failure. I suggest that the map's erotics articulate a fundamental and productive tension between the purported goal of a colonial map, the literal projection of knowledge and desire, and the persistent and self-aware failure of that projection, as characterized by the map's absences. A central question becomes how this failed orienting device of the fantasy map rambunctiously (dis)organizes, skips over, and fails to see its own imperial fantasies at multiple points in the map itself and in *Crusoe*, and how the simultaneous production and refutation of that failure produces a colonial system of nonsensical or disoriented erotics.

This chapter works to square the role of maps within eighteenth-century systems of hegemony-making with the odd symptomatic and elusive moments of queer eroticism that occlude some of *Crusoe*'s stranger passages. Such a method allows me to explore how these double failures ultimately register as anything but queer; the map's disorientation facilitates a systematized and naturalized perceptual fault in which erotic relations are first registered and then overlooked in order to "smooth" and project order onto the world. Though it's tempting to call these relations "queer," their strangeness actually produces their hegomonic power—faulty dynamics that with time become heterosexuality, racialized gender, and so forth.

The map powerfully conflates the viewer's literal and psychoanalytic gaze: the former observes the map's rendering of spatial relations, the latter theorizes vision as a vector for seeking and obtaining pleasure. That elision is particularly potent because it makes a rich set of visual metaphors available for analysis.[9] Consider a "saccade," the medical term for the shuddering movement of the eye while viewing objects in motion. Though it may not feel so, eyes actually jump—or saccade—between the object they're looking at and the environment, producing a smoother perception of the object's motion because of the visual breaks in viewing it. These breaks are vital to the perceptive process but occur both within and anterior to perception. "Saccade" becomes a persuasive metaphor for exploring scopophilic erotics and its necessary elisions because it bridges the perceptual and projective aspects of both the map and the narrative the map animates. Moreover, the term's pluripotent reach helps me read the eroticized fantasies underlying colonial scopophilic maps,[10] as well as the erotics of verisimilitude and referentiality embedded within the maps of *Crusoe*.

As Defoe shows, fictional travel literature was more than an exercise in expanding the colonial imagination or patterning the "empty space" of the frontier.[11] It is a new way of *seeing* the frontier such that the distinction between the apparent colony and the actual colony collapses. This impacts our understanding of early realist novels, because what results is a *perceived* verisimilitude that is ultimately not a product of a spatial or indexical relation but rather of forceful imposition or infrastructuring of projection. Maps are narrative devices that tell colonial stories, richly embellished with fantasies of ontological infrastructures of desire, identity, and time.[12] In exploring how fantasy maps are unqueered but left strange, it's possible to see how the early realist novel participates in this saccadic process of colonial projection.

If part of the colonial process is subjecting racialized Others to colonial regimes of sex-sexuality-gender, these maps fantasize about what erotics look like *in advance of* and *against the reality of* the colonial encounter. They foreclose the encounter's queerness, producing strange but now-familiar relations. Obviously, mapping as an act requires drawing boundaries, framing space and its antinomies, and ultimately *projecting* an ordered world. It's also a fantasy structure predicated on perceptual mechanisms that strategically do not perceive the world they pledge to render. This overlooking, or saccading, is how an erotics of nonrelation begins to speak through these spatialized, "mapped" fantasies.

Overlooking the Map

Though map technology existed long before Defoe's articulation of the fantasy map in *Crusoe*, as S. Max Edelson notes, in the early eighteenth century, the map rises to prominence and concatenates the needs of an expanding empire.[13] Maps manage projective mercantilist capitalism, data for an increasingly politically and spatially unruly empire undergoing a series of economic and social upheavals, and infrastructural demands for imperial totalizing projects. The map, in other words, is already considered a site where the needs and desires of empire coalesce and take shape.

Robinson Crusoe uses its map and its narrative mapping not as a literal perception of space but as part of a larger world-building project of reconciling or aligning *projection*, rather than *perception*, and reality. As Ala Alryyes writes on *Crusoe*'s cartography: "Although it may appear that geography is distinguished by an objective, neutral subject, a genealogy of geographical knowledge reveals that, in this age of conquest and colonialism, European polemics over the demarcations and legal representations of space were imbued with *polemos* itself, war and conflict."[14] Alryyes reads mapping in *Crusoe* as a knowledge-making project of empire, in which Crusoe's mastery of space is inextricably bound to his ability to wage war, producing orders of being that are relational insofar as they are spatialized. For Alryyes, Defoe-via-*Crusoe* also draws this power not just from mastery and aesthetics but through the ways that maps communicate verisimilitude.

Truth appears in multiple registers in Alryyes's reading, in which the mimetic representation of space (the ostensible purpose of a map) is subsumed by a larger realism defined by the "funny mirror of fiction" in which "verisimilitude . . . is perhaps beside the point. For Defoe is actually a 'realist of a larger reality.'"[15] Alryyes's reading uses the pseudoarchival map in *Crusoe* as an object of empire that speaks to its own of the realities of the colonial project conceived by Defoe.

Nevertheless, the map's *apparent* verisimilitude is a constitutive element of its ability to tell a larger truth: the realism of its construction is the engine of its metaphorical power. To Alryyes, Defoe's distorted map is still a map, except that this map traverses internal rather than external territory. Here, the openness of Defoe's map closes again as its coordinates become anchored in the metaphorical register, but their frames of reference still hold.[16]

Following Andrew Franta's *Systems Failure*, the map as it emerges in the early eighteenth century is in messy shape indeed—it's a bad object that is always already a target of empiricist suspicion yet becomes increasingly central to the project of Empire.[17] Franta's work historicizes a fundamental skepticism about systems: in this case, the map's ability to sustain its essential realism, or to reflect with some degree of verisimilitude the picture of the world it allegedly captures. Whereas the eighteenth century is often characterized as the era that developed the technologies of war, law, and rights discourses that inflect narratives of ongoing colonial expansion, what Franta demonstrates is that systems anxiety is non-teleological, and that maps as a projective element of fiction were already shot through with anxieties about the status of the embodied British subject.

These anxieties around what a map captures go beyond questions of spatial indexicality. The fantasy about what a map *reflects* (a picture of the world as it is) shifts—in Franta's reading as well as mine—to fantasies about what a map has the *capacity* to imagine. Franta reads this paranoid curiosity about maps' capacities from Borges back to Uncle Toby in *Tristram Shandy*: he points out that unspeakable spaces on the body or within the psyche can be externalized through the map's visualization of narrative. As these maps get more "realistic," they increasingly occlude an accurate perception of the terrain they index. This means that the map's bearing on reality, its increasing verisimilitude, in fact marks its departure from Alryyes's "realism of a larger reality."[18] The map emerges as a failing representational structure that, revealingly, does not need to be *accurate* but merely *forceful*. Franta and Alryyes both read maps as objects that transverse fiction and reality through their ability to forcefully index and coordinate points across these separate registers, regardless of accuracy.

The resulting maps depict *overlooked relations* which appear instead merely as *relations*. The ground they index is a projection of the eye/I of the cartographer, run through an apparatus that structurally erases the perceptual fault lines between what exists and what appears. This projective aspect of mapmaking is known as a "geographic imaginary"—a term that allows geographers to explore how subjectivity, desire, and projection bear on space.[19] Feminist and queer geography uses "geographic imagination" to explore how the erotic necessarily informs the construction of space and place.[20] In registering imagined spatial relations, cartographs become strange palimpsests that not only offer and efface the point of view from which the scopophilic gaze originates but also forcibly erase the desires and relations necessitating the map in the first place. The map, in the manner of a saccade, *appears* to be an inert object, though actually it is the product of a perceptive and projective process that can only produce the visible by overlooking and looking away from what is actually present and projecting a smooth space between projected points.

Overlooking the Boat

Crusoe's journeys abroad begin, crucially, by a primary encounter with Blackness: because Black life is often articulated in the colonial voice as absolute negation,[21] this encounter allows for the boundaries of fantasy and reality to be drawn and verisimilitude to be established. As the second son who must make his own fortune, Crusoe first joins the crew of a slave ship that is overtaken by Turkish pirates off the coast of the Moorish port of Salle. While his fellow sailors are sent "up the Country to the Emperor's Court," the captain of the pirate vessel instead retains his services as a slave.[22] Though Salle appears on the map, Crusoe never leaves the boat. Verisimilitude—the story's ability to say something real about the real world—is thus established here through nonrelation. Defoe establishes that this novel is "grounded" in the "real world" by gesturing toward a point on the map that is known to exist without Crusoe having to see it. The map in the novel—and the novel itself—is granted realism because of what Crusoe *doesn't* see and Crusoe is granted reliability as a narrator by *not encountering* the places he describes. Its externality to Crusoe's perception demonstrates a commitment to empiricism in much the same way the map does. His relationship to the "real" world is defined and upheld through a selective perceptual uptake and negation rather than constant encounter. The contact zones of the novel, like this ship outside Salle, become apertures through which Crusoe projects out knowledge that *appears* to be under his purview. But like the map, openness is projected and then forcibly saccaded over: the zones it observes are simultaneously known and unknown because of their strange way of seeing-as-elision.

This characteristically colonial double-failed saccadic desire extends throughout Crusoe's relationship with Xury. It's tempting but tricky to identify erotics in *Crusoe*—the text's lack of overt sexuality doesn't quite occlude the possibility of relations between Crusoe and others like Xury and later Friday; however, the confluence of emergent racialized sexual hierarchies and a shifting homosocial-homosexual paradigm *avant la lettre* often forces critics to look for erotics sublimated through other forces. For example, Joseph Campana identifies an emergent colonial sexual paradigm centering consumption and domination in dynamic tension with anxieties about *being* consumed and dominated. For Campana, Defoe's novel explores a subject who disavows desire and regulates attachment through asceticism, denial, and orality, which function as an extension of the book's (homo)erotics. In Crusoe's human encounters, including with Xury, "excessive attachment conspires with insupportable absence, provoking a kind of phantasmatic projection that threatens dispossession. Crusoe's response is to wish only for things he fantasizes he can tame and control, as in the case of Friday."[23] The resulting matrix of desire and fear that characterizes Crusoe's interactions with Friday and the figure of the "cannibal" that haunts the island is thus indicative of the novel's insistence on consumption and orality as an organizing principle of masculine desire in the eighteenth century, which then becomes articulated through contextual flows of power. Though not organized exclusively through genital contact and penetration, for Campana, this structure allows colonial subjects to render bodies into erotically consumable flesh—and of course, recognizing this process is key to understanding "not only the histories but the futures of sexuality."[24] In other words, Crusoe's joining together attachment and absence into a projective act that both necessitates and usurps control is symptomatic of the colonial encounter, both materially and figuratively.

However, there is another reading of Crusoe's encounters with Xury in which Crusoe's mapping I/eye does not need to perceive the ground but rather skips over it, or saccades, as a means of mastering it. Campana argues that Crusoe creates self-protective relations of domination and consumption in which the thing he desires is always an object of fear requiring subordination—he cites Kristeva's formulation of "phobia as a metaphor for want" as the operative mode of desire in this seemingly asexual text.[25] However, in taking together the sense of erotic domination from Campana with the function of the map as a style of projective fiction, a different erotic relationship between Crusoe and Xury reveals itself. In addition to rendering flesh consumable, territorializing borders, or emptying space through the logic of *terra nullis*, the ability of the "conquistador I/eye" to dominate a space through the nonrelation of the saccade manifests here textually as it does in the map visually.

The double-failure of the map's visualization of the frontier is reiterated in the double-failure of Crusoe's projected relationship with Xury. At first, Xury is characterized as a competent sailor and trader who expresses his dedication to Crusoe through words and deeds—an unquestionable asset to Crusoe throughout their shared journey. As Xury navigates (literally and metaphorically) the dangers of the open world, he pledges his loyalty to Crusoe and "smil'd in [his] Face and spoke so innocently that [he] could not mistrust him;" the two are consistently united in Crusoe's narration, which refers to them as "we" as they feel and struggle their way through an unknown coastline.[26] Crusoe is "off the map" by his own admission, and so the relationship between him and Xury, while by no means that of equals, is defined by a relational perception that allows Crusoe to observe, rather than project, the world he encounters.[27] Crusoe becomes accustomed to the saccadic nonrelation of the "map"—in other words, the failures of his projected system of relational meanings begin to become apparent as those connections are explored at greater length—as the perceptual apparatus of the eye/I is trained on this new space.

That is, however, until the saccade completes and the projective fiction of the map fails again: the first failure exposed the possibility of relation outside of the known points of triangulation, but this second failure "unqueers" that unknown space and occludes the possibility of a relationship between Crusoe and Xury. After weathering the unknown coastline, Crusoe begins to triangulate his location based *not* on what he sees, but rather what he expects to see. He writes:

I knew very well that the Islands of the *Canaries*, and the *Cape de Verd* Islands also, lay not far off from the Coast. But as I had no Instruments to take an Observation to know what Latitude we were in, and did not exactly know, or at least remember what Latitude they were in; I knew not where to look for them, or when to stand off to Sea towards them' otherwise I might now easily have found some of these Islands. But my hope was, that if I stood along this Coast till I came to that Part where the *English* Traded, I should find some of their Vessels upon their usual Design of Trade, that would relieve and take us in.[28]

Here, Crusoe's frame of reference shifts to a deliberate overlooking or non-relationship between the world he is seeing and the world that he is mapping onto it. Though Xury is included in Crusoe's desire to be rescued by English traders, he now begins a process of devaluation as the new coordinates of Crusoe's projected world take hold. Though Xury's perception of the world remains more accurate than Crusoe's—"Xury, whose Eyes were more about him than it seems mine were"—his ability to register and hold his gaze in this projected mapped fiction of Crusoe's perception wanes.[29]

This fault in colonial perception comes to its logical conclusion as Xury's ability to see *accurately* is superseded by Crusoe's ability to *not see* strategically. As the duo encounter a Portuguese vessel, these differences concretize as Crusoe's double-failed project "map" reinscribes the situation within a known frame of reference, forcibly unqueering the openness of the boat and remaking the scene into a familiar dynamic in which the nonrelation of what appears and what is perceived is central. In this scene, Xury calls out "*Master, Master, a Ship with a Sail*," and Crusoe writes, "the foolish Boy was frighted out of his Wits, thinking is must needs be some of his Master's Ships sent to pursue us, when, I knew we were gotten far enough out of their reach. I . . . immediately saw not only the Ship, but what she was, (*viz.*) that it was a *Portuguese* Ship, and as I thought was bound to the Coast of *Guinea* for *Negroes*."[30] In recognizing the ship's national origin, Crusoe reconciles the map of the world that he had been projecting and investing with his desires for navigating the openness of "unknown" space, a reconciliation based on the second perceptual failure inherent to the saccade. Not only does Xury *not* misrecognize the ship—the idea that it was Moorish is itself a projection of Crusoe's—but moreover, Xury identifies a larger shared homology between the vessels: they are both slave ships.

Xury's perception of the world is shown to be accurate and truthful in a way that does not usurp Crusoe's projection. However, the perceptual effect of Crusoe's saccading vision has already precluded Xury's accurate read because it allows Crusoe to navigate Xury's sale and barter for his own passage. It is here where the erotics of nonrelation come into full expression. Xury's perception of the Portuguese slaving vessel *cannot* be related to Crusoe's projection of its meaning—rather than being ignored, it cannot register within the saccade's perceptual mechanism due to its structural double-failures. Whatever relationship between Crusoe and Xury had existed is, from this point onward, necessarily contained within that strange nonrelation—that open space of the map between points originating within Crusoe's gaze. As such, the snap back of Crusoe's eye/I that completes the metaphorical saccade accounts for the lack of connection as well as the level of control over Xury's body and desires.

The ship's appearance reorients Crusoe's supposedly empirical perception, creating the saccadic fault that occludes the queer potentials of the open space and produces instead strange nonrelation between two characters. Whereas Crusoe had been able, in the queer uncoordinated space of the open map, to hold both Xury's desires and his own in view, the ship reoriented or restructured Crusoe's perception, rendering that open space unavailable for fantasy and desire. The ship's introduction occludes what had just been perceived before it and puts in its place a nonrelation between Crusoe and Xury, which enables the former to sell the latter. In effect, this creates an erotic infrastructure where the desiring body is also the projecting body is also the empirical body: to produce this body, the other participant in an erotic relation must be strategically overlooked or left in the queer open space between perceptual points. That space doesn't cease to exist, but it cannot operate the smooth functioning of the saccade, or the map, or the novel—the device registering perception. What it produces is (again) strange but definitely not queer. What potential there was for queerness—transgressive or disorienting relations—is lost in the perceptual jump between projected coordinates. The visual closure of the ship reorients—unqueers—that bizarre open unperceived space within the saccade. This comes to matter in the following passage, in which Crusoe's control over animal reproduction operates with this same logic of nonrelation and erotic control, though expression and enactment of explicit sexuality remain absent from the text.

Overlooking the Island

A great deal of work has been done on the ways that Crusoe's time on the island both illustrates and expands the colonial project's imbrication of space and place with sexual, gendered, and racialized infrastructures. Whereas critics like Campana and Hans Turley explore how Crusoe's colonial acts on the island are acts of force and assault—and they are—I want to suggest at the same time that the projective relationship that Crusoe establishes is an exercise in redrawing a fantasy coordinate system in which the land is remapped according to his fantasy of the space.[31] The violence in question is not only a matter of coercing the space to respond to colonial desire but of projecting a system that is fundamentally incapable of seeing coercion. In other words, though this portion of the novel is remarkably obsessed with cataloguing Crusoe's colonizing acts in intense detail (conveying an empiricist drive for verisimilitude), these projective acts are also indicative of a kind of erotic nonrelation made possible through the saccadic motion I've been describing. In particular, the reproductive politics of the island evidence the same sort of erotic double-failures we see at play in the map and on the ship. Though different than the erotic dynamics at stake between Crusoe and Xury, the unqueered occlusions of Crusoe's time on the island demonstrate yet another way that colonial worldbuilding operates as a kind of projective map-making project based in forceful and necessary perceptual faults.

In exploring the shipwreck, Crusoe finds himself cataloguing both present and absent items. However, for every lamentation of things lost, Crusoe projects an analogical alternative. Nothing appears that is not already a fantasy shaped by his needs. Even as Crusoe writes that "it was in vain to sit still and wish for what was not to be had," he nevertheless experiences just this phenomenon.[32] A coordinate system emerges in which the thing Crusoe fantasizes about appears, albeit in different form, before him. Seeking a place to bring a raft of supplies up the shore, Crusoe notes, "As I imagin'd, so it was, there appear'd before me a little opening of the Land, and I found a strong Current of the Tide set into it."[33] In another instance, Crusoe imagines himself to have stripped the ship bare of all provisions, yet finds a final stash of luxury, imperial goods—bread, spirits, sugar, and flour.[34] He imagines that his gun is the first ever fired on the island, and the native birds flee to confirm this belief.[35] What is being built—projected—here is not just the image of an Indigenous landscape that must be shaped through domination (under the guise of pedagogical intervention, as in Paul Kelleher's recent assessment, or other colonial modes) but a means of projecting out the world that Crusoe wishes to perceive—in a movement that maps over and excises the exigencies of the island. When things rise to interrupt the steady view of the map, threaten to interrupt the self-securing truth of its projection, they evidence the supplemental form of power in the erotics of nonrelation.

This takes its full expression, as well as its most overtly erotic politics, in how saccadic perception organizes—unqueers—Crusoe's treatment of the island's animals. As Kelleher writes in "A Table in the Wilderness," erotics in *Robinson Crusoe* emerges as part of the modern system of husbandry explored by the novel. Kelleher shows that a kind of sexuality in *Robinson Crusoe* is made visible through the pedagogical scene that emerges between Crusoe and Friday and articulates how Crusoe's transformative processes of mastery are all redoubled on his own body, particularly in the imposition (or rather, fantasy of imposition) of hunger and its relief. Kelleher contends that "in order for the human subject to arise and take its place in the world, the self must be rendered and handled as just another object to be shaped, mastered, and ultimately, 'husbanded'"—in other words, this novel explores how an imperial subject emerges through how they impose their own regulations on themselves.[36] Kelleher focuses on Crusoe's domestication of the island's wild goats, which cannot be accomplished via outright violence but instead relies on the imposition of hunger. Through this, Kelleher argues, Crusoe is constituted as a subject via his self-enforced proximity to goat-ness. The erotics that Kelleher reads appear to be less reciprocal and more reflexive, as "the domination of others, in Defoe's imagination, necessarily entails practices of self-mastery and self-formation."[37] Kelleher shares a focus on consumptive erotics with many of the other writers on *Crusoe*'s sexual politics. Though hunger is certainly a helpful proprioceptive metaphor through which to read the novel's erotics, one intriguing aspect of consumption is its self-evident materiality. Consumption creates both absences and wastes: it brings the consuming body into the world in a tangible, interactive way. Saccadic nonrelation might help account for the strange rifts that occur in the materiality of the world that Crusoe interacts with but fails to form relations toward. When taken alongside consumption as a metaphor, saccades suggest a mode of interaction with other lands and peoples that is ultimately self-securing, hiding away the important material relations that converge on the perceiving/projecting eye/I and account for its power.

The reproductive cycles of the island become indicative of this nonrelation: the longer Crusoe lives there, the more he carries out the double-failed perception that first perceives and then elides its novel spaces. Throughout the novel, Crusoe continues to find and kill female animals, particularly pregnant ones, including a sea turtle with a clutch of eggs, domestic cats, and a poultry hen with chicks.[38] Crusoe takes particular note of killing female species and their "useless" flesh: both she-goat and wild cat become environmental feminine excess. In a land with no observed potential for human reproduction, this exertion of control over other creatures' reproduction becomes an extension of Crusoe's assertion of a sex-gender (and species) hierarchy. It essentially remaps lines of husbandry and futurity to become circuited exclusively through Crusoe's fantasies about how reproduction works. Unlike consumptive moments—or moments that express Crusoe's fear of being consumed—there is no material linkage or chain here between what is taken and what is expended: instead, the perceptual break occurs here again as queer lifeways are perceived, overlooked, and then culled. In a sense, the process of saccadic projection is becoming more efficient, as Crusoe becomes more adept at occluding his own perceptions and foreclosing the queer openings he finds around him.

More projected coordinates take hold and occlude the island's queer failures to conform to Crusoe's initial "map." Crusoe recasts himself as the island's father: his refusal to salvage women's clothes from the wreck, and the notable absence of other male animals on the island despite obvious reproduction establish Crusoe as the spatial and relational patriarch-cartographer of the island (as well as its rightful steward, as Kelleher points out).[39] Though he eventually domesticates some of the fowls and goats that populate the island, his early time there is defined by the need to control and curtail reproductive cycles that fail to map onto his structures of desire.

And yet, Crusoe's cats, rather than the goats, play out the full sense of erotic nonrelation. Crusoe finds domestic cats on the island who then have kittens. In addition to the original dog who had survived the shipwreck, he calls these once-familiar creatures his "Family" and notes that he was "much surpriz'd with [their] Increase."[40] Becoming overrun, he culls these so-called family members.[41] This is surprising: not only is the act constructed as filicide, but "[he] had killed a Wild Cat, as [he] call'd it . . . I thought it was quite differing Kind from our *European* Cats, yet the young Cats were the same kind of House breed like the old one." Moreover, both cats he found were females.[42] Crusoe's "family" of cats seems guilty of adulterous miscegenation and/or lesbian parthenogenesis—

producing impossible offspring that went against all colonial logics of sex and sexuality, not to mention flouted his fatherly reign. Crusoe's imposed domestic relationship was initially a cognate to family and reproductive structures, but in mapping this fantasy onto his encounter with aberrant practice, it proved impossible to substantiate.

As Gabriel Rosenberg reminds us in "How Meat Changed Sex," animal husbandry expresses its erotics not just in the more abstract realm of biopolitical control of nonhuman subjects but also quite literally as sexual acts taken to ensure the production of new meat animals.[43] Though Rosenberg's analysis is more concerned with animal husbandry at the scale of industrial capitalism, the salient point about the erotic structure of animal (re)production remains. Furthermore, what Rosenberg makes visible is the idea that animal husbandry bears an erotic nonrelation to bestiality *despite*, and not *because* of the congruence of sexual acts between them. I suggest that erotic nonrelation is produced in the way that the laws around animal reproduction occlude—or map the space between and so necessitate a saccade over—these sexual homologies in animal-human sexual practices of both sorts. Though it operates more abstractly than the scopophilic desires that shape his relationship with Xury, what we see clearly between these two examples is the immense power that saccades offer to the perceiving/projecting eye/I.

In one sense, by remapping the cats from members of the house to vermin, Crusoe demonstrates the ultimate extension of colonial power: not just control over life, but control over the system that confers the ability or right to be seen as living at all. Much like Crusoe's episode with Xury, the cats also demonstrate a period within the saccade in which a relationship characterized by an openness and inability to bear projection produces a queer and disoriented erotics—before the saccade "closes" and the profusion of feeling and affiliation is martialed again. It is this power to remap the cats that accounts for Crusoe's power over Friday, Xury, and the rest of the island's inhabitants and life forms. Even Friday's designated "name"—an arbitrary temporal marker—functions as a projective means of remapping him into colonial systems of relation.

Unmapping

This instance of mapping, compounded as it is with other acts of projective fiction-making in this text, reaffirms King's contention that "the mapping of Blackness and Indigeneity is an attempt to spatially fix and capture forms of Black fugitivity and Indigenous resistance that elude the British and present an existential threat throughout the eighteenth-century Atlantic world."[44] In reading eighteenth-century maps as instances of colonial spatializing logics that designate Blackness as a "chaotic space" and Indigeneity as "anaspatial," King articulates the ways that "Black and Indigenous 'livingness' forced . . . British settlers' cartographic attempts to write themselves into being through anti-Black and anti-Indigenous violence to continually adjust and remain under revision."[45] In other words, King shows how the real-life project of the colonial map does what I have explored here—functions as a projective fiction that allows the Transparent I/eye to project, over/see, and produce subjects according to its desires, which necessarily contain an erotic component.[46]

I conclude by returning to the unsettling nature of this particular map and its fantasy status. As King observes, all colonial maps are necessarily fantasy structures with embedded erotics, regardless of whether they are meant to achieve a degree of verisimilitude with the real world or not. The failures of Crusoe's various "maps" in this story underscore these points and reaffirm the currents of Black and Indigenous thought in which "living otherwise" is both the object of colonial repression and its refutation. However, in exploring *Robinson Crusoe*'s depiction of an erotics of nonrelation, I hope to re-see a valence of King's argument. The saccadic motion of my reading metaphorizes a process that is considered a natural, involuntary part of seeing clearly. By reading maps as fantasy structures that have the power to repattern relations through the language of the saccade, I highlight how this process of overlooking is naturalized and thus invisibilized. Whereas metaphors of consumption, pedagogy, or BDSM erotics take for granted that there is a material series of consequences predicating a violent and domineering system, the metaphor of the saccade and the unqueering of the map suggest that a key part of the colonial process is the construction of a system in which the projecting/perceiving eye/I can occlude its own erotic investments—and pleasures—from the world it doubly fails to perceive. The saccadic looking-away-from the queer open places of these "maps" (whether metaphorical or literal) precludes the possibility of engagement, care, or substantive relation. What's left is a nonrelated gap held in constant place by the eye/I that is structured to overlook it. Perhaps sexuality here is resettled, then, rather than simply unsettled. The occluded queer failures tug uncomfortably at the edges of its vision in naturalized processes of forcibly overlooking them. The easiness of perceiving Crusoe's island on the map imperceptibly skips over a vertiginous expanse of projected-over relations that, try as we might, we cannot see.[47]

NOTES

1. Tiffany Lethabo King, *The Black Shoals: Offshore Formations of Black and Native Studies* (Durham, NC: Duke University Press, 2019).

2. Anne McClintock explores a similar text in the opening of *Imperial Leather: Race, Gender and Sexuality in the Colonial Contest* (New York: Routledge, 1995), though her map claims far less representative verisimilitude.

3. Sara Ahmed, *Queer Phenomenology: Orientations, Objects, Others* (Durham, NC: Duke University Press, 2006), 162.

4. Sara Ahmed, *Queer Phenomenology*, 165.

5. Since McClintock's *Imperial Leather*, Richard Braverman's *Plots and Counterplots*, and Edward Said's *Orientalism*, this linkage has been explored extensively. This essay takes for granted the interrelationship of those terms when approached from a postcolonial stance. See Braverman, *Plots and Counterplots: Sexual Politics and the Body Politic in English Literature, 1660–1730* (Cambridge: Cambridge University Press, 2005); and Edward Said, *Orientalism* (New York: Vintage, 1979).

6. Ahmed, *Queer Phenomenology*, 165.

FANTASY MAPS AND PROJECTIVE FICTIONS

7. Melissa K. Downes, "Erotic Bo(u)Nds: Domination, Possession, Enclosure and the Self in Daniel Defoe's *Robinson Crusoe*," in *The Erotic in Context*, ed. M. Soraya García-Sánchez, Cara Judea Alhadeff, and Joel Kuennen (London: Brill Publishers, 2010), 171–182 (171).

8. Downes, "Erotic Bo(u)Nds," 171.

9. This also follows King's analysis of the productive slip between "I" and "eye." See King, *The Black Shoals*, 88–89.

10. Cartographic imaginaries have been explored at length within the Black radical tradition, as in King, *The Black Shoals*, 74–110; Dionne Brand, *A Map to the Door of No Return* (New York: Vintage, 2002); Christina Sharpe, *In the Wake: On Blackness and Being* (Durham, NC: Duke University Press, 2016), 13–19; and Katherine McKittrick, *Demonic Grounds: Black Women and the Cartographies of Struggle* (Minneapolis: University of Minnesota Press, 2006).

11. In *The Black Shoals*, King refers to the Blackened and Indigenized spaces on maps as "chaotic space" and "anaspace," respectively (77–78).

12. On Indigenous place-based knowledge as a vector for engaging with decolonial sexuality and human-being, I am thinking with Zoe Todd, "An Indigenous Feminist's Take on the Ontological Turn: 'Ontology' Is Just Another Word for Colonialism," *Journal of Historical Sociology* 29, no. 1 (March 2016): 4–22; Mark Rifkin, *When Did Indians Become Straight?* (Oxford: Oxford University Press, 2010); Catherine E. Walsh and Walter Mignolo, *On Decoloniality: Concepts, Analytics, and Praxis* (Durham, NC: Duke University Press, 2018); King, *The Black Shoals*; C. Riley Snorton, *Black on Both Sides: A Racial History of Trans Identity* (Minneapolis: University of Minnesota Press, 2017); and Sylvia Wynter and Katherine McKittrick, *On Being Human as Praxis* (Durham, NC: Duke University Press, 2014).

13. S. Max Edelson, *The New Map of Empire: How Britain Imagined America before Independence* (Cambridge, MA: Harvard University Press, 2017).

14. Ala Alryyes, "Defoe's *Robinson Crusoe*: 'Maps,' Natural Law, and the Enemy," *Eighteenth-Century Life* 44, no. 3 (September 2020): 51–74 (52).

15. Alryyes, "Defoe's *Robinson Crusoe*," 58.

16. This dynamic between projection and displacement through appeal to a larger I/eye is echoed in Hans Turley's work about how Defoe displaces Crusoe's anxieties about normative sexuality through an appeal that I'd characterize as "upward" toward God rather than "outward." This saccadic motion and its relation to the project of verisimilitude in this text is characteristic of both Turley's and my reading. See Hans Turley, "The Sublimation of Desire to Apocalyptic Passion in Defoe's Crusoe Trilogy," in *Imperial Desire: Dissident Sexualities and Colonial Literature*, ed. Philip Holden and Richard J. Ruppel (Minneapolis: University of Minnesota Press, 2003), 3–20.

17. Andrew Franta, *Systems Failure: The Uses of Disorder in English Literature* (Baltimore, MD: Johns Hopkins University Press, 2019).

18. Alryyes, "Defoe's *Robinson Crusoe*," 58.

19. Jen Jack Gieseking, "Geographical Imagination," in *The International Encyclopedia of Geography: People, the Earth, Environment, and Technology*, ed. D. Richardson, N. Castree, M. Goodchild, A. Jaffrey, W. Lui, A. Kobayashi, and R. Marston (New York: Wiley Blackwell, 2017), 1–8.

20. As Gieseking argues: "Studies around cognitive and mental mapping reveal how situated and specific the geographical imagination is to a person, and also related to a person's race, class, gender, sexuality, and sense of embodiment and privilege" ("Geographical Imagination," 3).

21. A great deal of scholarship in Black studies works through this claim and its consequences, especially in conversation with Sylvia Wynter. See, for instance, the work of Alexander Weheliye, *Habeas Viscus: Racializing Assemblages, Biopolitics, and Black Feminist Theories of the Human* (Durham, NC: Duke University Press, 2014); and Calvin Warren, *Ontological Terror: Blackness, Nihilism, and Emancipation* (Durham, NC: Duke University Press, 2018).

22. Daniel Defoe, *Robinson Crusoe*, ed. Thomas Keymer (New York: Oxford University Press 2008), 18.

23. Joseph Campana, "Cruising Crusoe: Diving into the Wreck of Sexuality," in *Queer People: Negotiations and Expressions of Homosexuality, 1700–1800*, ed. Chris Mounsey and Caroline Gonda (Lewisburg, PA: Bucknell University Press, 2007), 159–179 (167).

24. Campana, "Cruising Crusoe," 175.

25. Kristeva, quoted. in Campana, "Cruising Crusoe," 171.

26. Defoe, *Robinson Crusoe*, 22.

27. "I knew not what, or where; neither what Latitude, what Country, what Nations, or what River." (Defoe, *Robinson Crusoe*, 22).

28. Defoe, *Robinson Crusoe*, 25.

29. Defoe, *Robinson Crusoe*.

30. Defoe, *Robinson Crusoe*, 29.

31. Turley, "The Sublimation of Desire," 3.

32. Defoe, *Robinson Crusoe*, 43.

33. Defoe, *Robinson Crusoe*, 45.

34. Defoe, *Robinson Crusoe*, 49.

35. Defoe, *Robinson Crusoe*, 48.

36. Paul Kelleher, "A Table in the Wilderness: Desire, Subjectivity, and Animal Husbandry in *Robinson Crusoe*," *Eighteenth-Century Fiction* 32, no. 1 (Fall 2019): 9–29 (20).

37. Kelleher, "A Table in the Wilderness," 15.

38. Defoe, *Robinson Crusoe*, 74, 88.

39. Kelleher, "Animal Husbandry in *Robinson Crusoe*," 27.

40. Defoe, *Robinson Crusoe*, 88.

41. Crusoe "came to be so pester'd with Cats, that [he] was forc'd to kill them like Vermine, or wild Beasts, and to drive them from [his] House as much as possible" (Defoe, *Robinson Crusoe*, 88).

42. Defoe, *Robinson Crusoe*, 88.

43. Gabriel Rosenberg, "How Meat Changed Sex: The Law of Interspecies Intimacy after Industrial Reproduction," *GLQ: A Journal of Gay and Lesbian Studies* 23, no. 4 (October 2017): 473–507.

44. King, *The Black Shoals*, 85.

45. King, *The Black Shoals*, 77–78.

46. I draw this formulation from Snorton's use in *Black on Both Sides*. King also points out how these fantasies are related to the fantasy of Black fungibility. See Snorton, *Black on Both Sides*, 8–11; and King, *The Black Shoals*, 21–26.

47. This coincides with the work of Zakiyyah Iman Jackson, *Becoming Human: Matter and Meaning in an Antiblack World* (New York: New York University Press, 2020); Jayna Brown, *Black Utopias: Speculative Life and the Music of Other Worlds* (Durham, NC: Duke University Press, 2021); and Katherine McKittrick, *Dear Science and Other Stories* (Durham, NC: Duke University Press, 2021). My hope, drawing on Fred Moten and Stefano Harney's logic from *The Undercommons*, is to write endnotes to be capacious and vibrant spaces under and around the text, where a writer invites in alternatives, messiness, and where academic thought begins to undiscipline itself. I hope this note holds open this space and invites in as much as it can hold. See Fred Moten and Stefano Harney, *The Undercommons: Fugitive Planning and Black Study* (New York: Minor Compositions, 2013), 106–107.

PART IV

Racializing Affect, Queering Temporality

CHAPTER 8

Dark and Delayed Labor

SEX WORK AND RACIALIZED TIME IN EIGHTEENTH-CENTURY LONDON

Nour Afara

She who will always dazzle with the charms of her person, or surprise by the force of her genius, without allowing the least indulgence to sickness, indolence, or stupidity, is a slave to that vanity which she thinks exalts her to a kind of empire.
—Anonymous, The Histories, Vol. I[1]

Both volumes of *The Histories of Some of the Penitents in the Magdalen-House, as Supposed to Be Related by Themselves* (1760) are a collection of fictional stories about Magdalen inmates framed as a nonfictional series of memoirs offered by the imprisoned. The Magdalen House detained prostitutes, as well as women who were allegedly at risk of becoming sex workers because of extramarital liaisons, with the express purpose of rehabilitating them and training them in virtuous types of labor. As Jennie Batchelor and Megan Hiatt point out in their edition of *The Histories*, much of the public discourse on the inmates in mid-eighteenth-century Britain came from those involved in the governance of Magdalen House, rather than the inmates themselves: "The glimpse we do obtain of the inmates' lives illuminates the differences between the fictional and the nonfictional attitudes to prostitutes, as signified by their different approaches to autobiography," including provisions in the rules for the Magdalen House that allowed inmates to take an assumed name.[2]

The blurred boundaries between nonfictional discourses on sex work and the novelistic structure of *The Histories* are reflected in the title itself: "Supposed to be related by themselves." That is, *The Histories* purports to offer testimony from a "feminocentric community," similar to Sarah Scott's *Millenium Hall* (1762), on the conditions that pushed inmates into sex work.[3] Supporters of this institution during the mid-eighteenth century maintained that women turned to prostitution out of economic necessity—what we categorize today as survival sex work. However,

The Histories provide alternative justifications for joining the trade, consequently humanizing the inmates and depicting the sex trade as a line of work that any woman could potentially "fall" into.

My analysis of The Histories takes up the text's representation of racialized sex workers, in particular, as subjects who speak their experiences but are nonetheless portrayed as resistant to the temporalized labor values of sobriety, frugality, thrift, and hard work—in other words, as idle. In this way, my essay's exploration of racialized subjects within a purported memoir is in conversation with Jeremy Chow and Riley DeBaecke's explication of Olivia Fairfield's letters in The Woman of Colour (1808), which follows this chapter, where the novel's epistolary conventions significantly foreground the interior life of a woman of African descent.

This chapter examines two case studies from The Histories through the lens of Christina Lupton's work on temporal striations and coordinates to recover evidence of an idleness rhetoric that "sticks" to racialized sex workers even in such efforts as The Histories to humanize the narrators within.[4] My aim is to develop a novel theoretical approach by applying time theory and affect theory to eighteenth-century formations of race and understandings of labor as it was completed by dark-skinned sex workers. In one entry from the first volume of The Histories, for instance, the job descriptions of two "brown complexion[ed]" women are explained, and we begin to see social tensions emerge.[5] The narrator is a sex worker whose subjectivity is unsettling because she exaggerates her "exotic" physical features with makeup and trades sex for money. Her sister, who is disabled, however, excels in the domestic sphere where she completes "valid" women's work.

While I explore the social tensions between the sisters' different workforces and embodiments in more detail later, for now they serve as an example of how urgently examinations of race are needed in studies of eighteenth-century sex work.[6] Records from the period that detail the lives of sex workers elide racialized lived experiences entirely, and thus the workers are typically assumed to be white. By attending to racialized sex work using idleness rhetoric and theories of temporal delays, I argue that we can recover evidence of these women and provide a fuller record of eighteenth-century economies of sex work, especially as they are informed by conversations in critical race and disability studies. As a whole, Unsettling Sexuality moves away from traditional queer and gender studies to call out the rampant Eurocentricity that has shaped these fields. For example, this chapter asserts that affect is constructed across identity categories, thereby pushing back against whitewashed sentimentality to privilege the histories of underexamined racialized subjectivities. Accordingly, my chapter's focus on racialized embodiment and sexuality serves as a rejection of studies of sex work that position white women as the exclusive or primary laborers of this trade. While queer approaches to precarious labor are robust, they often elide racialized sexuality,[7] and this chapter seeks to remedy this opacity by contending that racialized affects queer normative notions of sentimentality.

Eighteenth-century conceptions of productivity and labor, especially as they are applied to sex work, are complicated by dark-skinned laborers because they were, in racist fashion, thought to operate through *slowed time*. For instance, pejorative descriptions of idleness and lethargy like those noted in the epigraph taken from *The Histories* were widely ascribed to dark-skinned people and the type of labor they were (in)capable of producing.[8] As subjects who have historically been assigned the designations of "idle" and "lazy" because of their complexion and other biologically determined assumptions, in a trade that hardly "counts" as work, their status as laborers needs further elucidation. Scholarship about sex work in this period—most notably by Laura J. Rosenthal and Karen Harvey—centers white women and their place as laborers in the face of precarity.[9] While I am motivated by its insights, this body of scholarship typically refers to dark-skinned prostitutes in passing, offering a few pages in a book otherwise filled with white people, and I endeavor to make these understudied women the focus of my chapter.

Because of the elastic state of race throughout the eighteenth century, sex workers could experience both a fall from virtue and a fall into various racial categories depending on who might be observing or employing them.[10] While eighteenth-century narratives are occupied with the distinction between and overlap of Blackness and Asianness, my work highlights nuance in how Brownness and Beigeness were represented and conceptualized. Indeed, my work draws from theories and histories by Gretchen Gerzina, Stephen Ahern, and Sowande' M. Mustakeem on colorism, sex work, and slavery.[11] Thinkers of the period had trouble with the slipperiness of race, and their misguided understandings of other cultures led to "misleading dichotomies that . . . inhibit our interpretation of written . . . texts and distort our understanding of the history of racialized thinking."[12] Only by making important connections between representations of temporality, idleness, race, and labor can we fully understand eighteenth-century sex work as it was negotiated by women of color.

RACIALIZED LABOR AND IDLE FEMININITY

Throughout the eighteenth century, idleness was a quality often assigned to laborers who did not conform to white, European expectations of productivity and/or hetero- and chrono-normative ways of understanding "quality" work. I open with observations made about Khoikhoi peoples by European travel writers in the seventeenth century to demonstrate how the same pejorative linguistic connection between laziness and racialized labor traveled throughout the eighteenth century, and indeed into these memoir documents. Christopher Fryke infamously composed nineteen categories called "Account of the Hottentots" and perpetuated these racists labels by focusing on the Khoikhoi women's "idleness" (noting that they sleep all day, lay all over each other, choose not to work) and "primitiveness" (living "like hogs," utilizing a language that sounds like turkey noises, displaying their sexual organs openly).[13] These "observations" construct a racialized identity that revolves around idleness and primitiveness as signifiers of inferiority, inadequacy, and lack of progress—antinomies of the constructed ideals of whiteness (i.e., activity, progress, hard work, and so on).[14] Racialized subjects, often regarded as idle or in a state of perpetual sloth, were "sentenced" to this state of being based solely on observations of their mannerisms and assumptions tied to their melanin. In this same vein, observers perceived sex work as a leisurely or effortless form of labor, despite the difficult working conditions. John Ovington perceived the Khoikhoi to be "a very lazy people [who] choose to live . . . poor and miserable, than to be at pains [effort] for plenty."[15] Further, he decided that "their native inclination to idleness and a careless life, will scarce admit [hardly allow] of either force or reward for reclaiming them from that innate lethargic humour."[16]

I compare these eighteenth-century sex workers to the Khoikhoi women because the latter group serves as an earlier example of racialized subjects whose labor was deemed insufficient and consequently regarded as idle. This comparison likewise documents how we might understand the genre of memoir as one that accounts for, and is interwoven with, first-person narratives, natural histories, and novels. In *The Anxieties of Idleness*, Sara Jordan compiles extensive primary evidence from the seventeenth to the late eighteenth centuries on the treatment and observation of the Khoikhoi and notes the pervasive reports of African idleness.[17] European discussions of the grotesque racialized subject typically focused on physical embodiment (e.g., nudity, filth, anomalous genitalia, strange eating habits), which are relayed to descriptions of racialized sex workers. Jordan asserts that such characterizations were deeply associated with presumptions regarding racialized idleness and an innate inability to "keep up" with normative lifestyles, and, consequently, normative time.[18] In what follows, I offer two case studies from *The Histories* to account for a rhetorical connection that exists between designations of idleness and abjection that are recurrently racialized—a rhetorical connection complicated by the text's status as novelized nonfiction. In so doing, I examine how observations of melanated skin provide alternative approaches to understanding eighteenth-century labor, femininity, and sex work.

Case Study 1: Brownness and the Façade of Vivacity

The person who, according to the regulation agreed upon, was to have the precedency in talking of herself; a valuable privilege! was about three and twenty; tall and genteel; her complexion was brown, but her features good.
—*Anonymous*, The Histories, Vol. 1[19]

A trend across all entries included in the volumes of *The Histories* is that nearly all of them are "race neutral," a term I borrow from critical race theory.[20] This term refers to situations, works of literature, conversations, and the like, wherein whiteness is presumed. To assume whiteness often positions it as a baggage-free political standing that perpetuates racist ideologies including ones about labor and physical energy. As such, these entries either make no mention of race—gesturing toward a racial neutrality in how women

DARK AND DELAYED LABOR

sex workers were perceived in eighteenth-century London—or they discuss at length the fairness of skin and the lightness of eyes, which remain tied to whiteness.

One entry deviates from this trend by signaling attention to the woman's melanin: her "complexion was brown."[21] This woman's brownness becomes inextricably linked to her labor, overall exertion, and vocational motivation. Because race was relatively fluid during this period, mentions of brownness were nonspecific and could refer to myriad racial configurations. Roxann Wheeler, for instance, accounts for "the emergent character of race" in the long eighteenth century and clarifies that the categories that determine whether a person belongs to various groups extend beyond mere complexion.[22] When looking for race, as this chapter shows, we can also search for ideas, behaviors, and descriptions that are invariably connected to race, thus making known how race, affect, and labor become mutually constitutive. What further racializes the narrator's self-portrait is her disclosure of Turkish sexual partners and, crucially, a moment wherein she compares her beauty to that of a Persian monarch.[23] The racialization of the language present in this entry pushes readers to assume that she shares the ethnic heritage of those she strives to emulate. The memoir itself thus becomes a medium by which to understand how embodiment, race, and transnational belonging become narrativized, a set of questions also taken up by Humberto Garcia in chapter 3.

Given that most scholarship on evidence of race in eighteenth-century London centers on Black[24] and Chinese[25] women, this entry provides some evidence for the presence and activity of other women-of-color sex workers who remain understudied. The lack of substantial biographical information on this narrator indicates her perceived averageness. In other words, her lived experience, her struggles in the trade, and the complications that her race brings on are quotidian. However, this lack of information and its potential insignificant nature makes this entry especially worth examination. Wheeler reminds us that "the deployment of racial discourse mattered in relation to populations other than Africans," and this variety of discourse analysis brings to the forefront evidence of women of other cultures laboring in the London sex trade in this period.[26] Searching for evidence of even more diversity in this labor force is crucial for recent work on mixed-heritage identities borne of the transatlantic slave trade and the burgeoning sex trade in London. Situating this allegedly Persian lady in A. B. Wilkinson's research on "mixed blood," for example, illuminates eighteenth-century attitudes about those groups "in-between" Blackness and whiteness—the Beigeness that I suggested earlier—and why they were thought to have come from a "slavish sooty race of mixed-heritage offspring."[27] Whether this woman is of mixed heritage is irrelevant, but what is important is that she represents a racial liminality.

The synopsis, which comes from a different voice than the woman's, articulates the woman's brownness. It identifies the woman as a "lady of quality" and describes her wealthy family.[28] At the start of her letter, she notes that her high social standing is something from which she benefited, but she does not elaborate. We can infer from the series of events that follow that the social perks she capitalizes on are material rather than social because "[her] father was a very rich trader in a country town [and] it rendered him one of the principal people in it—an advantage that [she] partook in."[29] This is a particularly useful case because it is written as a sort of comparative study: we not only follow our lady's journey through the pains of her labor but also follow it in tandem with a description of her homely sister, who, "like most girls, had been taught to think marriage the ultimate end of her creation" and therefore seems to be her perfect opposite both in physicality and in personality.[30] The sister's disability is emphasized by the narrative, highlighting a further binarism: sex working/able-bodied/immoral labor versus homemaking/differently-abled/virtuous labor. The "brown"-complexioned woman gives insight into how color is deployed to her advantage by using makeup and embellishments luxurious enough to only be accessible to women of high class. Further, the able-bodied sister stands in direct opposition to her trade because it produces an acute social tension: she is at once normatively able-bodied for futurist purposes and held back in a regression of sorts because of her occupation. Beautifying the exotic/othered body is part of her business model and parcel of her success as a laborer in the sex trade.

Our narrator is conventionally beautiful because she gestures to the parade of men she seems to always have at her disposal—none of them husband material, according to her sister. That the woman describes her sister as being physically disabled in a way that makes her unattractive to potential suitors additionally emphasizes a study in contrasts that seems to diametrically position race and disability.[31] She notes that her sister's aspirations center on "shining in domestic life," from which she receives a great deal of moral judgement regarding the way she chooses to live her life.[32] The narrator's sister seems unaware of her trade and is likewise unfamiliar with the narrator's employment through sex work as a marriage-finding mechanism. The narrator is convinced, however, that her approach to love and admiration is not only the ideal method for attracting the "superior sex" but also "the ultimate end of her being," meaning that she feels she has no other choice; if she wants to find a permanent partner, she could not "wait till that superior sex should please to accept [her] [because that] might never happen at all."[33] Readers are provided with a comparison between the sisters, a simultaneous disdain for the more virtuous and "boring" approach to men completed by her disabled sister, and an extensive discussion of the labor involved in performing pleasure with each man that passes through her life.

These investments of time and labor gesture to the sister's disapproval of the alleged and false loophole the sex worker employs for marital aspirations. Throughout the entry, the narrator receives unrelenting criticism from her sister, who warns her that "beauty soon grows familiar to the lover; fades in his eyes, and palls upon his sense"; this communicates the age-old moral in which relying on good looks to secure a mate and thus bypassing the true labor of virtue and courtship will result in failure.[34] If we understand this loophole to be a way for our narrator to skip the niceties of polite courtship and cut to the step of intimate acquaintance with possible suitors, it might seem that she is avoiding the "real work" of a relationship that might lead to the hetero-domestic marriage plot—at least from her sister's perspective. Here, we witness the stereotype that sex work is allegedly non-work: if courtship truly is "real work," then sex work completed to seek out a husband must be "harder work" because there are higher stakes involved (as countless other eighteenth-century novels detail), endangering the worker from the questionable men she might need to entertain.

This rhetorical loophole, however, becomes null and void because the narrator returns home daily "weary of the labour [she] had gone through, in exhibiting all my charms," and suffers from unseen labor that she endures in her quest to find an ideal mate.[35] This labor is only unseen by those not privy to her sexual activities. While in the throes of passion, the narrator remains in the trenches of romantic labor and the narrative in turn demonstrates a progressive conjugality to the entwinement of courtship and sex labor. In short, the narrator purposely mixes business with pleasure. She labors in a mentally and physically exhausting trade as an already mentally and physically exhausted subject due to her racialized status, which is itself a form of "real" labor, pushing to succeed despite systemic obstacles.

The narrator's alternative approach to labor and subsequent exhaustion exemplifies how she operates within her own temporal coordinates. For this, I draw from Lupton's work on temporal coordinates and eighteenth-century conceptions of labor and leisure to ask whether certain subjects operate at different temporal coordinates from others depending on the color of their skin.[36] The narrator's approach to marriage differs from that of her sister and is framed as "less work," but studying her alternative positionality proves otherwise. While both sisters are presumably equally racialized, the narrator's disabled sister serves as a foil to illustrate how valid women's labor (the domestic variety) is exalted and sex work is moralized and shunned. Most important to this analysis are Lupton's theorizations of temporal striation.[37] For Lupton, whereas temporal coordinates are the literal placement of a subject—as in where one lives, works, and socializes—temporal striation refers to the subjective experience of this placement—as in why one lives in that place, how one makes a living, and with whom one socializes. While both the narrator and her sister inhabit the same place, they labor in different spaces and have different motivations for their labor, which produce different social circles. For example, while we know her sister remains at home and works on her "good housewifery," the narrator "did nothing but carry [her]self to places where [she] might be seen."[38] Put somewhat differently, the sisters again become diametrically situated wherein the sister's housewifery promotes stasis within the private sphere and the narrator's sex work demands her mobility among the public: she must "carry [her]self to places where [she] might be seen."[39] While the two women in this entry ostensibly share the same temporal coordinates and striation at the start of their lives, these coordinates and striations progressively drift through labor, ability, and age.

The labor completed by the narrator here is framed as "slowed down" because of her alternate striations. The narrator notes that the "first part of the business of every day was adorning [her] person."[40] We are given a description of her extensive preparation process, attempting to replicate the heavy-handed beauty regime of a Persian monarch on her person and of her "never-ceasing labour."[41] The language employed is notably racialized insofar that she highlights the importance of disallowing oneself "the least indulgence to sickness, indolence, or stupidity."[42] Those who fail do so, she adds, are "slave[s] to that vanity which she thinks exalts her to a kind of empire."[43] Monika Fludernik draws on the influential work of Emily Anglin and Sarah Jordan, who remind us that "idleness is often ascribed to the social and racial other."[44] This work channels the alleged indolence of Indian bodies and is apropos of this case study because Fludernik both analyzes how British nabobs understood and mimicked local styles of living in "the Orient" and discusses how descriptors of indolence were inextricably tied to these racialized bodies. By applying Fludernik's thinking to this case, readers witness an internal tension in the narrator: she seems to be aware of the pejorative connotations of indolence and laziness and how she is at risk of having those affects ascribed to her—arguably more risk than typical for a sex worker because of her Othered status.

The narrator's anxieties about being perceived as indolent are more fraught when we consider the consequences faced should her "laziness" be exposed. She "sometimes confines [her] spirits . . . in spite of a depression . . . affecting vivacity and mirth, to show the brightness of [her] eyes."[45] Unlike Fludernik's context that centers on British colonizers' appropriation, romanticization, and simultaneous condemnation of Oriental indolence, the stakes are much more severe for this narrator because her services will no longer be in such great demand if she reveals "how tired" she is despite "acting a part quite contradictory to the turn of [her] mind at that time."[46] This alternative timeline is allegedly slower and less productive. This temporally augmented work ethic is thoroughly discussed: the difficulty keeping up with the demand of her labor market, the façade of her overall "vivacity," and the recurrent theme of fooling clients into thinking she is brimming with motivation.[47] There is a vivid fear that her true affective state might be exposed because of her exhaustion, thus unifying affective labor's ties to sex work. The risks of the trade are "rubbing off" on her physical, and emotional, states. She must hide the consequences of affective labor if she hopes to keep up with the demands of her workforce.

While the narrator states outright that her beautification routine is laborious and exhausting, she insists that it is nevertheless necessary to give the impression that this otherwise tiring work is effortless and enjoyable. She describes the "first part of the business . . . [as] adorning [her] person [like] a Persian monarch," an invocation that conjures dark complexion, Oriental otherness, and geographic displacement.[48] Afsaneh Najmabadi has shown that in eighteenth-century Iran, a heavy amount of makeup, prominent eyebrows, and "Venus-shaped" curvaceous bodies were particularly desirable.[49] The narrator implicitly emulates this beauty standard, which contrasts the Anglicized beauty standards of the period. She essentially elevates the exoticism of her sex work and its success by amplifying her status as Other. Making herself more visibly Othered allows her to entice customers and therefore increase her chances of securing a permanent partner through business acumen. As such, when considering her complexion, body shape (which could be read as an "adornment" of its own if her body is not naturally full), and particular use of makeup, we can conclude that her beautification process is indeed mentally laborious and physically taxing. This "Persian" lady feigns aesthetic effortlessness and presents in direct opposition to the socially desired norms of British eighteenth-century beauty and labor standards.

Alongside London's desirability for and fetishization of whiteness, eighteenth-century makeup trends *required* whiteness as a base. For example, shiny "lead white [face paint], favoured for its opacity" was applied across the entire face and shoulders "to attain the fashionable white complexion" and so that the blush or rouge that was applied in a large circular shape on the cheeks would stand out starkly on the skin.[50] Even if the sex worker applied the same blush on her complexion, it would have been a heavy-handed application to appear as visible as it would on paler skin. The ability to show blush on one's face indicated a certain capacity to empathize, and therefore the person in question was deemed trustworthy. A person with a darker complexion, on whom blush would be harder to detect, was thought to be, as a result, untrustworthy.[51] Brian Cummings adds that the act of blushing was thought to "come naturally" and, crucially, that it "could not be willed or learned."[52] Building on Cummings, this definition of blush entirely precludes our Persian lady because she assembles her blush in an exaggerated manner for hypervisibility. Hypervisiblity works doubly if not triply for the narrators whose melanin, physiology, able-bodiedness, and affective labors emphasize her difference.

Case Study 2: Brownness and Acquired Indolence

This housekeeper was one who, as I learned from the lady I have mentioned as my neighbour, had, during the continuance of her youth, lived with Mr. Merton in another capacity; nor had her office ceased till he married me.

—Mrs. Merton, The Histories, Vol. 2[53]

The affective labors undertaken by the supposedly Persian lady are not unlike those experienced by service workers of the time. Domestic laborers required a bedside manner like that of a sex worker; the difference is that instead of enthusiastically bedding a client, the worker must cheerfully freshen the linens and maintain a socially acceptable level of decorum. This entry from volume two of *The Histories* magnifies the complicated relationship between the narrator, Mrs. Merton, and her husband's racialized housekeeper. We learn that the housekeeper was formerly Mr. Merton's kept mistress, and as such she harbors ill will toward Mrs. Merton, "behaving to her with continual insolence" after being demoted to this service work position.[54] Mrs. Merton also admits that she is outraged at the housekeeper for exposing her affair with a Captain Turnham to her husband.[55] She does not feel shame about her affair, explaining that she could not possibly lose her virtue twice over. Because she is already married to Mr. Merton, she gestures to the social value of virginity, suggesting that there is no longer anything to save or conceal from other men. She inadvertently highlights the power imbalance in their labor/employment agreement and, crucially, the temporal lag that the housekeeper experiences through her demotion by attempting to shift sympathy to herself. This power imbalance is exacerbated when Mrs. Merton suggests that this temporal lag is caused by the housekeeper's "indolence" and "corpulency"—both synonyms for idleness as an affective trait—thus gesturing to a sort of physical decay that the housekeeper could not avoid experiencing despite her physically and emotionally taxing labor.[56]

The narrator's language racializes the housekeeper by linking opinions on her allegedly lacking work ethic to idleness and disability rhetoric. She explains in a commonsensical tone that the reason this worker lost her position as Mr. Merton's kept mistress is because "her bloom was past, corpulency had impaired her ..., her indolence was so great, [and] she was extravagant, wasteful, and idle."[57] Here, her language is socially loaded: she raises classist, sexist, and racist connotations, which amplify the accusations of the housekeeper's purported idleness. The narrator displays a recurrent displacement of responsibility, but what remains consistent is her rage toward the housekeeper and her conviction that she underperforms her duties because of her indolence.[58] Mrs. Merton's description of her housekeeper reveals a different type of sex work—one that takes place in the domestic

DARK AND DELAYED LABOR

sphere and involves only one man—that consists of the same physical and emotional expectations of any streetworker. Commentary on her "bloom" and "corpulency" juxtaposes what the housekeeper was upon employment and what she became upon demotion: first beautiful, young, energetic, even excelling at her job, and eventually ugly, old, indolent, and lazy. Unlike the previous case study in which the virtuous sister is physically disabled, this housekeeper lacks virtue and is "degraded into a servant" as a result of disability.[59] The racialized personality traits—idleness, ugliness, indolence—are only ever attributed to the housekeeper when Mrs. Merton observes her. Just the visibility of her complexion in combination with her status as "ex" prompt Mrs. Merton to derogate her thusly.

While the concept of resilience has only recently been discussed in the academy as a racist and anti-Indigenous concept, it is also inextricably tied to class. Pejorative theories of resilience have long been used to justify the mistreatment of the working classes through ideologies of bootstrapping, suggesting they exist in those social tiers because of a lack of will, and thus absolving bodies in power of responsibility for those precariously employed groups.[60] The narrator opens by gendering the concept of resilience and how women should never "give up" on their targets despite the impediments of social obstacles.[61] She "never stop[ped] at the first imprudence [when beginning her affair with] Captain Turnham [despite] great difficulty" in avoiding the housekeeper during her evening outings.[62] The story's presumably white narrator identifies herself as resilient, and the obstacle in question is her racialized housekeeper. She continues explaining her plight, defending that she "did not see why [she] would deny [herself] and her lover so great a pleasure [from] professing [their] mutual love" without "receiving punishment of [her] crime from "[her] housekeeper."[63] She narcissistically frames her hardship as challenging and painful, ignoring the loss of work and status experienced by the racialized service worker. Mrs. Merton makes herself the victim, capitalizing on her housekeeper's precarious employment status and ultimately reversing the linguistic use of resilience for her own gain.

Typically, we would look to the housekeeper's life events and observe a robust ability to persevere through her sex working "contract," her demotion, and her new lady's displaced rage toward her—all of these textbook examples of working hard in the everyday, demonstrating the opposite of an idle subjectivity.[64] Instead, readers are presented with a case wherein the narrator vehemently defends her own resilience in attempting to live with her husband's ex-mistress while maintaining her own extramarital affair. If we are to follow the narrator's argument that her housekeeper failed to retain her status as mistress because of corporeal idleness (sluggish disposition, gaining weight), a state she pejoratively equates with disability, and now continues to fail at her job as a service worker, does this demotion signal an affective dilution or does idleness rhetoric pervade all her employment positions? Here, "affective dilution" suggests that the housekeeper's racialized designation as idle might become un-stuck to her or at least less significant to her subjectivity because she is no longer a kept mistress/sex worker. If we consider that these pejorative descriptions are only applied to the housekeeper upon sight (Mrs. Merton seeing her for the first time and having to live with and observe her), and that the requisites of her labor call for able-bodiedness in the way of youth and beauty, then it is possible that these affects remain sticky because of the white gaze making these assignations.

The housekeeper's alleged social abjection ultimately leads to her demotion: this "fall" occurs not only as the result of Mr. Merton's marriage but also because of her alleged physical decay.[65] The fall signals the temporal lag that defines her subjectivity; in other words, her demotion and aging body literally set her back—a literal time lag. Eighteenth-century opinions on women's aging positioned it as a type of deformity or disability, something that James Bryan Reeves criticizes as a "deficient understanding of time."[66] Per Lupton's theorizations, then, the housekeeper experiences a shift in temporal coordinates and striations, one that sets her on a different, "sickly," and slowed down life path.[67] But what of the racialized complications effected by this case study? This temporal disjuncture acknowledges that physical and social factors are tied to the housekeeper's complexion and work ethic that ultimately slow her down. Ultimately, the housekeeper's previous status as a kept mistress was instrumental to her social and financial progress—the only mechanism for her upward mobility, which, in its absence, triggers a derailment of her set temporal coordinates and journey up the social ladder.

Theorizing Racialized Sex Work: Affordances for Future Scholarship

The Magdalen housekeeper's intense resentment toward the narrator is, as a result, well-founded because she loses work, reputation, and status. Because she had already given up her virtue by engaging in sexual relations with Mr. Merton, she was ostensibly *saved* from that fall when granted a formal mistress position.[68] As such, in her demotion, she has been *unsaved*—socially tossed to the curb, but with a housekeeper's income. Her rage is rooted in the loss of all her hard work invested over the years, not only while in service but also presumably in emotional labor as mistress.[69] It is by mapping her shifting coordinates and striations, as well as tracking the racialized language used to describe her alleged idle work ethic and indolent personality, that we find evidence of her labor in an otherwise race-neutral collection. This labor expended over a period that the narrator identifies as "several years" long demonstrates a degree of industriousness that is in stark opposition to the assumed state of idleness with which the narrator imbues her.

By rereading eighteenth-century records about sex workers, I have sought to recover evidence of racialized laborers in the sex trade. If we continue to map temporal coordinates (workers' lives) and striations (workers' social movements) and read them alongside historically racialized affects, we can imagine a more comprehensive vision of eighteenth-century conceptions of race, labor, sex, and sexuality. I ask in closing, how might we use these narrative hints to enflesh a broader conception of race, affect, and sex work as it is obscured by race-neutral archives?

NOTES

1. Anonymous, *The Histories of Some of the Penitents in the Magdalen-House: As Supposed to Be Related by Themselves: In Two Volumes* (London: Printed for John Rivington in St. Paul's Church-yard, and J. Dodsley in Pall-Mall, 1760).

2. Jennie Batchelor and Megan Hiatt, "Introduction," in *The Histories of Some of the Penitents in the Magdalen House: As Supposed to be Related by Themselves: In Two Volumes* (London, Routledge, 2006), ix–xxiii (xiii). They note that an early 1917 history of the Magdalen House written by the Rev. H.F.B. Compston contains an evocative but no doubt apocryphal story that inmates within the Magdalen House wore signs that said, "Tell your story to no one" (xiii).

3. Batchelor and Hiatt, "Introduction," xiv.

4. Christina Lupton, *Reading and the Making of Time* (Baltimore, MD: Johns Hopkins University Press, 2018). "Stickiness" is a concept discussed by Sara Ahmed in *The Cultural Politics of Emotion* (New York: Routledge, 2014). She describes the ways that emotions are tied to particular words and discourses that can operate across different contexts. In this way, "traces" of affective-discursive regimes from a particular context can be mobilized and used in other contexts. Through this phenomenon we can begin to parse the ways in which the discourses and affects tied to decadence in the eighteenth-century London sex trade evolved.

5. Anonymous, *Histories*, 1:128.

6. Faiza Ali and Jawad Syed, "The White Woman's Burden: From Colonial Civilisation to Third World Development," *Third World Quarterly* 32, no. 2 (March 2011): 349–365; and Sarah Jordan, *The Anxieties of Idleness: Idleness in Eighteenth-Century British Literature and Culture* (Lewisburg, PA: Bucknell University Press, 2003).

7. See, for instance, Eva Pendleton, "Love for Sale: Queering Heterosexuality," in *Whores and Other Feminists*, ed. Jill Nagle (New York: Routledge, 1997), 73–82; Corina McKay, "Is Sex Work Queer?" *Social Alternatives* 18, no. 3 (July 1999): 48–54; Michael Warner, *The Trouble with Normal: Sex, Politics, and the Ethics of Queer Life* (Cambridge, MA: Harvard University Press, 1999); and Brooke M. Belosko, "Queer Theory, Sex Work, and Foucault's Unreason," *Foucault Studies* 8, no. 23 (2017): 141–166.

8. See Sowande' M. Mustakeem, *Slavery at Sea: Terror, Sex, and Sickness in the Middle Passage* (Champaign-Urbana: University of Illinois Press, 2016); and Nour Afara, "Forever Idle: The Resilience of Colonial Ideas on Black Bodies," *Alternate Routes: A Journal of Critical Social Research* 31, no. 1 (2020): 183–205.

9. See Laura J. Rosenthal, *Infamous Commerce: Prostitution in Eighteenth-Century Literature and Culture* (Ithaca, NY: Cornell University Press, 2006); and Karen Harvey, *Reading Sex in the Eighteenth Century: Bodies and Gender in English Erotic Culture* (Cambridge: Cambridge University Press, 2008).

10. See Gretchen Gerzina, *Black London: Life before Emancipation* (New Brunswick, NJ: Rutgers University Press, 1995); Felicity A. Nussbaum, "Introduction: The Politics of Difference," *Eighteenth-Century Studies* 23, no. 4 (Fall 1990): 375–386; Londa Schiebinger, "The Anatomy of Difference: Race and Sex in Eighteenth-Century Science," *Eighteenth-Century Studies* 23, no. 4 (Fall 1990): 387–405; and Rose A. Zimbardo, "African-American Culture in the Eighteenth Century," *Eighteenth-Century Studies* 27, no. 4 (Fall 1994): 527–531.

11. Stephen Ahern, ed., *Affect and Abolition in the Anglo-Atlantic, 1770–1830* (New York: Routledge, 2013).

12. Felicity A. Nussbaum, "Between 'Oriental' and 'Blacks so Called,' 1688–1788," in *The Postcolonial Enlightenment: Eighteenth-Century Colonialism and Postcolonial Theory*, ed. Daniel Carey and Lynn Festa (Oxford: Oxford University Press, 2013), 137–166 (138).

13. Gitanjali Shahani, "Food, Filth, and the Foreign: Disgust in the Seventeenth-Century Travelogue," in *Disgust in Early Modern English Literature*, eds. N. K. Eschenbaum and B. Correll (New York: Routledge, 2016), 106–123 (116).

14. See Hortense J. Spillers, "Mama's Baby, Papa's Maybe: An American Grammar Book," *Diacritics* 17, no. 2 (Summer 1987): 64–81.

15. J. M. Coetzee, "Idleness in South Africa," *Social Dynamics: A Journal of African Studies* 81 (1982): 1–3.

16. Coetzee, "Idleness in South Africa," 28.

17. Jordan, *The Anxieties of Idleness*, 135.

18. Jordan, *The Anxieties of Idleness*, 135.

19. Anonymous, *Histories*, 1: 53.

20. See Sunil Agnani, *Hating Empire Properly: The Two Indies and the Limits of Enlightenment Anticolonialism* (New York: Fordham University Press, 2013); Emmanuel Chukwudi Eze, ed., *Race and the Enlightenment: A Reader* (Malden, MA: Blackwell Publishing, 1997); Schiebinger, "The Anatomy of Difference," 387–388; and Devin Vartija, "Revisiting Enlightenment Racial Classification: Time and the Question of Human Diversity," *Intellectual History Review* 31, no. 4 (August 2020): 1–23.

21. Anonymous, *Histories*, 1:128.

22. Roxann Wheeler, *The Complexion of Race: Categories of Difference in Eighteenth-Century British Culture* (Philadelphia: University of Pennsylvania Press, 2000), 31.

23. Anonymous, *Histories*, 1:135.

24. See Lyndon J. Dominique, *Imoinda's Shade: Marriage and the African Woman in Eighteenth-Century British Literature, 1759–1808* (Columbus: The Ohio State University Press, 2012); and Catherine Molineux, "Hogarth's Fashionable Slaves: Moral Corruption in Eighteenth-Century London," *English Literary History* 72, no. 2 (Summer 2005): 495–520.

25. See Vanessa Alayrac-Fielding, "'Frailty, Thy Name Is China': Women, Chinoiserie and the Threat of Low Culture in Eighteenth-Century England," *Women's History Review* 18, no. 4 (September 2009): 659–660; and Elizabeth Kowaleski-Wallace, "Women, China, and Consumer Culture in Eighteenth-Century England," *Eighteenth-Century Studies* 29, no. 2 (Winter 1995): 153–167.

26. Wheeler, *The Complexion of Race*, 9.

27. A. B. Wilkinson, *Blurring the Lines of Race and Freedom: Mulattoes and Mixed Bloods in English Colonial America* (Chapel Hill: University of North Carolina Press, 2020), 173.

28. Anonymous, *Histories*, 1:129.

29. Anonymous, *Histories*, 1:129.

30. Anonymous, *Histories*, 1:129.

31. Jason Farr's examination of Scott's *Millennium Hall* explains how the eighteenth-century novel conceived of disability, and more specifically, how socially constructed bodily standards oppressed disabled people—very much like the Persian narrator's sister and her everyday limitations and aspirations. See Jason Farr, *Novel Bodies: Disability and Sexuality in Eighteenth-Century British Literature* (New Brunswick, NJ: University of New Jersey Press, 2019).

32. Anonymous, *Histories*, 1:130–131.

33. Anonymous, *Histories*, 1:130–131.

34. Anonymous, *Histories*, 1:138.

35. Anonymous, *Histories*, 1:137.

36. Lupton is interested in how one makes time for reading, either by forcing it into a tight schedule or by having ample time for it in a life of leisure. She suggests that in the former option, for "more compartmentalized lives—ones that would allow temporally designated zones of intense engagement with books as an alternate to work" that they necessarily operate at different temporal coordinates than those individuals in the latter group. Lupton, *Reading and the Making of Time*, 36.

37. Lupton, *Reading and the Making of Time*, 34–38.

38. Anonymous, *Histories*, 1:132.

39. Anonymous, *Histories*, 1:132.

DARK AND DELAYED LABOR

40. Anonymous, *Histories*, 1:135

41. Anonymous, *Histories*, 1:135

42. Anonymous, *Histories*, 1:136.

43. Anonymous, *Histories*, 1:136.

44. Monika Fludernik, "The Performativity of Idleness: Representations and Stagings of Idleness in the Context of Colonialism," in *Idleness, Indolence and Leisure in English Literature*, ed. Monika Fludernik and Miriam Nandi (London: Palgrave Macmillan, 2014), 129–153.

45. Anonymous, *Histories*, 1:137.

46. Anonymous, *Histories*, 1:137.

47. Anonymous, *Histories*, 1:137.

48. Anonymous, *Histories*, 1:135.

49. Afsaneh Najmabadi, "Gendered Transformations: Beauty, Love, and Sexuality in Qajar Iran," *Iranian Studies* 34, no. 1–4 (2001): 89–102.

50. Aimée Marcereau DeGalan, "Lead White or Dead White? Dangerous Beauty Practices of Eighteenth-Century England," *Bulletin of the Detroit Institute of Arts* 76, no. 1–2 (2002): 38–49 (41).

51. Brian Cummings, "Animal Passions and Human Sciences: Shame, Blushing and Nakedness in Early Modern Europe and the New World," in *At the Borders of the Human: Beasts, Bodies and Natural Philosophy in the Early Modern Period*, ed. Erica Fudge, Ruth Gilbert, and Susan Wiseman (London: Palgrave Macmillan, 1999), 39–45.

52. Cummings, "Animal Passions and Human Sciences," 44–45.

53. Anonymous, *Histories*, 2:146.

54. Anonymous, *Histories*, 2:147.

55. Adding to the precarity this housekeeper faces is the fact that she is not given a name at any point in the narrative, and as such, her entire existence is her occupation.

56. Anonymous, *Histories*, 2:146.

57. Anonymous, *Histories*, 2:146–147.

58. Anonymous, *Histories*, 2:146.

59. Anonymous, *Histories*, 2:146.

60. Kay Aranda, Laetitia Zeeman, Julie Scholes, and Arantxa Santa-María Morales, "The Resilient Subject: Exploring Subjectivity, Identity and the Body in Narratives of Resilience," *Health: An Interdisciplinary Journal for the Social Study of Health, Illness and Medicine* 16, no. 5 (September 2012): 548–563; Mark Neocleous, "Resisting Resilience," *Radical Philosophy* 178 (March/April 2013): 2–7; and Paul Pierson, "The New Politics of the Welfare State," *World Politics* 48, no. 2 (January 1995): 143–179.

61. Anonymous, *Histories*, 2:143.

62. Anonymous, *Histories*, 2:143–144.

63. Anonymous, *Histories*, 2:145.

64. Pun intended with the use of the term "textbook," as this case is taken from a conduct book.

65. Here, I am referring to the etymology of decadence, circa 1500 (closely linked to idleness in historical studies about Blackness and Brownness and work ethic, see note 4).

66. James Bryant Reeves, "Untimely Old Age and Deformity in Sarah Scott's *Millennium Hall*," *Eighteenth-Century Fiction* 27, no. 2 (Spring 2014): 229–256.

67. Reeves, "Untimely Old Age and Deformity," 256.

68. Anonymous, *Histories*, 2:150.

69. We can read the housekeeper's rage through Audre Lorde's descriptions of "metabolizing hatred" or being "force-fed" racist hatred. Lorde suggests that the racialized subject learns to deal with this hatred despite its indigestibility. Similarly, the housekeeper in this case is forced to hate Mrs. Merton because of the mistreatment she receives from her and learns to deal with this oppression in her everyday life. See Audre Lorde, "Eye to Eye," in *Sister Outsider: Essays and Speeches* (Berkeley, CA: Crossing Press, 1984), 144–175, especially 152; and Shiloh Whitney, "Affective Indigestion: Lorde, Fanon, and Gutierrez-Rodriguez on Race and Affective Labor," *The Journal of Speculative Philosophy* 30, no. 3 (August 2016): 278–291.

CHAPTER 9

Unsettling Happiness

BLACKNESS, GENDER, AND AFFECT IN *THE WOMAN OF COLOUR* AND ITS MEDIA AFTERLIVES

Jeremy Chow and Riley DeBaecke

The good woman is good in part because of what she judges to be good, and hence how she aligns her happiness with the happiness of others.
—Sara Ahmed, The Promise of Happiness[1]

The pursuit and attainment of happiness is too often regarded as a foregone conclusion attended by privilege. "The eighteenth century made happiness into something that can be obtained in this life, or in the course of history, through progress," Flavio Gregori observes.[2] That the eighteenth-century novel replicates such appeals to happiness is unmistakable. We need only think of the white heroines penned by Samuel Richardson, Charlotte Lennox, Frances Burney, Ann Radcliffe, and Maria Edgeworth. As Melissa Adams-Campbell contends, mid-century marital legal reform and the literary genres that take up these concerns "assure[d] British women that their courtship customs (and the recent legal changes regulating marriage) secure[d] them more advanced institutions and more personally satisfying intimate relations than anywhere else in the world."[3] Consider the narrator of Edgeworth's *Belinda* (1801), who suggests of the heroine's domestic happiness, "Every body must ultimately judge of what makes them happy, from the comparison of their own feelings in different situations. Where there was so much happiness, no want of what is called *pleasure* was ever experienced."[4] Despite Belinda's initial assurance that Clarence Hervey is unsuitable as a husband, their marriage is foretold from the first volume. Edgeworth's novel articulates the twinned goals of happiness and pleasure that accompany companionate marriage, a concern of Ziona Kocher, Ula Lukszo Klein, and Cailey Hall in this collection, or, a "social *ideal* within a discursive tradition of novels and conduct books targeted at Anglophone women readers."[5]

The eighteenth-century novel's appeal to happiness, however, only underscores its universalizing tendencies, which too often coalesce with utilitarian impulses exemplified by the words of Jeremy Bentham, "It is the greatest happiness of the greatest number that is the measure of right and wrong."[6] Happiness, to no surprise, is never available to everyone. And in eighteenth-century fiction, this happiness is recurrently tied to the role of the heroine; indeed, as Sara Ahmed identifies, "The good woman is good in part because of what she judges to be good, and hence how she aligns her happiness with the happiness of others."[7] This totalizing tendency of happiness unwittingly reveals "that some forms of happiness are better than others," and its repeated invocation serves to hold harmless sociocultural systems that make happiness elusive for the oppressed and marginalized.[8]

This chapter explores such elusive and oftentimes subversive representations of happiness as they are navigated by mixed-race women in the anonymously written *The Woman of Colour* (1808) and Amma Asante's film *Belle* (2013), which we place into conversation. The former is an epistolary novel that narrates the trials and tribulations of Olivia Fairfield, a mixed-race heroine born of a white English enslaver and a Black enslaved mother. Fairfield must leave her Jamaican home and community in search of an English cousin, Augustus, whom she must marry in order to benefit from her late father's bequeathal. *Belle* is a historical biopic that channels similar tropes and fictionalizes the life of Dido Elizabeth Belle, also born of a white English enslaver and Black enslaved woman, who must navigate Georgian aristocracy under the protectorate of her father's family. The family is headed by William Murray, the first Earl of Mansfield, who is also, as the film highlights, lord chief justice of England.

In navigating both representations, we respond to the façade of universal happiness situated by the rise of the novel and "its insistence on the marriage plot" to suggest how such novels, and later filmic adaptations, occlude and preclude the types of happiness that are experienced by, or unavailable to, racialized bodies.[9] As Tara Bynum writes of the archive, "It's not always easy to imagine good feelings in the lives of Black persons."[10] In correspondence, we are not interested in hierarchizing happiness, which may only reinforce the utilitarian notion that some happinesses are more desirable and sanctioned than others. Instead, we want to uncover happinesses otherwise, akin to Shelby Johnson's invocation of an "archive of the elsewhere" in chapter 2, that must better account for the experiences of mixed-race women, who are often also understood as Black.

We examine, first, *The Woman of Colour* with a careful eye to how happiness is defined by and besets Olivia Fairfield alongside her lived experience as a mixed-race heroine, and her deliberate failure to fulfill the heteronormative marriage plot. Second, we trace how differential notions of racialized happiness are depicted by *Belle*. Dido Elizabeth Belle's image graces the cover of Lyndon Dominique's edition of *The Woman of Colour*.[11] *Belle* imagines a trajectory by which to envisage *The Woman of Colour*'s media afterlives, especially as it portrays Dido's path to happiness differently from Olivia's in the novel.[12] Whereas the film centers the marriage plot as the determinant of Dido's happiness, the novel reminds us of Olivia's willingness to redefine the eighteenth century's notions of sexual autonomy outside of the marriage plot. In reading *The Woman of Colour* and *Belle* together, we emphasize the subversive and tacit feminist and queer of color potentialities that buck the heteronormativity of the marriage plot. We also uncover how racialized affects—happiness in particular—are regarded by coherent narratives that are historically disparate. This effort unsettles the whitewashed obligations of happiness that saturate the eighteenth-century novel and offers "Blackened happiness" as a heuristic to understand the variegated appeals and rejections of happiness modeled by Olivia and Dido.

Blackening happiness, like Sofia Prado Huggins's method of reading *The Woman of Colour* "slantwise," commingles "unrealized possibilities, unanswered questions, and open endings" to consider how mixed-raced women mobilize racialized affect to achieve happiness on their own terms.[13] By unsettling and Blackening happiness, we uphold differential media, audiences, and genres as vital to enfleshing how we might understand divergent affects and their correlative sexual autonomies as they are composed by intersectional lenses. We thus refuse to indemnify aspirations and subscriptions to normative, monolithic affects that may only reinforce the marginalization of women of color.

The Blackening of Happiness

Our attention to happiness in *The Woman of Colour* and *Belle* cannot be unfixed from negotiations of "erotic autonomy." For M. Jacqui Alexander, from whom we draw this concept, erotic autonomy "signals danger to the heterosexual family and to the nation" and "brings with it the potential of undoing the nation entirely, a possible charge of irresponsible citizenship, or no responsibility at all."[14] Alexander's erotic autonomy concatenates with Audre Lorde's imagining of the erotic to cement community, endow capacities of feeling and joy, and mobilize a recognized self-empowerment that refuses to be tyrannized.[15] With Alexander and Lorde as central interlocutors, we account for how what we call "unsettling happiness" participates in reframing the eighteenth-century novel's commitment to a marriage plot that is exclusively about white hetero-domesticity. Unsettling happiness identifies how characters read as Black women endure and engender new parameters for understanding happiness in the long eighteenth century.

We see happiness as *affect*, a capacious term that signifies how emotion, feeling, and intersubjectivity are represented and simultaneously socialized and politicized. This chapter, in turn, converses with Nour Afara's and M. A. Miller's preceding chapters to offer the study of affect as one that can participate in anticolonial praxes of unsettling. Negative affects and their attendant (re)actions have garnered significant attention, for example, from Lorde, Sianne Ngai, Cathy Park Hong, and Sue J. Kim, and, in extension, we are interested in the myriad affective components of happiness, which are not strictly positive or utopian.[16] Examining happiness as racialized, specifically Black or mixed-race, affect is a means to apprehend diverse emotionality that remains inextricably linked to politicized, intersectional identities.

Tyrone S. Palmer susses out the relationship between theories of Blackness and affect and observes that they are uneasy bedfellows that render Black affect an *"unthinkability"* given Blackness's ostracism, at best, and expungement, at worst, alongside structures of onto-epistemological humanity.[17] By reading for happiness as a Blackened affect within *The Woman of Colour* and *Belle*, we transhistorically unsettle happiness and refuse to accept such an affective metric as cursory, innocent, or universal. The promise of happiness, which in its concomitance with a white supremacy that insidiously persists today and is inherited from its eighteenth-century mobilization (see, for example, *The Declaration of Independence* or Alexander Pope's *An Essay on Man*), encodes a colonial politics dead set on maintaining differential affects and acceptability politics. We take seriously the emancipatory potential of racialized affect, epitomized here by happiness, to reject projections and totalizing appeals to happiness that only resituate supremacist values.[18]

The Blackening of happiness centralizes the experiences of mixed-race women who are read as Black, but it does not minimize how unsettling happiness might be lionized by other global majority identities. We employ Blackening in concert with Black feminist and queer of color traditions that detail how Blackness becomes constructed as a social index. In *The Woman of Colour*, Blackening accounts for the novel's shifting contours of racial identification and the ways in which Olivia's color and gender abut, confirm, and reject how she is read by other characters.[19] Like Palmer, who has suggested that Black affect may be an impossibility that demarcates how Blackness as nonbeing (because of an enduring historio-socio-cultural anti-Blackness) is likewise excluded from frameworks of affect and emotion, we read the novel's prescription of Olivia's hetero-domestic happiness as an impossibility because she agentively refuses its normative structures of happiness.[20]

To experience the Blackening of happiness in *The Woman of Colour* is to understand a differential, racialized affect that Olivia's experience might uncover and to then imagine how the novel's conclusive remarks on happiness can remake her encounters with domestic happiness. In a powerful farewell speech to Augustus, Olivia informs him that she will abjure him, for both of their sakes, and cites the Bible, "look[ing] forwards to that eternally happy state where there is neither 'marrying nor giving in marriage.'"[21] That Olivia returns to Jamaica (the site of her birth and her mother's enslavement) at the novel's end and is not affixed to any paternalist entity suggests that the Blackening of happiness accounts for racialized affects that are freighted with histories of enslavement, patriarchal ghosts, and the prospect of singledom. In Rebecca Anne Barr's words, "The open-ended conclusion of *The Woman of Colour* confronts readers with the insufficiency of white sentiment to provide justice or to effect meaningful change."[22] The failures of white sentiment and the resulting differential affects endow Olivia with an erotic autonomy that successfully dislocates her from the hetero-domestic marriage plot.

Blackening happiness is, de facto, a political gesture; it recognizes how subaltern identities can forge their own pathways to happiness that are in conversation with but different than the whitewashed monolith. Xine Yao has recently turned to the prospect of unfeeling to uncover a dissident literary politics. Yao heralds disaffection to name and disavow the monolith and projection of white feelings on all persons and, within the long nineteenth century to which Yao turns, rejects whitewashed appeals to sentimentality.[23] The conceptual framework we pioneer here, like Yao's, honors the work that Black feminist and queer intellectuals like Sylvia Wynter and Katherine McKittrick, Jennifer Morgan, Jessica Marie Johnson, Tiffany Lethabo King, and Imani Perry have spearheaded by identifying how African diasporic and Black bodies remain, in perpetuity, outside of the realms of white acceptability.[24] Hortense Spillers's Black vestibulary exemplifies this invocation: "The black person mirrored for the society around her what a human being was *not*."[25] Systems of enslavement, which are channeled by *The Woman of Colour* and *Belle*, keep racialized bodies in abeyance from white acceptable modes of gender, sexuality, affect, and embodiment. As Yao succinctly prognosticates, "affect studies has a race problem" that Lauren Guilmette typifies as the "coloniality of the affects" and Michalinos Zembylas understands as the "invalidation of emotional expressions of peoples from non-White racialized groups."[26] The Blackening of happiness recognizes these differential politics and upholds these differences to imagine alternative opportunities for politics, being, and affect.

Coloring Contingent Happiness

As *The Woman of Colour* opens, Olivia is on a ship bearing her northward to England. She contemplates the prospects dictated by her father's will: marrying the cousin to whom she is affianced, Augustus Merton, or taking the risk of depending solely on his brother and sister-in-law. Despite the paternalism of her father that places her in this uneasy predicament, Olivia constantly worries for Augustus's happiness and prioritizes it over her own. In Olivia's efforts to honor her father's "guardian spirit," her happiness hinges on the will, desire, and happiness of paternalistic others.[27] Even with her £60,000 dowry, Olivia's happiness remains contingent on a masculine protectorate that assures readers that a woman's happiness relies on being shuttled from father to husband.

The novel, as mentioned, is organized as a series of letters, including dense packets sent by Olivia to Mrs. Milbanke in Jamaica and a few interpolated letters by Augustus and his family. Olivia's letters often emerge in the novel as interrupted and continued narratives extended over several days and sent to Mrs. Milbanke in sheafs. At the close of her first epistle, Olivia questions why she must abandon Mrs. Milbanke in search of her cousin, only to quickly check this glimmer of authentic feeling by reminding herself that "it was the will of *him* who always studied the happiness of his child."[28] The italicized "him" posthumously deifies her father, who arbitrates her past, present, and future. In "stud[ying] the happiness of his child," Mr. Fairfield "cultivated" the best possible odds for Olivia's happiness, attempting to insert her into a hetero-domestic marriage plot for which she is ill-fitted.[29] Throughout the first volume, Olivia articulates and puppets genres of contingent happiness—indeed, Ahmed identifies the etymologies of "contingent" and "happiness" as interwoven—that are predicated on and whitewashed by the eighteenth-century domestic novel.[30] Yet, Olivia's placement within the epistolary novel ultimately allows her to upend the allegiances of the genre's form by remaining unmarried at the novel's end.

Whereas the introductory epistle locates Olivia's happiness within the confines of her father's wishes, at the start of the second sheaf of letters—with Olivia now introduced, albeit tumultuously, to the Mertons and married to Augustus—this paternalistic, contingent happiness transfers to Augustus. To Mrs. Milbanke, Olivia writes, "Yet, believe me, my beloved friend, I am happy; and the attention and indulgence of my husband exceeds my highest expectations.—And yet, I had formed high expectations of the character of Augustus Merton (Fairfield he is now become). If I can be instrumental to *his* happiness, I shall have reason to bless my father for my happy lot."[31] It is impossible to disregard the narrative similitude that opens the first and second packets of epistles. In the substitutive family romance of the second one, Augustus assumes the role of the father, even in name, likeness, and title (the £60,000 dowry is now his).[32] That Augustus adopts the surname Fairfield upon marriage to Olivia demonstrates a further enlargement of the patriarchal will (and surrogacy), which positions him also as an enslaver in Jamaica (and retroactively positions Olivia's mother, who is both his mother-in-law and aunt, as defunct property). The repeated use of an italicized "his" echoes the deification of the father, and like the father who bestows happiness on Olivia, readers understand Augustus as a similar, if not identical, paternal figure on whom Olivia's happiness depends. The affirmation of "I am happy" accords a socialized statement in which the expectation of happiness accompanies marital bliss and "brutal," as Barr notes, paternalistic oversight.[33] Olivia's announcement performs a narrative conformity that is only short-lived.

Olivia's private declaration of her instrumentality to Augustus's happiness defines her happiness as a mixed-race woman as something that must be tokenized. "Token" here works in multitudes: first, etymologically, a token is a didactic sign that serves for instruction. Olivia as the hyperattentive wife instructs others how to achieve domestic bliss (which is upturned shortly after, and so the subversion of this domestic bliss remains a viable reading too) and thereby becomes a token of happiness for both readers' and Augustus's narcissistic pleasures. Second, the etymology of "token" likewise realizes an exchangeable good enfolded in commodification. Exogamy traditionally requires the exchange of women to institute social harmony and renders Olivia's dowry and marriage to Augustus as primarily transactional in nature. Unbeknownst to readers in volume one, Augustus struggles to please his own father (paternalistic, contingent happiness returns) as he navigates the marriage economy, and Olivia assumes the form of his "political currency," to borrow from Frank Wilderson, or, a token whose acceptance elevates Augustus's station.[34] "Token" can, furthermore, be read alongside affective vertices in that it acknowledges how Augustus's "attention" and "indulgence," demonstrating his satisfaction, are the means by which Olivia's happiness is forged. This exchange of emotion holds captive Olivia's happiness, binding it to the economy of the marriage plot in which she is traded. Finally, in that Olivia's contingent happiness is instrumental to her husband's, we bear witness to a more contemporary understanding of tokenization in which she becomes a racialized token rent by her husband's and father's desires for domestic stability.

The confirmation of domestic stability is further verified by Olivia when she notes in a subsequent letter, "I have got a fine Utopian scheme of domestic happiness in my head, and the *country* must be the birth-place of it."[35] What follows Olivia's admission is a list of duties, avocations, and outings that can subtend her "felicity," and yet, the utopianism of her claim foreshadows the quick stillbirth of her scheme. We invoke stillbirth in correspondence with Olivia's identification of the country as a primal scene of domestic happiness (later reinforced by Dido's relationship with John in *Belle*), which prematurely perishes because of Augustus's deceit and Olivia's consequent rejection of their marriage. While utopianism incites fanciful and imaginative pleasures, its etymology reminds us that it is literally (and literarily) a "no/n place" and so too must be Olivia's domestic happiness. Kerry Sinanan reads *The Woman of Colour*'s utopianism to situate how "the power of the novel, then, lies in the promise it holds to reach forward into a more multicultural future in which gender and race might not be such oppressive structures as they are in 1808."[36] Our reading, however, like Kristina Huang's and Jennifer Reed's, considers utopianisms foreclosed rather than liberated: Olivia's aspirations of domestic happiness are utopian in that they are stillborn and never fully realized because she ultimately rejects their immuring logic.[37] *The Woman of Colour* creates a path of agency for Olivia that is rarely allowed Black and mixed-race women in the novel of sentiment.

Eighteenth-century narrative domesticity recurrently corresponds with visions of the country as the paradigmatic site of conjugality. In *The Woman of Colour*, however, the country is not so much an originary point of connubial happiness as a geography that homes domestic happiness's *failures*. Indeed, Dido, Olivia's enslaved attendant (not to be confused with the Dido of *Belle*) wistfully parallels the country to the Fairfield plantation as she and Olivia describe their distaste for London life, foreshadowing the racism and deceit they experience in their idyllic abode. By figuring the country as the site of domestic happiness, Olivia aligns her own domestic happiness (and its contingency on an honest and good-intentioned husband/father) with the marriage plots that have preceded *The Woman of Colour*. In reading volumes one and two, distinct yet coordinated epistolary packets, we witness how the first volume consolidates the utopian imaginary of the hetero-domestic marriage plot, and the second volume revamps it.

Curiously, Olivia concludes the continuation of her epistle with a question rather than a statement—by our account, the only time this happens in the entire novel.[38] Upon thanking the Almighty as "bestower of such felicity," Olivia concludes,

"Say, dear madam, is such a plan likely to be realized by your
OLIVIA FAIRFIELD?"[39]

Olivia's genre-breaking enjambed signature furthermore calls into question the
utopianism of domestic felicity. The question mark functions as an epistolary cliff-
hanger and undermines the narrative of domestic happiness in which Olivia feels
interpolated. The interrogative likewise pinpoints Olivia's questioning of identity,
her own as well as that of the others, such as Augustus, who assume the Fairfield
surname as proprietary exchange. Political affects that undercut the law of the
father scaffold the deployment of the question mark here. Jennifer DeVere Brody
magnifies punctuation to argue that grammatical performances animate an archive
of feeling that politicizes aesthetics and induces layers of textual embodiment.[40]
Olivia's question mark follows suit in that it espouses ways of being and reading
that react to and fundamentally *question* the marriage plot.

OLIVIA'S BLACKENED HAPPINESS

At the conclusion of volume one, Olivia engineers a new metric of happiness that
serves as a guiding framework for the remainder of the novel. Olivia writes, "Happy
is it, when, with no overstrained fastidiousness, we can consent to take the world
as we find it, when we endeavour to mend where it lies in our power, and firmly
resolve not to make it worse by our *example*."[41] Her prophetic prose, while border-
ing on self-flagellatory, sparks a new design for happiness: a Blackened happiness
reflective of her experiences as a mixed-race woman rather than beholden to generic
(in terms of the novel as genre and with regard to the word genre's etymological
root, from which we also obtain "gender") conventions that have so far restrained
happiness's possibilities. By consenting "to take the world as we find it," Olivia telegraphs a shift in the contingent and formulaic experiences of happiness that col-
ored her journey through volume one. Accepting the world as she experiences it—in
a few short letters, she divulges to Mrs. Milbanke that with Augustus outed, she is
now "your late *happy* Olivia"—our heroine inspires modes of reading happinesses
otherwise.[42]

Olivia discloses that Augustus had been clandestinely wed to Angelina (who
has also borne him a child) and thus finds herself dependent on Mr. George
Merton, Augustus's brother. Such calamity, superficially, throws Olivia back into her
precarious position as a young, unmarried (widowed or falsely married) mixed-
race woman who relies on paternalistic guardianship. However, Olivia rejects this
precarity and alchemizes her autonomy from the ashes of misfortune. As Huggins
notes, "By claiming the status of widowed wife at the end of the novel, Olivia . . .
use[s] this ambivalent position to advance [her] financial and social freedom."[43]
In attempting to reconcile her relationship with Augustus and Angelina, Olivia
uses her newfound "mobility and freedom of the idealized, self-possessed individual" to gift Angelina "the jewels which had been presented to me on my marriage
by Mr. Merton," and twice wishes Augustus happiness:[44] "I feel not the slightest

spark of resentment towards you; that I will fervently beseech Heaven for your future happiness, and pray that you may forget that there exists such a being as myself!" and "May heaven protect, and bless you all! May my fervent prayers be heard for your happiness!"[45] While Augustus identifies these martyr-like gestures as "unexampled magnanimity," Olivia reveals two interconnected realizations: first, that happiness derives from her exemplary nature, as in the passage that concludes volume one, and second, that the happiness she wishes Augustus, Angelina, and their son (also Augustus) is unavailable and undesirable to her.[46] Such happiness is unwanted by Olivia because she does not wish to occupy "the role of plunderer," as Sinanan suggests.[47] If in the previous packets of epistles, Olivia characterizes a genre of happiness that upholds domesticity, then in wishing the Mertons happiness, she suggests that the whitewashing of domestic felicity is something achievable to them: they are the target audience and vehicles for apprehending a domestic happiness bequeathed by the eighteenth-century marriage plot.

Olivia, in turn, proposes a novel framework of happiness that accounts for her experience as a mixed-race woman and rejects the hetero-domestic, whitewashed marriage plot. The penultimate epistle announces Olivia's return to Jamaica to reunite with Mrs. Milbanke. The former writes:

> YES! My beloved friend, I am coming to you. I wait but for you to suggest a scheme which my heart has long anticipated. Your letter is arrived and Dido is already packing up with avidity. We will revisit Jamaica. I shall come back to the scenes of my infantine happiness–of my youthful tranquility. I shall again zealously engage myself in ameliorating the situation, in instructing the minds– in mending the morals of our poor blacks. I shall again enjoy the society of my dear Mrs. Milbanke–I shall forget the lapse of time which has occurred since I parted from her, and shall again be happy! Eager to be with you once more, I almost count the tardy minutes as they move along.[48]

Happiness appears twice here: first in an appeal to Jamaica, and second in the announcement of a reunion with Mrs. Milbanke. We focus on the former here.[49] Olivia identifies Jamaica as the site of "infantine happiness," which may superficially be read as a sort of regression. This happiness also seems bound up in the "zealous" engagement with ameliorating the conditions of "our poor blacks." Such a remark ostensibly aligns Olivia's happiness with patrimonial modes that characterize volume one. While Olivia is not a faultless character (see the lack of detail about Dido's uncertain manumission, for instance[50]), to think of her happiness as regressive or ameliorationist, as Natalie Zacek contends, is to denounce both her progression as a character and her abolitionist sentiments throughout the novel. Zacek explains that the ameliorationist argument "proposed that, if planters could no longer purchase new labourers via the transatlantic slave trade, they would have to treat those they possessed with greater care."[51] Instead, understanding Jamaica as a place of Olivia's alternative happiness (which she articulates in the first epistle)[52] is to imagine how it embodies a site of transgressive Black geography, as Katherine McKittrick and Clyde Woods conceive of it, in which we "see place as the location of co-operation, stewardship, and social justice rather than just sites to be dominated, enclosed, commodified, exploited, and segregated."[53]

To read the return to Jamaica as a Black geography that might endow Blackened happiness, we recognize, is challenging because it requires that we juggle multiple readings of the novel and Olivia's character at once alongside ongoing legacies of enslavement that cannot be romanticized. For Huggins, "Olivia's return to Jamaica at the end of the novel can be read as an empowering move that rejects the patriarchal and imperialist powers that have dominated her life up until this point."[54] We also recognize that Olivia will continue to benefit from her father's wealth, potentially supporting Zacek's contention that Olivia follows the ameliorationist argument. The novel's ending makes murky Olivia's complicity with enslavement, and this is made all the more uncertain by her precarious position as a woman of color and the inevitable limits of her agency therefrom. The promise of Jamaica for Olivia is, without question, one bound up in these convoluted textures, and while we are mindful of the shortcomings of her Edenic rhetoric, what remains is an opportunity for Olivia to leave England and the novel unmarried, on her own terms.

The Woman of Colour's domestic marriage plot showcases generic innovation in which the return to Jamaica, as Black geography, "revisits" an experience of happiness in which Olivia is *not* pawned off as a transactional token to accede to the marriage plot. The concluding "Dialogue between the Editor and a Friend" outwardly rejects this rhetorical and material transaction, as Olivia does when she refuses a second marriage proposal by the milquetoast Honeywood. When the Friend questions why "you have not rewarded Olivia even with the usual need of virtue–*a husband*!," the Editor counters, "Virtue, like Olivia Fairfield's, may truly be said to be its own *reward*."[55] Through her pursuit of a Blackened happiness, Olivia models experiences of happiness that are denuded from a marriage plot that primarily commodifies women.

BELLE AS FILMIC AFTERLIFE

This section turns to Amma Asante's *Belle* (2013) as a future vision of *The Woman of Colour* that recasts some of the racialized affective tropes we have so far charted. *Belle* is not a filmic adaptation of *The Woman of Colour*; we consider it a filmic afterlife that networks racialized affects that are at once encoded and rewired given the book and film's historical, audience, and generic differences. Theorizing this afterlife is a means to access myriad racial temporalities bound up in histories of enslavement—efforts that have been pioneered by Saidiya Hartman and Alys Eve Weinbaum.[56] A period piece derived from Misan Sagay's screenplay, *Belle* imagines how the unsettling of happiness manifests through characters read as mixed-race or Black women in contemporary film.

Although the film conceptualizes Dido's *un*happiness through the lack of belonging, its solution to her negative affect is to funnel her through the marriage economy. While the romantic tropes of eighteenth-century British aristocracy might be more digestible to modern audiences than the aristocracy's contributions to the slave trade, *The Woman of Colour*'s attention to geographies of happiness (and retreat) for mixed-race women primes similar innovation in film. Dido Elizabeth Belle's happiness channeled through patriarchal hetero-domesticity solidifies the supremacy of the marriage plot and contributes to the collective discouragement of alternative Blackened happinesses for mixed-race women. We magnify Dido's failed and successful marriage proposals to better ascertain how filmic appeals to the marriage plot participate in racialized affects and are enmeshed with invocations of happiness.

As Dido (played by Gugu Mbatha-Raw) comes of age, she forges her way into circles that educate her about the slave trade and the 1781 murder of enslaved west Africans en route to Jamaica aboard the *Zong*. Whereas *The Woman of Colour* downplays West Indian enslavement, *Belle* centralizes the slave trade from the vantage point of England. Dido's search for happiness—that is, in pursuit of erotic autonomy—radicalizes and effectively makes her a token of exchange for the debate leading up to the hearing on the *Zong*, presided over by her uncle, Lord Mansfield, chief justice of England (Tom Wilkinson). Her presence as a mixed-race woman in his household arouses suspicions of bias. She also serves as the mode of transport through which Lord Mansfield's private documents on the case are communicated to her romantic interest, fellow abolitionist John Davinier, and the "radicals" advocating for the indictment of the shipping syndicate. Dido exists as a strategic pawn who triangulates political, romantic, and social spheres. She finds conclusive happiness as Davinier's wife, yet only after she nearly falls victim to a condescending marriage offer by Oliver Ashford (James Norton), who is willing to "forgive" her melanin in pursuit of her dowry, a trope implicitly installed by *The Woman of Colour*. In this way, both Dido Elizabeth Belle and Olivia Fairfield narrowly escape the pitfalls of undesirable heteronormative marriage, but their eventual outcomes of happiness diverge.

While the word "happiness" and its semantic associations litter *The Woman of Colour*, they are noticeably absent from *Belle*, the word appearing only five times in the screenplay[57] and twice in the movie itself. Lady Mansfield (Emily Watson) voices both filmic utterances, underlining the racio-sexual tensions fraught in the Mansfields' reluctance to allow Dido sexual autonomy by participating in the same marriage economy and courtship rituals as her white cousin, Elizabeth Murray (Sarah Gadon). Before accepting an abrupt proposal by Oliver, Dido wavers under his pleading stare as her familial reputation, dowry, and distaste for his "forgiving" attitude toward her converge in a storm of conflicting emotions, resonating with Palmer's statement that "incorporation into 'citizenship' and 'personhood' is predicated on a denial of the past—a disavowal of blackness itself."[58] Dido, eager to marry and avoid a life of solitary housekeeping, silently realizes that her ticket to "citizenship" and "personhood" in aristocratic English society is to refuse her own Blackness alongside a man who denies it. She later proudly claims her maternal heritage, but in this pivotal moment, she hesitates because she does not fit the stereotypical molds of whiteness and femininity that characterize the ideal

Georgian aristocratic wife. By contrast, Olivia avows her love for her mother and the gift of melanin from the novel's start.

As the subject of a marital request from a white man who, along with her entire family, expects her to comply, Dido is "trapped in [an] interaction ritua[l] in which [she has] little power" and "experience[s] negative emotional energy, such as fear, anxiety, shame, and guilt," as Ulla Berg and Ana Ramos-Zayas posit.[59] Emotional energy opens up a cornucopia of negative feelings to induce Dido's "self-protective" interiority that, as Bynum contends, communicates "what and who matters" to her.[60] Some of her fear and anxiety undoubtedly stem from her knowledge that if she refuses the hand of the "only gentleman that will consider [her]," she will be forced to assume Lady Mary's (Penelope Wilton) position of housekeeper at Kenwood, possessing the keys to the closed doors of the home, yet unmarried and longing for marriage forevermore.[61] In other words, the alternative for Dido is to possess the keys to the house but not domestic happiness. Dido feels the prospective familial shame and guilt that would accompany her rejection of Oliver's hand; to comport herself to Oliver's happiness would signify a familial obligation that, like Olivia's in *The Woman of Colour*, is contingent on paternalism. The film renders genres of happiness through obligations to familial and social structures from which Dido is precariously sidelined.

Dido experiences affect differently than her white counterparts, thereby reifying how "White European bourgeois understandings of affect" have "been used to justify racialization."[62] Her reaction to Oliver's proposal is scrutinized, and her "Black affect becomes irrelevant and powerless as a result of colonial violence."[63] Her feelings are dictated by Lady Mansfield, recasting the contingent happiness of the father as the contingent happiness of the surrogate white mother. Dido is powerless in the Georgian marriage economy, and her acquiescence to Oliver's proposal is both expected and necessary to foster a future prescribed, whitewashed happiness that is seen as her sole opportunity to avoid domestic work.

This contingency wields a trifold conditionality in what Ahmed calls "conditional happiness," which embodies the widely accepted form of happiness striven for today.[64] Its stipulations are: first, such a happiness must implicate a "relationship of care and reciprocity," and although Dido's engagement to Oliver may give all appearances of fulfilling such an aspiration, the fact remains that Lord Ashford purchases Oliver a commission in the navy, indicating his eventual departure from Dido.[65] The bleeding ink of paternalism stains this marriage contract. It not only signals a similar career from which Dido's father never returns but also means that Oliver will not be available to care for Dido should she need security, protection, and a caretaker of her physical health as the Mansfields believe she will. A second stipulation is that Dido's reaction to Oliver's offer and her subsequent questioning of Lady Mansfield and the prudence of her decision render the marriage contract's "terms of conditionality unequal."[66] The happiness of others precedes Dido's, as it does for Olivia in *The Woman of Colour*. Third, Oliver introduces himself to Dido in this scene by subtly imploring her to express her reciprocated happiness in accepting his hand in marriage, indicating that his happiness is contingent on her consent. Dido is trapped in a web of conditionality in which she "can only be happy if they are happy."[67]

Dido knows that declining Oliver's hand jeopardizes her social survival, for "the inability or refusal to engage in 'proper' affective performances often becomes a mark of social marginalization," as Analiese Richard recognizes, especially in Dido's constant state of hypervisibility as the sole (by the film's purview) mixed-race woman in the English aristocracy.[68] "I cannot," she begins, hesitating, "think of anything . . . more wonderful!"[69] Dido's consent becomes an affective performance; she ventriloquizes white economies of affect. In the face of her whitewashed world, Dido's Blackness, as Palmer might say, "overdetermines everything, rendering even 'happiness' illegible."[70] The compound emotions and considerations she processes before her acceptance make happiness more unintelligible for her, and Dido ultimately transitions into a requisite heteronormativity.

SPATIAL HAPPINESSES

In contradiction to Dido's forged happiness with Oliver, ensuing scenes of authentic happiness shared between Dido and John Davinier are notably set outdoors, where they freely walk the streets of London. Asante's choice subtly transmits to viewers how Blackened happiness is a feeling born at the intersection of love, nature, and agency. Dido actively seeks pleasure in this way, "insist[ing] on [her] presence" in a tumultuous, racist political economy and making real the "very possibility of a deep, deep joy."[71] For Bynum, reading Black interiorities requires reading for pleasure and joy because "there is no way to truly read individual suffering without also asking questions about pleasure."[72] In their strolls, John visibly shares Dido's happiness, and their interactions are much less rigid than the ones dictated by courtship etiquette. John welcomes Dido into masculinized circles of law, and as the film mounts to its climax in the courtroom, Dido becomes increasingly confident in discussing the *Zong* case and her position in Georgian society with Lord Mansfield. In an admittedly, though reframed, paternalistic fashion, John introduces Dido to the world from which Lord Mansfield previously sheltered her.[73]

The standard marriage economy underserves Dido's needs, just as it does for Olivia, and John is willing to diverge from etiquette norms to deliver himself and Dido toward, by the film's purview, mutual happiness. His public pronouncement of his love for Dido following their clandestine liaisons paves the road to marriage. Augustus, quite oppositely, never publicly proclaims his affection for Olivia in this fashion. Olivia is aware, as Kathleen Lubey stresses, that marriage "does not guarantee affection and that her primary function is to transfer capital."[74] Instead, Olivia's aspirations to please Augustus, as well as her desire for confidence, dominate her utopic descriptions of happiness, even as he conceals secrets.

Charting these contrasts reveals that John and Augustus's comparative trustworthiness ultimately determines the fate of their relationships. Dido cannot trust Oliver to embrace her fully, so John takes his place; Olivia, however, can trust neither Augustus nor Honeywood to satisfy her. Dido and Olivia together unsettle the white economies of affect by demanding trust in environments that are inherently hostile to them. As in Ruth Wilson Gilmore's definition of abolition geography, Dido and Olivia "make freedom provisionally, imperatively, as they imagine home against . . . racial capitalism."[75] Trusting the men with whom they choose to bond to promote their best interests is an indispensable part of that liberation. Both the pursuit of a desirable marriage (for Dido) and the decision to remain unmarried (as Olivia models) represent crosshatched representations of abolitionist Black geographies subversively located within the borders of colonization (at home and abroad).

When publicizing the film, Sagay wrote, "From the start I avoided all the clichés, like the black character who earns the acceptance of the white characters through superhuman feats of generosity and saintlike goodness."[76] We cannot help but notice how Sagay's statement aligns with the characterization of Olivia Fairfield; yet, Olivia builds on her innate goodness in an autonomous search for Blackened happiness away from the domestic sphere of the hetero-domestic marriage plot. *Belle*, however, makes a conscious choice to finalize happiness within the structures of heteronormative marriage to a white man. This romantic ending parallels—rather than diverges from—the romantic ideals of the Georgian era. Sagay's desire to "write a love story" is translated by Asante as a commitment to the marriage plot.[77] Love and marriage (and the happiness they invoke) are inextricably sutured. Our concern remains though: the film's perpetuation of white, heteronormative ideals of happiness, that Olivia outwardly rejects in *The Woman of Colour*, perhaps speaks to the film's success in that such a clichéd ending is marketable to film-going audiences invested in such ideals.[78] Olivia's story, on the other hand, "end[s] with freedom—from her father's will, English society, financial constraint, marriage, and motherhood—freedom to be active."[79] Assuredly, Dido's happily-ever-after is free from financial constraint, but all of the aforementioned factors tug at her freedom in ways that Olivia disavows.

Although we acknowledge that Dido may have fewer geographies of retreat than Olivia, we still wonder: What might it mean to audiences if Dido refuses to condone the happinesses spoon-fed her and instead *paths*, to return to Ahmed's creative denominalization discussed in the introduction, alongside Olivia? In what ways do our continued commitments to the marriage plot suggest that refusals to abide are ostensibly tragic in their own right? Can we instead read against the grain to view *Belle* as a tragedy of happiness, its contingencies, and our collective complicities in creating an echo chamber constructed by white economies of affect? How might we continue to imagine how regimes of affect and race are mutually constitutive?

To consider racialized affects and their correspondence with the hetero-domestic marriage plot is to refuse the whitewashed universality of happiness, which in its continued circulation is tantamount to coerced bootstrapping. What we have demonstrated here is that mixed-race women, who are read as Black, imagine alternative horizons for happiness that do not require their subjugation to domesticity. Olivia and Dido pioneer modes of Blackened happiness that are subversive, non-reductive, and non-commodifiable. How can we reduce the appeals to totalizing emotionality to better account for situated knowledges? Through unsettling happiness, we wish to rectify the whitewashed monolith of universal affects to witness other horizons that honor women of color in the eighteenth century and beyond.

NOTES

1. Sara Ahmed, *The Promise of Happiness* (Durham, NC: Duke University Press, 2010), 55.

2. Flavio Gregori, "Happiness (and Unhappiness) in Eighteenth-Century English Literature," *English Literature* 2, no. 1 (July 2015): 5–16 (7).

3. Melissa Adams-Campbell, *New World Courtships: Transatlantic Alternatives to Companionate Marriage* (Hanover, NH: Dartmouth College Press, 2015), 22–23.

4. Maria Edgeworth, *Belinda*, ed. Linda Bree (Oxford: Oxford University Press, 2020), 198.

5. Adams-Campbell, *New World Courtships*, 4.

6. Jeremy Bentham, *Fragment on Government* (Oxford: Clarendon, 1891), 93.

7. Ahmed, *The Promise of Happiness*, 55.

8. Ahmed, *The Promise of Happiness*, 12.

9. Adams-Campbell, *New World Courtships*, 7.

10. Tara A. Bynum, *Reading Pleasures: Everyday Black Living in Early America* (Champaign: University of Illinois Press, 2023), 14.

11. Scholars debate the attribution of the 1779 painting. Recent forensic and archival research conducted for BBC's *Fake or Fortune* series 7, episode 4, "A Double Whoddunit," suggests that Johann Zoffany was not the painter, as the frame label suggests, but rather David Martin. For a history of the portrait, see Jennifer Germann, "'Other Women Were Present': Seeing Black Women in Georgian London," *Eighteenth-Century Studies* 54, no. 3 (Spring 2021): 535–554.

12. The portrait of the real-life Dido Elizabeth Belle Lindsay and her cousin Elizabeth Murray inspired *Belle* screenwriter Misan Sagay, who observed it at Scotland's Scone Palace in 2004. It is speculated that the author of *The Woman of Colour* drew inspiration from this painting too.

13. Sofia Prado Huggins, "Reading Slantwise: Dido in *The Woman of Colour* (1808)," *Eighteenth-Century Fiction* 35, no. 1 (Winter 2023): 27–42 (28).

14. M. Jacqui Alexander, *Pedagogies of Crossing: Meditations on Feminism, Sexual Politics, Memory, and the Sacred* (Durham, NC: Duke University Press, 2005), 22–23.

15. Audre Lorde, *Sister Outsider: Essays and Speeches* (Berkeley, CA: Crossing Press, 1984).

16. Lorde, *Sister Outsider*; Sianne Ngai, *Ugly Feelings* (Cambridge, MA: Harvard University Press, 2005); Cathy Park Hong, *Minor Feelings: An Asian American Reckoning* (New York: One World, 2021); Sue J. Kim, *On Anger: Race, Cognition, Narrative* (Austin: University of Texas Press, 2013).

17. Tyrone S. Palmer, "'What's More than Feeling?': Theorizing the Unthinkability of Black Affect," *Critical Ethnic Studies* 3, no. 2 (Fall 2017): 31–56 (33).

18. Ulla Berg and Ana Ramos-Zayas contend that race cannot be delinked from affect (and vice versa) because of neoliberalism; to do so is only to play into white supremacist epistemologies that sideline racialization (from affect) or affective comportment (from constructions of identity). See Berg and Ramos-Zayas, "Racializing Affect: A Theoretical Proposition," *Current Anthropology* 56, no. 5 (October 2015): 654–677.

19. Olivia identifies herself in *The Woman of Colour* as a "mulatto West Indian" (92) and "yellow" (79) or "olive" (53), respectively, in contrast to "black" like her attendant Dido (79). However, by her own epistolary account (as well as the other epistles enfolded in the narrative), she is exclusively read as Black by her English interlocutors, especially Augustus, who writes, "I beheld a skin approaching to the hue of a negro's" (102) and Mrs. George Merton who, with anti-Black repugnance, refers to Olivia as "Miss *Blacky*" (101). See Anonymous, *The Woman of Colour: A Tale*, ed. Lyndon J. Dominique (Peterborough, ON: Broadview Press, 2008).

20. Tyrone Palmer, "Otherwise than Black: Feeling, World, Sublimation," *Qui Parle* 29, no. 2 (December 2020): 247–283.

21. Anonymous, *The Woman of Colour*, 154.

22. Rebecca Anne Barr, "Sentiment and Sexual Servitude: White Men of Feeling and *The Woman of Colour*," *Eighteenth-Century Fiction* 35, no. 1 (January 2023): 81–102 (102).

23. Xine Yao, *Disaffected: The Cultural Politics of Unfeeling in Nineteenth-Century America* (Durham, NC: Duke University Press, 2021).

24. Sylvia Wynter and Katherine McKittrick, "Unparalleled Catastrophe for Our Species? Or, to Give Humanness a Different Future: Conversations," *Sylvia Wynter: On Being Human as Praxis* (Durham, NC: Duke University Press, 2014), 9–89; Imani Perry, *Vexy Thing: On Gender and Liberation* (Durham, NC: Duke University Press, 2018); Tiffany Lethabo King, *The Black Shoals: Offshore Formations of Black and Native Studies* (Durham, NC: Duke University Press, 2019); Jennifer Morgan, *Reckoning with Slavery: Gender, Kinship and Capitalism in the Early Black Atlantic* (Durham, NC: Duke University Press, 2020); and Jessica Marie Johnson, *Wicked Flesh: Black Women, Intimacy, and Freedom in the Atlantic World* (Philadelphia: University of Pennsylvania Press, 2020).

25. Hortense J. Spillers, *Black, White, and in Color: Essays on American Literature and Culture* (Chicago: University of Chicago Press, 2003), 155.

26. Yao, *Disaffected*, 9; Lauren Guilmette, "Unsettling the Coloniality of the Affects: Transcontinental Reverberations between Teresa Brennan and Sylvia Wynter," *philoSOPHIA* 9, no. 1 (January 2019): 73–91; and Michalinos Zembylas, "Sylvia Wynter, Racialized Affects, and Minor Feelings: Unsettling the Coloniality of the Affects in Curriculum and Pedagogy," *Journal of Curriculum Studies* 54, no. 3 (July 2022): 336–350 (337).

27. Anonymous, *The Woman of Colour*, 68.

28. Anonymous, *The Woman of Colour*, 53.

29. Anonymous, *The Woman of Colour*, 53.

30. Sara Ahmed identifies happiness as etymologically originating from the premise of contingency, which we see recast by Olivia's characterization of her father. See Ahmed, "Killing Joy: Feminism and the History of Happiness," *Signs* 35, no. 3 (Spring 2010): 574. Nancy Armstrong characterizes the types of whitewashed domesticity, immanent in the eighteenth-century's rise-of-the-novel discourses, that we see subverted by *The Woman of Colour*. Armstrong, *Desire and Domestic Fiction: A Political History of the Novel* (Oxford: Oxford University Press, 1987).

31. Anonymous, *The Woman of Colour*, 94.

32. On first meeting Augustus, Olivia writes, "The likeness to [my father] is very strong, and his voice has the very tones which used to bless my ear!" (Anonymous, *The Woman of Colour*, 72).

33. Rebecca Anne Barr, "From Romance to Decolonial Love in *The Woman of Colour*," *Studies in Religion and Enlightenment* 2, no. 2 (Fall 2021): 41–44 (42).

34. Frank B. Wilderson muses over Saidiya Hartman's case for the absence of "consent as a possession of the slave" in *Afropessimism* (New York: Liveright, 2021), 191. He argues that "Black people are political *currency*, not political subjects" in the context of the electoral college (198).

35. Anonymous, *The Woman of Colour*, 99.

36. Kerry Sinanan, "Introduction—A Roundtable on *The Woman of Colour* (1808)," *Studies in Religion and the Enlightenment* 2, no. 2 (Fall 2021): 39.

37. Kristina Huang, "'Ameliorating the Situation' of Empire: Slavery and Abolition in *The Woman of Colour*," *Eighteenth-Century Fiction* 34, no. 2 (Winter 2022): 167–186; and Jennifer Reed, "Moving Fortunes: Caribbean Women's Marriage, Mobility, and Money in the Novel of Sentiment," *Eighteenth-Century Fiction* 31, no. 3 (Spring 2019): 509–528.

38. Olivia concludes four letters with exclamation points, but no others with question marks.

39. Anonymous, *The Woman of Colour*, 99.

40. Jennifer DeVere Brody, *Punctuation: Art, Politics and Play* (Durham, NC: Duke University Press, 2008).

41. Anonymous, *The Woman of Colour*, 125.

42. Anonymous, *The Woman of Colour*, 136.

43. Huggins, "Reading Slantwise," 32.

44. Huggins, "Reading Slantwise," 32; Anonymous, *The Woman of Colour*, 149.

45. Anonymous, *The Woman of Colour*, 152, 155.

46. Anonymous, *The Woman of Colour*, 153.

47. Kerry Sinanan, "'The Wealth of Worlds': Gender, Race, and Property in *The Woman of Colour*," *Studies in Religion and the Enlightenment* 2, no. 2 (Fall 2021): 53–56 (56).

48. Anonymous, *The Woman of Colour*, 188.

49. Were additional space afforded, we would speak to the reunion between Olivia and Mrs. Milbanke, which underscores a type of queer interracial kinship that is characterized as "happy" by Olivia.

50. Nicole N. Aljoe, Kerry Sinanan, and Mariam Wassif note in the Introduction to *Eighteenth-Century Fiction* 35, no. 1 (Winter 2023), that Dido is still legally enslaved until, should she live beyond the novel's end, the British Slavery Abolition Act of 1833. Notably, however, "Olivia is not Dido's owner" (10), although the lack of discussion on the subject leads us to believe that Dido is still legally considered the property of the Fairfield family.

51. Natalie Zacek, "Favoured Isles: Selfishness and Sacrifice in the Capital of Capital," *Eighteenth-Century Fiction* 35, no. 1 (Winter 2023): 113–132 (131).

52. Olivia writes, "I sometimes think, that had my dear parent left me a decent competence, I could have placed myself in some tranquil nook of my native island, and have been happily and usefully employed in meliorating the sorrows of the poor slaves who came within my reach, and in pouring into their bruised souls the sweet consolations of religious hope! But my father willed it otherwise—Lie still, then, rebellious and repining heart!" (Anonymous, *The Woman of Colour*, 55–56).

53. Katherine McKittrick and Clyde Woods, "No One Knows the Mysteries at the Bottom of the Ocean," *Black Geographies and the Politics of Place*, ed. Katherine McKittrick and Clyde Woods (Chico, CA: AK Press, 2007), 1–11 (6).

54. Huggins, "Reading Slantwise," 40.

55. Anonymous, *The Woman of Colour*, 189.

56. See Saidiya Hartman, *Lose Your Mother: A Journey along the Atlantic Slave Route* (New York: Farrar, Straus and Giroux, 2007); and Alys Eve Weinbaum, *The Afterlife of Reproductive Slavery: Biocapitalism and Black Feminism's History of Philosophy* (Durham, NC: Duke University Press, 2019).

57. Misan Sagay, *Belle*, "Best Original Screenplay." Film, DJ Films Limited (2012): 31, 46, 61, 63, 83.

58. Palmer, "'What's More than Feeling?,'" 48.

59. Berg and Ramos-Zayas, "Racializing Affect," 663.

60. Berg and Ramos-Zayas, "Racializing Affect," 663; Bynum, *Reading Pleasures*, 13.

61. Sagay, *Belle*, "Best Original Screenplay," 85.

62. Zembylas, "Sylvia Wynter, Racialized Affects, and Minor Feelings," 337.

63. Zembylas, "Sylvia Wynter, Racialized Affects, and Minor Feelings," 341.

64. Ahmed, "Killing Joy: Feminism and the History of Happiness," 578.

65. Ahmed, "Killing Joy: Feminism and the History of Happiness," 578.

66. Ahmed, "Killing Joy: Feminism and the History of Happiness," 578.

67. Ahmed, "Killing Joy: Feminism and the History of Happiness," 579.

68. Analiese Richard, "Commentary on Berg and Ramos-Zayas, 'Racializing Affect: A Theoretical Proposition,'" *Current Anthropology* 56, no. 5 (October 2015): 670.

69. Sagay, *Belle*, "Best Original Screenplay," 62.

70. Palmer, "'What's More than Feeling?,'" 46.

71. Bynum, *Reading Pleasures*, 15–16.

72. Bynum, *Reading Pleasures*, 15–16.

73. Dido's increasing agency and character growth corresponds with Steven Wise's claim that the real-life Dido occasionally worked as Lord Mansfield's amanuensis, indicating an unusually high level of trust in Black women at the time. See Steven Wise, *Though the Heavens*

May Fall: The Landmark Trial That Led to the End of Human Slavery (Paris: Hachette, 2005).

74. Kathleen Lubey, "*The Woman of Colour*'s Counter-Domesticity," *Studies in Romanticism* 61, no. 1 (Spring 2022): 113–123 (114).

75. Ruth Wilson Gilmore, "Abolition Geography and the Problem of Innocence," in *Futures of Black Radicalism*, ed. Gaye Theresa Johnson and Alex Lubin (London: Verso, 2017), 224–241 (238).

76. Misan Sagay, "Bringing Slavery into the Heart of Jane Austen," *HuffPost*, July 2, 2014, https://www.huffpost.com/entry/bringing-slavery-into-the-heart-of-jane-austen_b_5255127.

77. Sagay, "Bringing Slavery into the Heart of Jane Austen."

78. Asante admits that "this is an unashamedly commercial movie" that she "wanted to tell . . . through the lens of a Jane Austen world." Amma Asante, "Interview [Part 4]: Amma Asante, Director, 'Belle.'" By Scott Myers, May 1, 2014, https://gointothestory.blcklst.com/interview-part-4-amma-asante-director-belle-594c45f9d3db.

79. Lyndon J. Dominique, "Introduction," *The Woman of Colour: A Tale*, ed. Lyndon J. Dominique (Peterborough, ON: Broadview Press, 2007), 11–42 (39).

Coda

EIGHTEENTH-CENTURY LONGING

Eugenia Zuroski

In its commitment to a revived pursuit of queer horizons in an age of decolonial dreams, this collection of essays is dedicated to longing—not as an object of theory, but as practice. As such, it formally resists *conclusion* as it is oriented away from and beyond closure. But the *con-* is very much part of what these pages set in motion: the sense of "being with," the technique of collecting together. In the collective's final pages, then, this coda asks how we might practice coming together in an opening rather than an enclosure; how we might collect our energies around indeterminate desires rather than shared objects of pursuit; how we might move together in an undoing, rather than a doing, of something.

The thread that holds this collection together might be this question: How can those of us practicing eighteenth-century studies *long together*? This is perhaps the quintessential eighteenth-century studies question two decades into the twenty-first century, when multiple generations of scholars have come to take for granted that the century in which we specialize is notoriously "long." The eighteenth century has been long for so long, one might say, that its length has lost its charm, which in the context of academic fields means that the coherence of its explanatory power is failing.

Is the eighteenth century that we study too long? Has it gone on quite long enough already? Or does it invite us to reconsider how to long through and beyond it? In *On Longing: Narratives of the Miniature, the Gigantic, the Souvenir, the Collection*, Susan Stewart focuses on the state of longing to ask: "How can we describe something? What relation does the description bear to ideology and the very invention of that 'something'?"[1] In the detailed study of modern subject formation that this question engenders, Stewart shows descriptive narrative to be a particular concern of European imperial powers of the long eighteenth century, in their various quests for the semantic closures that would make newly "discovered" worlds make sense, and place the colonial subject in meaningful relation to these "new" worlds, through logics of measurement, aesthetic judgment, commercial circulation, and property. Colonial descriptive narrative is a technique, in other words, for yielding both the "something" that promises to satisfy longing and the "someone" defined by such longing. It doesn't extinguish desire but maps it onto identifiable, enclosed territories that can be assessed, governed, disciplined, and accounted for—that can tell you what something, or someone, *is*.

The call back to eighteenth-century studies' queer horizons is a call away from the territorializing projects of the eighteenth century, and back to the indeterminate coordinates of longing as a utopian, not imperial, practice. In "Something's Missing: A Discussion between Ernst Bloch and Theodor W. Adorno on the Contradictions of Utopian Longing" (1964), Bloch and Adorno think together about the tension between utopian longing and the forms of cultural and technological invention that are generated historically in the social pursuit of utopian futures. When the moderator opens the discussion by asking about the "depreciation" of the concept of utopia in their own historical moment, Adorno answers by invoking a fairy tale:

> I would like to remind us that numerous so-called utopian dreams—for example, television, the possibility of traveling to other planets, moving faster than sound—have been fulfilled. However, insofar as these dreams have been realized, they all operate as though the best thing about them had been forgotten—one is not happy about them. As they have been realized, the dreams themselves have assumed a peculiar character of sobriety, of the spirit of positivism, of boredom. What I mean by this is that it is not simply a matter of presupposing that what really is has limitations as opposed to that which has infinitely imaginable possibilities. Rather, I mean something concrete, namely, that one sees oneself almost always deceived: the fulfillment of the wishes takes something away from the substance of the wishes, as in the fairy tale where the farmer is granted three wishes and, I believe, he wishes his wife to have a sausage on her nose and then must use the second wish to have the sausage removed from her nose.[2]

I take Adorno's theoretical point here—that as a principle of social and especially of technological progress, utopian thinking must habitually disavow its own utopian longing as a way of committing to each new reality that is brought into being. These ideological commitments to the reality of the present are wedded to registers of minor aesthetics and low affect (in this case, "sobriety," "positivism," "boredom") that, as Sianne Ngai has argued, rehearse the fundamental social relations of late capitalism as a matter of just how things are.[3] The substance of the utopian dream, in other words, is the audacity to dream at all. One simply cannot hope for what has already arrived, and one must acknowledge the arrival by pretending the magical thinking of hope has nothing to do with it.

I return to this passage again and again, not to revive my understanding of the politics of dreams but to think about the sausage. Why does the farmer wish to have a sausage on his wife's nose? One explanation, supported by his "having to" use the second wish to undo the first, is that he is simply testing the wish-granting technology—a sausage suddenly appearing on his wife's nose being the most outlandish, least possible thing he can think of in the moment. Another is that he is simply hungry—too hungry to "think straight," as it were. As Adorno and Bloch both acknowledge in their conversation, wishes are forms of desire and are therefore categorically erotic, even if—perhaps especially if—they cannot be narratively "accounted for." What we do know is that under some confluence of pressures and imaginings, the wish that leaps first to the farmer's expression is *for his wife to have an edible phallus on her face*. In the way of fairy tales, which is also the way of dreams, the farmer's inarticulable longing takes the comedically absurd form of a literal "longing" in the elongation of his wife's nose. That this particular wish's fulfillment mandates its immediate reversal tells a story not merely about utopia's tense relationship with the real, but specifically about queer desire's radical capacity to shock its own dreamers—the way it can make one feel "deceived" by one's own wishes in the moment of their expression—and its profound incapacity to settle for what is shown to be possible.

I was introduced to the concept of the "queer horizon," like so many of us, by José Esteban Muñoz, with whom Jeremy and Shelby opened, and whose appearance has been peppered throughout, this collection. We conclude with it here—as queer bookends might. In "Queerness as Horizon," Muñoz insists that queerness is a site of collective hope on the order of utopia, that "Queerness is utopian, and there is something queer about the utopian."[4] To embrace it as such is to understand, and to accept, that *queer* exists somewhere beyond the possibility of embrace—that it is never the here and now, but the "then and there" of Muñoz's title, or, both more and less precisely, the "not-quite-conscious" theorized by Bloch in *The Principle of Hope*. This is not to say that queerness and utopia never find material form, but rather, that understood as two aspects of the same phenomenon, queer/utopia names a refusal to stop dreaming at the moment of fulfillment.

In his conversation with Adorno, Bloch too locates the "richly prospective doubt [of the satisfactions of the present] and the decisive incentive toward utopia" in the two-word sentence by Brecht, "Something's missing": "What is this something? If it is not allowed to be cast in a picture, then I shall portray it as in the process of being (*seiend*). But one should not be allowed to eliminate it as if it really did not exist so that one could say the following about it: 'It's about the sausage.'"[5] In the margin of my copy of "Something's Missing," my notation of this passage consists of a bunch of excited scrawls and exclamation marks around "the sausage," followed by a somewhat more subdued, "Wait, what sausage??" Bloch clarifies as he goes on, invoking "the old peasant saying, there is no dance before the meal. People must first fill their stomachs, and then they can dance . . . only when all the guests have sat down at the table can the Messiah, can Christ come."[6] His point, as I understand it, is that "the sausage" (whichever sausage) is necessary but only because people have to eat, have to survive, in order to make themselves available to the miracle of utopia, the not-yet-here, the not-(about)-sausage. "It's about the sausage" is the mantra of pragmatism, "something's missing" the plaint of the utopian. And yet, in the tale of the farmer and his wife, the sausage *is* the something that is missing, except for the brief, miraculous moment when it is not. And the sausage is the thing that is eliminated in the farmer's immediate disavowal of queer desire made manifest. Utopia, then, both is and is not about the sausage. The sausage itself is not about the sausage. Because in queer/utopia, a sausage is never just a sausage.

Read as a fable of queer/utopian yearning, the tale of the sausage is not only about the (unrealized) possibility of owning one's most outlandish desires but also about the importance, in the process of such forthright yearning, of taking responsibility for the things one actually does in the messy material pursuit of the missing thing. Rather than be allowed to wish it away, what if the farmer had to deal with the sausage, had to reckon with the conflagration of desires and impulses that brought the sausage about, and, most importantly, had to address the consequences of the sausage's manifestation for the person most directly affected by it, his wife?

Bloch offers a brief history of Euro-Western utopian projects that clarifies why any present commitment to queer/utopian futurity must similarly grapple, earnestly and intensely, with the imperial history of utopian ventures past: "At the very beginning, Thomas More designated utopia as a place, an island in the distant South Seas. This designation underwent changes later so that it left space and entered time. Indeed, the utopians, especially those of the eighteenth and nineteenth centuries, transposed the wishland more into the future. In other words, there is a transformation of the topos from space into time."[7] This philosophical transformation does not belong merely to a "history of ideas" but to the history of European empire. The eighteenth- and nineteenth-century transposition of utopian imaginings from geographical space to historical time corresponds to the actual expansion of colonial occupations into the "distant South Seas" and myriad other global sites fantasized by European cultures as versions of heaven on earth. More's elaborate pun in the term *utopia*, whose Greek etymology refers both to "good place" and "*no* place," registers the fundamental tension between utopian longing and geographic *settling*, a tension that impels the voracious colonial appetites of the long eighteenth century.[8] Like the sausage on the farmer's wife's nose, perhaps, the realities of colonial occupation didn't correspond to the utopian yearnings that motivated the grand project of imperial expansion. By relocating the dreams of empire from space to time, colonial cultures were able to embrace occupation as a pragmatic reality—"how things are" and what "must be done" to keep them that way—while projecting their utopian desires into the future, where they cannot be reached by journey but only by settlement: the dedicated, which is to say violent, development of the here and now into something else.

As this collection shows, any present commitment to queer horizons and the utopian longings that move us toward them must therefore begin with an *unsettling*. This is distinctively, though not exclusively, a project for eighteenth-century studies, because eighteenth-century culture is where the utopian dreams of European global expansion turned starkly into the establishment of settler colonial nation-states upon mythologies of economic and historical necessity (later "manifest destiny"), not the extravagant urges of utopian hope. As each of the essays gathered here reveals in its own way, the queerness of empire's utopian urges doesn't disappear in the projects of colonization and settlement, but is dispersed into various explanatory and descriptive narratives that wrangle indeterminate longing into specific subjectivities animated by specific affordances within specific political orders. These specificities are the eighteenth century's ideological enclosures of meaning, the empire's "somethings" drawn in detail and arranged meticulously to make a colonized world make sense. And, for this reason, they are what anticolonial eighteenth-century studies must reopen and unmap in the revitalization of queer hope. "Hope," Bloch says toward the end of his conversation with Adorno, "is not confidence. If it could not be disappointed, it would not be hope.... Otherwise, it would be cast in a picture. It would let itself be bargained down. It would capitulate and say, that is what I had hoped for."[9] Hope, in other words, remains unsettled because it does not settle. To unsettle the orders of sexuality that take shape through the eighteenth century's colonizing projects is to say: This is *not* what we hoped for, this is *not* who we hope to be.

The queer horizons toward which this collection orients itself are focal points that reopen the possibility of being outside of or beyond colonization. (Re)turning to the queer horizon in the wake of European empire is a commitment, or a compulsion, to want more and to want otherwise, without disavowing that which one *once wanted* and now no longer wants, and without promising not to want differently going forward. As Jeremy and Shelby write in the introduction, the directionality indicated by queer horizons is, by Enlightenment measures of space and time, baffling: "A queer horizon can be behind, besides, adjacent, and in front of us. Other queer directions and prepositions abound. We seek them out here. A queer horizon does not exist in a single temporality. It is not linear. It is not hierarchical. It is not an ontology. It defers stable signification." A queer horizon prompts us to move in convoluted, seemingly contradictory ways because moving toward it entails revisiting where one has been, how one has come, what has been done, and what needs undoing. There is no "ground to cover," but there is immense work to be done, which this collection concludes with by way of invitation. As the poet Canisia Lubrin writes in "Dream #29" of *The Dyzgraph*st*, the queer dream of undoing empire is located in

> these hours where finally
> we demand
> the fucked-with be unfucked-with[10]

A dedicated longing away from imperial worldmaking leads us simultaneously backward and forward, in time and in space, along laborious dreamways of unfucking-up every territory—material, conceptual, embodied, and subjective—conscripted into empire's self-narrative. We are being prompted, here, to—finally—unfulfill each colonial wish as we go long, together.

NOTES

1. Susan Stewart, *On Longing: Narratives of the Miniature, the Gigantic, the Souvenir, the Collection* (Durham, NC: Duke University Press, 1993), ix.

CODA

2. Ernst Bloch, *The Utopian Function of Art and Literature: Selected Essays*, trans. Jack Zipes and Frank Mecklenburg (Boston: MIT Press, 1988), 1.

3. Sianne Ngai, *Our Aesthetic Categories: Zany, Cute, Interesting* (Cambridge, MA: Harvard University Press, 2015).

4. José Esteban Muñoz, *Cruising Utopia: The Then and There of Queer Futurity* (New York: NYU Press, 2009), 26.

5. Bloch, *The Utopian Function*, 15.

6. Bloch, *The Utopian Function*, 15.

7. Bloch, *The Utopian Function*, 3.

8. I am grateful to the anonymous reviewer who called my attention to More's pun and observed that "More's *Utopia* registers the settler desire to move into territories where things are supposedly better than they are 'here' . . . this becomes one of the settler justifications for colonialism. How, then, would queer longing unsettle this colonialist impulse?" Let's find out!

9. Bloch, *The Utopian Function*, 16.

10. Canisia Lubrin, *The Dyzgraph*st* (Toronto: McClelland & Stewart, 2020), 82.

Notes on Contributors

NOUR AFARA is a policy analyst at the Missing and Murdered Indigenous Women and Girls Secretariat within Crown-Indigenous Relations and Northern Affairs Canada. She completed her doctorate in English at the University of Ottawa in 2023. Her research explores racialized sex work, labor policy, affect, and time theory, and has appeared in *Alternate Routes: A Journal of Critical Social Research*.

JEREMY CHOW is assistant professor of English at Bucknell University in Lewisburg, Pennsylvania. Chow is the editor of *Eighteenth-Century Environmental Humanities* (2023) and the author of *The Queerness of Water: Troubled Ecologies in the Eighteenth Century* (2023). As a cultural critic, Chow examines the connections among literary and media studies; theories of race, sexuality, and queerness; and the environmental humanities.

RILEY DEBAECKE works as a climate change and corporate sustainability consultant at Environmental Resources Management, in Washington, DC, to aid the transition to a low-carbon economy. She graduated from Bucknell University in 2023. Her honors thesis examined the steep challenges and ethical impasses that accompany researching the endemic sexual violence against Black and mixed-race women in an eighteenth-century archive of enslavement.

HUMBERTO GARCIA is professor and Vincent Hillyer Chair of Literature at the University of California in Merced. He studies eighteenth- and nineteenth-century British literature in a global context, with an emphasis on Anglo-Islamic relations in this period. Among his publications are *Islam and the English Enlightenment, 1670–1840* (2012) and *England Re-Oriented: How Central and South Asian Travelers Imagined the West, 1750–1857* (2020).

TESS J. GIVEN is a doctoral candidate in the English Department at the University of Indiana in Bloomington. Their work explores the novel as a transhistorical medium for theorizing character, world-building, and subjectivity. They focus mainly on the early eighteenth-century novel and its resonances within contemporary science and speculative fiction through a queer, posthumanist, and feminist science studies methodology.

CAILEY HALL is assistant professor of English at Oklahoma State University in Stillwater. Her research and teaching interests include long eighteenth-century Anglophone literature, environmental and health humanities, food studies, gender and sexuality studies, and romance novels. She is working on a book, "Gut Reading: Literature, Environmental Culture, and the Alimentary Body."

SHELBY JOHNSON is assistant professor of English at Oklahoma State University in Stillwater, where she researches and teaches sexuality, race, and environmental studies in the long eighteenth century. Her book, *The Rich Earth between Us: The Intimate Grounds of Race and Sexuality in the Atlantic World* (2024), argues that figures of a gifted earth organize a set of worlding practices that ground and animate anticolonial intimacies.

ULA LUKSZO KLEIN is associate professor of English and director of women's and gender studies at the University of Wisconsin in Oshkosh. She has published *Sapphic Crossings: Cross-Dressing Women in Eighteenth-Century British Literature* (2021). Her current research interests focus on trans histories of the Chevaliere d'Eon, queer and trans celebrity, and feminist and women's issues in the long eighteenth century.

ZIONA KOCHER is a postdoctoral lecturer at the University of Tennessee in Knoxville, where they study queerness in the long eighteenth century. Their dissertation, "Breeches: Theatrical Cross-Dressing and Queer Embodiment, 1675–1745," explores the embodiment of gender/sexuality on stage as carefully constructed "gender collages." They were awarded the 2022 Catharine Macaulay Prize and have received fellowships from the Lewis Walpole Library and the University of Tennessee Humanities Center.

M. A. MILLER is assistant professor of gender, race, and health in women's, gender, and sexuality studies at Washington State University in Pullman. They have recent and forthcoming publications in *Victorian Studies, Nineteenth-Century Literature, MELUS, European Romantic Review, The Edinburgh Companion to Queer Reading,* and *The Routledge Handbook of Trans Literature*. They are currently working on two monographs, "Trans*-imperial Ecologies: Cultivating the Ideal Trans Subject" and "Gender Unconformities: Deep Time's Racial Matters."

EUGENIA ZUROSKI is professor of English and cultural studies at McMaster University in Hamilton, Ontario. She is the author of *A Taste for China: English Subjectivity and the Prehistory of Orientalism* (2013). Her forthcoming book, *A Funny Thing: The Undisciplined Eighteenth Century* argues for the emergence of politically relevant forms of "funniness" in eighteenth-century literature, aesthetics, and subjectivity. She also serves as the editor of *Eighteenth-Century Fiction*.

Index

Note: Italicized page numbers refer to figures

Abbas I, Shah, 64
abolitionism, 170, 172, 175
Ackermann, Rudolph: *La Belle Assemblée: or Court and Fashionable Magazine*, 62; *Repository of Arts, Literatures, Commerce, Manufactures, Fashions and Politics*, 62
Adams, Abigail, 41
Adams-Campbell, Melissa, 162
Adorno, Theodor, 15, 181–184
Afara, Nour, 164
affect: asexual, 79–92; Black, 165–176; emancipatory potential of racialized, 165–176; queer, 80–92; white economies of, 173–175. *See also* happiness
Ahad-Legardy, Badia, 104
Ahern, Stephen, 149
Ahmed, Sara, 104–105, 159n4, 167, 173, 175, 177n30; *Living a Feminist Life*, 7; *On Being Included*, 1, 5–6; *The Promise of Happiness*, 162–163; *Queer Phenomenology*, 51n20, 131
Alexander, M. Jacqui, 164
Alryyes, Ala, 133–134
ameliorationism, 170–171
American Revolution, 14, 39, 42–43, 45–46, 49
Anglin, Emily, 154
animal husbandry, 139–141
Aravamudan, Srinivas, 33n1
archives, eighteenth-century, 11, 15; Indigenous, 45; race-neutral, 159
Armstrong, Nancy, 177n30
Arondekar, Anjali, 103–104; "There Is Always More," 95

Arvas, Abdulhamit, 6
Asante, Amma: *Belle*, 15, 163–176
asexuality, 11, 14; Black erotics of, 123–124; Black ontologies of, 124; queer friendship and, 79–92; queerness of, 114. *See also* sexuality
Austen, Jane, 96–98; *Mansfield Park*, 56; *Northanger Abbey*, 101; *Pride and Prejudice*, 97, 101; *Sanditon*, 96–97
Azoulay, Ariella Aïsha, 10

Bacon, Nathaniel, 21, 23–24, 26–29
Bacon's Rebellion, 21, 24, 26
Baker, Samuel, 120; map of St. Christopher, 121
Bakhtin, Mikhail, 51n20
Barker, Joanne, 28
Bassi, Laura, 102
Batchelor, Jennie, 147
Beach, Adam, 33n1
Becoming Jane (Jarrold), 97
Behn, Aphra: *Oroonoko* (novel), 21, 23, 33n1; *The Widow Ranter* (play), 13, 21–33, 31
Bell, John, 64
Bell, Mary Ann, 64, 66
Bell's Weekly Messenger, 69
Bentham, Jeremy, 163
Berg, Ula, 173, 176n18
Berkeley, Governor William, 26
Bertram, Edmund, 57
Best, Stephen, 103–104
Binhammer, Katherine, 11
biopolitics, 24
biopower, 24
Black, Christopher Allan, 127n37

Black, Scott: *Without the Novel*, 106n11, 106n25

Black Atlantic, 11

Blackness, 12, 151, 174; and affect, 165; and Asianness, 149; Crusoe's primary encounter with, 135; mapping of, 141

Black women. *See* women

Bloch, Ernst, 15, 181–182; *The Principle of Hope*, 182

Bly, Mary, 107n28

Bodenhorn, Barbara, 46

Borges, Jorge Luis, 134

Borot, Luc, 22–23

Bowen, Scarlet, 22

Brecht, Bertolt, 182

breeches parts, 26, 36n39

Bridgerton (Van Dusen), 97–98, 106n12

Britain: power abroad of, 28; queerness in early nineteenth-century, 98. *See also* England

British Slavery Abolition Act (1833), 178n50

Brody, Jennifer DeVere, 169

Brooks, Joanna, 49

Brooks, Lisa, 47

Brothertown, 45, 47, 49

brownness, 150–152

Brummell, Beau, 62, 70

Burney, Frances, 162

Bynum, Tara, 163, 173–174

Byrd, Jodi, 25, 29, 40, 45

Calvin's Case (1608), 23

Campana, Joseph, 135–136, 138

capitalism: animal husbandry at the scale of industrial, 141; fundamental social relations of late, 181; global expansion of agricultural, 114; maps as management of projective mercantilist, 133; nascent global, 111; production of, 117–118

Caribbean, 14–15, 113–125

Carr, Nicole, 128n59

Catlin, George: *Dance to the Berdache* (painting), 2

Cerankowski, KJ, 114, 118

Chaplin, Sue, 90–91

Chaskin, Hannah, 22

Chen, Mel, 117

Chow, Jeremy, 8, 148, 184

citation: circulation of, 7; intersectional, 2; praxis of, 1

citizenship: American, 23; concept of universal, 23; incorporation into, 172; transgender, 21–33

Coates, Ta-Nahisi, 17n17

Cole, Alyssa, 96; *That Could Be Enough*, 100

Colebrook, Claire, 33, 48

colonialism: Indigenous experiences under, 52n42; mapping in the age of conquest and, 133; settler, 8, 11–12, 21–33, 45; as subjecting racialized Others to colonial regimes of, 133. *See also* colonization; imperialism; settler expansion

coloniality, 4; of being, 9. *See also* decoloniality

colonization: and imperial expansion, 23, 183; logics of, 118, 141; and settlement, 18, 184; violence of, 29. *See also* colonialism; imperialism

Cooper, Danielle, 80

corsets, 66–68, 70

cross-dressing, 13, 24, 27–29, 33; in Restoration theater, 26

Cummings, Brian, 155

Cvetkovich, Ann, 80, 108n48

dandyism, 63, 68–71

death, 47–48

Death Book of the Society of Universal Friends, 39–41, 43–45

DeBaecke, Riley, 148

decadence, 159n4, 161n65

Declaration of Independence, The, 165

decoloniality, 1, 9, 16; feminist, 9; intimacy and, 12; recovery of, 40. *See also* coloniality

Defoe, Daniel: *Robinson Crusoe*, 15, 129–42

Degooyer, Stephanie, 23

Dinshaw, Carolyn, 11, 48

Dominique, Lyndon, 163

Downes, Melissa K., 131

dreams, 48–49; decolonial, 180

Driskill, Qwo-Li, 29

Eaton, Sara, 33n1

ecocriticism, 14

ecologies: asexual, 111–125; racial and sexual difference as the products of, 12

Edelman, Lee, 116

Edelson, S. Max, 133

Edgeworth, Maria, 55–57, 59, 62–63, 71, 162; *Belinda* (novel), 37n68, 79, 162

Elmer, Jonathan, 33n1

embodiments: settler colonialism with whiteness and queer, 18n43, 33; racial, 9, 49, 147–159, 166

England, 13, Regency, 55–71, 96–98. *See also* Britain

Enlightenment, 8

enslavement: of African labor, 111, 114–122, 124, 127n37; complicity with, 171; ; fugitive

INDEX

persons of, 114; grieving Black, 13; systems of, 166. *See also* slavery
epistemologies: global Indigenous, 11; structures of onto-epistemological humanity, 165; white supremacist, 176n18
equestrian, 62–63
erotic autonomy, 164, 172. *See also* happiness
erotics: of compostability, 119–123; of nonrelation, 132–133, 137–142; queer, 132–142. *See also* homoeroticism; sexuality
ethics: of compost, 128n48; environmental, 12
eugenics, 111

Faderman, Lillian: *Surpassing the Love of Men*, 80
fairy tales, 69, 181–182
Farr, Jason, 160n31
fashion: cross-dressing, 69; female, 55–71
Fath 'Ali Shah, 14, 55, 58
Female American, The (Winkfield), 28
femininity: able-bodied, 69; eccentric, 62; foreign ideals of beautiful, 66; ideals of white, 29, 67, 70, 172–173; racialized labor and idle, 149–150, 156–158. *See also* women
feminism, 80; Black, 128n58, 165–166; decolonial, 9; romance readers' embrace of, 107n28. *See also* women
Ferguson, Margaret, 30
Ferguson, Roderick, 8
fictional travel literature, 132
Fielding, Theodore Henry: "No. [1, 2] of a Series of Views in the West Indies" (engraving), *122*
film, 163, 171–176
Fludernik, Monika, 154
Foucault, Michel, 25, 35n22
Frangos, Jennifer, 22, 34n4
Franta, Andrew: *Systems Failure*, 134
Freeman, Elizabeth, 41; *Beside You in Time*, 7
Freud, Sigmund: *Three Essays on the Theory of Sexuality*, 126n14
friendship: companionate, 88; queer, 14, 79–92
Frye, Northrop, 101
Fryke, Christopher, 149

Gallagher, Catherine, 104
Gamble, Joseph, 22
Garcia, Humberto, 151
gender: colonial racialization of, 49; early American norms of, 14; European ideals of, 71; illusory nature of, 26; nonconfor-

mity of, 62; racialized, 132; representations of, 10; tenuous binaries of, 26–27. *See also* sexuality; transness
genocide, 25
geography: Black, 170–171; feminist and queer, 134
George III, King, 55–56, 58, 63
George IV, King, 56
Gerzina, Gretchen, 97, 149
Getsy, David, 22, 33
Giffney, Noreen, 125n6
Gilmore, John, 126n19
Gilmore, Ruth Wilson, 175
girdles, 66
Given, Tess, 5
Goldberg, Jonathan, 6
Grainger, James: *The Sugar Cane* (poem), 15, 111–125
Gregori, Flavio, 162
Grimaldi, Joseph, 69–70
Grimaldi, Joseph Samuel William, 69
Guilmette, Lauren, 166
Gumbs, Alexis Pauline, 12
Gupta, Kristina, 81

Haggerty, George: *Queer Friendship*, 79
Halberstam, Jack, 100, 107n37
Hall, Alexis, 96
Hall, Cailey, 162
Hall, Radclyffe: *The Well of Loneliness*, 99
Hall, Thomas/Thomasine, 22
Halperin, David: *One Hundred Years of Homosexuality*, 11
Hanson, Elizabeth Hanna, 82, 87
happiness, 162–176; as affect, 164–176; Blackened, 163–166, 169–176; colonial politics of the promise of, 165; coloring contingent, 166–169; conditional, 173–174; domestic, 170–171, 173; façade of universal, 163, 175; infantine, 170; spatial, 174–176. *See also* affect; erotic autonomy
Harlequin and Cinderella; or, the Little Glass Slipper (pantomime), 58, 68–70
Hartman, Saidiya, 11, 171, 177n34
Harvey, Karen, 149
Herschel, Caroline, 102
heteronormativity, 4, 5, 70; of colonial records, 7, 43; of hetero-domestic marriage, 97, 163–176
heteropatriarchy, 10
heterosexuality: cisgender, 114; compulsory, 22, 117; and monogamy, 33; and reproductive futurity, 32, 116; romance novels and, 107n28; as system, 131. *See also* sexuality
heterotopia, 24–26
Hiatt, Megan, 147

INDEX

hierarchies: emergent racialized sexual, 135; patriarchal, 85; sex-gender, 140

Hird, Myra J., 125n6

Histories of Some of the Penitents in the Magdalen-House, as Supposed to be Related by Themselves, The (fictionalized collection of memoirs), 15, 147–154, 159n2

homoeroticism, 117–118, 135. *See also* erotics

homonationalism, 34n5

homonormativity, 4, 5, 105

Hong, Cathy Park, 164

Howitt, Samuel: "Ladies Evening or Opera Dress" (engraving), 65

Huang, Kristina, 168

Huggins, Sofia Prado, 164, 169, 171

Human Rights Campaign (HRC), 35n27

Hunt, Sarah, 11

hypervisibility, 155

identities: assumptions made about asexuality and related queer, 92n9; Indigenous nonbinary and transgender, 13

ideologies, 180; of bootstrapping, 157; of race and empire, 62, 184; racial, 51n10, 150

imperialism, 33, 184; British colonialism and, 131; history of European, 183. *See also* colonialism; colonization

Indigenous peoples, 4, 28; Algonquian, 46–49; Cherokee, 29; Chumash, 52n42; colonial laws and treaties erasing the sovereignty of, 45–46, 49; Cree, 2; displacement of, 13–14, 42, 47; Doeg, 26; dogs and wolves in the cultures of Northeast, 48, 53n64; Esselen, 52n42; Haudenosaunee, 42–43, 45; land theft from, 14; Mattaponi, 21; Mohawk, 43; Mohegan, 45, 47; Montauk, 46, 49; Narragansett, 42; obliteration of, 32, 46–47; Oneida, 49; oral traditions of, 12; Pamunkey, 21, 26; perspectives on non-normative personhood of, 39; Powhatan, 21, 36n51; Seneca, 43; Stockbridge-Munsee, 49; Susquehannock, 26; Wampanoag, 42. *See also* Native Americans

intimacies, 9–13; biographical, 66; Indigenous, 13; as methodology, 114; queering of Indigenous, 46; settler regulations of, 49; soil, 119–125

Iran, 155

Jagose, Annamarie, 118

Jamestown, 21–33

Jenkins, Henry, 98

Johnson, Jessica Marie, 11, 166

Johnson, Shelby, 163, 184

Johnson, Walter, 126n22

Jones, Sir Harford, 58

Jordan, Sara: *The Anxieties of Idleness*, 150, 154

Juster, Susan, 41

Kafantaris, Mira Assaf, 98

Kaul, Suvir, 30

Kay, John, 59, 61

Kelleher, Paul, 81, 140; "A Table in the Wilderness," 139

Khoikhoi peoples, 149–150

Kim, Sue J., 164

King, Tiffany Lethabo, 2, 12, 40, 129, 141–142, 144n46, 166

King Philip's War (1675–76), 42

Klein, Ula Lukszo, 162

Kocher, Ziona, 5, 114, 162

Kramer, Kaley, 90

Kristeva, Julia, 136

La Belle Assemblée, 57, 64, 66, 69; "A Portrait of Delarom" (stipple with engraving), 67

labor: affective, 154–156, 161n69; of beautification, 155; domestic, 156–157; eighteenth-century conceptions of, 148–149; racialized, 149–159; valid or invalid types of, 15, 150. *See also* sex work

Lady's Magazine, The, 61

LaFleur, Greta, 12

Lanser, Susan S.: *The Sexuality of History: Modernity and the Sapphic*, 11, 80

Larson, Scott, 42

Lee, Ann, 41

Lee, Wendy Anne, 81

Lennox, Charlotte, 162; *The Female Quixote*, 101

Levellers, 23

Linnaeus, Carl, 111

Lloyd, Vincent, 51n10

London, 147–159, 168, 174

Lorde, Audre, 128n58, 161n69, 164

Love, Heather: *Underdogs: Social Deviance and Queer Theory*, 11

Lowe, Lisa, 114; *The Intimacies of Four Continents*, 10

Lubey, Kathleen, 174

Lubrin, Canisia: "Dream #29" (poem), 184

Lugones, María, 9

Lupton, Christina, 82, 87, 148, 153, 158, 160n36

Lush, Rebecca, 29

Mahmood, Saba: *Politics of Piety*, 74n48

Manion, Jen, 6; *Female Husbands: A Trans History*, 99, 102

maps: colonial spatializing logics, 141; fictionalized, 15, 129–142; as management

INDEX

of capitalism, 133; "A map of the world, on which is delineated the voyages of Robinson Cruso [sic]," *130*
marginalia, 7
marriage, 14–15, 69–71, 79; as compulsory sexuality, 82–92, 167; eighteenth-century legal reform of, 162; financial advantages of, 99, 167, 172; happiness within the structures of heteronormative, 175; monogamous heterosexual, 57, 71, 90, 97, 102; as patriarchal system, 86, 99, 172; rise of companionate, 81, 83, 97, 107n32. *See also* sexuality
Marx, Karl, 119
masculinity: elite Persian, 59, 70; genteel British, 56, 70; racialized, 56
McGurl, Mark, 107n32
McKittrick, Katherine, 12, 166, 170; *Dear Science and Other Stories*, 7
McMahon, William, 123–124; survey map of St. Kitts, *123*
Menon, Madhavi, 6, 44
Middle Passage, queer imaginings of the, 12
Mignolo, Walter, 9
Milan, Courtney, 96
Milks, Megan, 114
Miller, D. A., 97
Miller, Derrick R., 48
Miller, M. A., 5, 164
Miranda, Deborah, 13, 52n42
Mirza Abul Hassan Khan, 14, 55–59, *60*, 61–64, 66, 69–71, 75n69
Miss Austen Regrets (Lovering), 97
modernity: colonial, 8, 9; European, 57
Mohegan Indians v. Connecticut (1705–1773), 45
Monkman, Kent: *Welcoming the Newcomers* (mural), 2, *3*, *4*, 7
More, Thomas: *Utopia*, 183, 185n8
Morgan, Dawn, 25
Morgan, Jennifer, 12, 166
Morgensen, Scott Lauria, 40
Morning Post, 59, 61
Morris, Robert, 43
Morrisseau, Norval, 8
Moten, Fred, 41
mourning, 13
Mowry, Melissa, 24, 35n17
Moyer, Paul B., 42
Muñoz, José Esteban: *Cruising Utopia: The Then and There of Queer Futurity*, 2, 5, 41, 99, 104, 182
Mustakeem, Sowande' M., 149

Najmabadi, Afsaneh, 57, 155
narrative: as queer union, 90–92; transness as a racial, 25. *See also* novels

nationalism, 24
nationality, 26
Native Americans: tobacco and, 25; two-spirit, 2, 12, 16n3, 52n42. *See also* Indigenous peoples
Nelson, Melissa K., 12
Ngai, Sianne, 164, 181
Nicolazzo, Sal, 8
novels: eighteenth-century proto-feminist, 98; epistolary, 167–169; epistolary fiction and romance, 14, 79–92; happiness in eighteenth-century, 162–176; mid-eighteenth-century conduct books and, 87; queer historical romance, 95–105; queer romance, 13–14, 105n4; romance, 97–99, 101–102, 106n11, 106n19, 107n28, 107n32; sentimental, 83. *See also* narrative

O'Brien, Jean, 45
Occom, Samson, 13–14, 38–50, 53n64; "Account of the Montauk Indians," 46; *Sermon on the Execution of Moses Paul*, 39
Orientalism, 57–58, 73n27, 155
Ovington, John, 150
Owen, Ianna Hawkins, 124, 127n33

Palmer, Tyrone, 165, 174
Peiser, Megan, 8
Perrault, Charles: "Cendrillon," 69
Perry, Imani, 166
Peterkin, Joshua: *A Treatise on Planting*, 111, 113
philosophy: "common sense" in eighteenth-century British, 16n9; eighteenth-century literature and, 81
Pickering, Timothy, 43
Pinkerton, John, 120
plantation economy, 113–125; development of monocrop production within the, 115–120, 123–124; emergence of homoeroticism out of the transatlantic slave trade and, 117. *See also* slavery
Pocahontas mythology, 26
poetry, English pastoral, 117
political economy, 174
Pope, Alexander: *An Essay on Man*, 165
popular culture, 96–98
Portrait of a Lady on Fire (Sciamma), 99
Przybylo, Ela, 80

queerness, 13, 25, 80, 98–99; as desire, 182–183; as hope, 184; as horizon, 180–184; imbrication of imperial whiteness and, 13; queer of color tradition, 165. *See also* sexuality
queer theory, 80

Quijano, Aníbal, 9
Quinn, Julia, 97; *Bridgerton*, 105n4
Qur'an, 58

race, 5, 23, 26; eighteenth-century formations of, 148–159; emergent character of, 151; representations of, 10; well-born, 32. *See also* racism
racism, 96–97; ideologies of, 150. *See also* race; white supremacy
Radcliffe, Ann, 162
Radway, Janice: *Reading the Romance*, 101–102
Rae-Prescott, Amanda, 96–97
Raleigh, Sir Walter: *The Discoverie of Guiana*, 29
Rambuss, Richard, 48
Ramos-Zayas, Ana, 173, 176n18
Rancière, Jacques, 100
Ranters, 26
Reed, Jennifer, 168
Reeves, James Bryan, 158
Regis, Pamela, 101
religious dissenters, 23, 26
resilience, 157
resistance: Black fugitivity and Indigenous, 141; to discourses of racial and national hegemony, 25; erotic, 12; human and more-than-human, 12
Restoration era, theater of the, 26, 30
Rich, Adrienne, 80
Richard, Analiese, 174
Richardson, Robbie, 28
Richardson, Samuel, 162; *Clarissa*, 79, 81, 85; *Pamela*, 81, 97, 101
Rifkin, Mark, 6, 7, 9, 32, 40
Roach, Joseph, 47, 58
romanticism, 1, 24
Rosenberg, Gabriel: "How Meat Changed Sex," 141
Rosenberg, Jordy: *Confessions of the Fox*, 95, 108n46
Rosenthal, Laura J., 149
Rossini, Gioachino: *La Cenerentola* (opera), 69–70
Rowlandson, Mary, 42
Rubin, Gayle, 63
Rusert, Brit, 115
Rycroft, Eleanor, 59

saccade, 132, 134, 136–138, 140–142
Sagay, Misan, 171, 173, 176n12
Sampsonia, Teresa, 64
Sapphic Crossings (Klein), 24
Sargent Murray, Judith, 41
satire, 22, 67–68; cross-dressing, 70

Savery, William, 43
Saxton, Kirsten T., 22
Sciamma, Céline, 99
Scott, Sarah: *Millenium Hall*, 79, 89, 98, 147, 160n31
Sebastian, Cat, 96
Sedgwick, Eve Kosofsky, 57, 80; *Between Men*, 85
Seeman, Erik R., 46
sentimentality, 166
settler expansion, 8, 11–12, 21–33, 45, 183. *See also* colonialism
sexism, 9
sexuality: colonial logics of sex and, 141; compulsory, 6, 14, 80–92, 92n6; early American, 14, 41; environmental, 12, 14; Islamicate, 70–71; racialized, 5, 147–159; realities of female, 86–87; representations of, 10. *See also* asexuality; erotics; gender; heterosexuality; marriage; queerness
sex work: as non-work, 153; racialized, 15, 147–159. *See also* labor
Shakers, 41
Shakespeare, William: *Twelfth Night* (play), 37n66
Sharpe, Christina, 11
Sheridan, Frances: *The Memoirs of Miss Sidney Bidulph*, 11, 14, 79–92, 93n18
Shirley, Robert, 64
Silva, Cristobal, 116–117
Simpson, Leanne Betasamosake, 10
Sinanan, Kerry, 168, 170
slavery, 25, 149; British practice of selling enslaved Africans, 128n49; French West Indies slave plantations, 69; Portuguese slaving vessel, 137; transatlantic slave trade, 66, 151, 170, 172. *See also* enslavement; plantation economy
Snook, Edith, 25
Snorton, C. Riley: *Black on Both Sides*, 25, 33, 40, 144n46
Society of Universal Friends, 42–43, 49
"Something's Missing: A Discussion between Ernst Bloch and Theodor W. Adorno on the Contradictions of Utopian Longing" (Bloch and Adorno), 181–184
Southcott, Joanna, 41
space: Black, 129; Enlightenment measures of time and, 184; Indigenous, 129; noncolonial, 129; queer, 131–142
Spacks, Patricia Meyer, 84, 90
Spillers, Hortense, 11, 40, 119, 166
Stewart, Carol, 84–85
Stewart, Susan: *On Longing: Narratives of the Miniature, the Gigantic, the Souvenir, the Collection*, 180

sugarcane, 111–125, *112*; colonial propagation of, 115; cisgender and heterosexual rhetoric for describing the production of, 113, 117; intimacies of the cultivation of, 115–116; queer erotics of, 116–119
Sullivan, General John, 45

time: Enlightenment measures of space and, 184; racialized, 147–159; slowed, 149; straight, 2; Western understandings of, 11
Times, The, 63
Tinsley, Omise'eke Natasha, 12
tobacco, 25, 28
Todd, Janet, 37n60
tokenization, 167–168
trans doubling, 24–26, 35n24. *See also* transness
transexion, 22
transgender citizenship. *See* citizenship
Trans Historical: Gender Plurality before the Modern (LaFleur, Raskolnikov, and Kłosowska), 22
transness: as racialized category, 25, 29, 33; and reproducing empire, 30–33; transfeminate, 22. *See also* gender; trans doubling
transparency, 124–125; as an environmental concept, 125
Traub, Valerie, 6
Tristram Shandy (Sterne), 134
Tsing, Anna, 122, 126n14
Turley, Hans, 138, 143n16
Turner, J.M.W.: *The Slave Ship* (painting), 2

utopianism, 5, 168–169; Euro-Western projects of, 183; as longing, 181–183; queer, 16, 181; tense relationship with, 182–183

violence: anti-Black and anti-Indigenous, 141; anti-queer and transphobic, 13; colonial, 21, 29, 39, 113, 138–142, 173; eighteenth-century archives as constitutively shaped by, 11; imperial, 12, 21, 45
vom Bruck, Gabrielle, 46

Wagner, Sydnee, 29
Waite, Olivia: *The Lady's Guide to Celestial Mechanics*, 14, 96, 98–99, 102–105, 106n14
Walsh, Catherine E., 9
Washington Post, 101
Weinbaum, Alys Eve, 171
Wheeler, Roxann, 151
Whitefield, George, 48–49; "Christ the Best Husband," 48
whiteness, 4, 16, 23, 131; British imperialism and, 33; ideals of, 150–151, 155; as racial category, 32
white supremacy, 8, 25, 165. *See also* racism
Wichelns, Kathryn, 22
Wilde, Oscar, 99
Wilderson, Frank, 167, 177n34
Wilkinson, A. B., 151
Wilkinson, Jemima (Public Universal Friend), 38–43
Williams, Charles, 67; "British Graces, Attireing the Circassian Venus in the English Costume" (engraving), 67–68, *68*
Williamson, Margaret Holmes, 36n51
Wise, Steven, 178n73
Wollstonecraft, Mary: *Maria; or, The Wrongs of Woman*, 98
Woman of Colour, The (Anonymous), 13, 15, 148, 163–176, 176n19
women: the aging of, 158; Black, 12, 15, 168; Circassian, 56, 62–70, 74n54; erasure of Indigenous, 28; imperialist accounts of Indigenous, 29–30; as loud-mouthed and sexually liberated, 26–27; mixed-race, 13, 15, 163, 168, 172, 175; social value of the virginity of, 156; trans Black, 35n27. *See also* femininity; feminism
Woodard, Vincent, 117
Woods, Clyde, 170
Wynter, Sylvia, 12, 143n21, 166; "Novel and History, Plot and Plantation," 124

Yao, Xine, 166

Zacek, Natalie, 170–171
Zembylas, Michalinos, 166